ROSS KEMP ON
AFGHANISTAN

ROSS KEMP ON AFGHANISTAN

Ross Kemp

CHIVERS

British Library Cataloguing in Publication Data available

This Large Print edition published by BBC Audiobooks Ltd, Bath, 2010.
Published by arrangement with Penguin Books Ltd.

U.K. Hardcover ISBN 978 1 408 47816 5
U.K. Softcover ISBN 978 1 408 47817 2

Printed and bound in Great Britain by
CPI Antony Rowe, Chippenham and Eastbourne

To everyone in the armed forces
and their families

When you're wounded and left on
Afghanistan's plains
And the women come out to cut up what
remains,
Just roll to your rifle and blow out your brains
And go to your Gawd like a soldier.

Rudyard Kipling, 'The Young British Soldier',
from *Barrack-Room Ballads*, 1892

The Taliban are your problem. You are the
Taliban's problem. All of you are my problem.

An Afghan villager to the author,
summer 2008

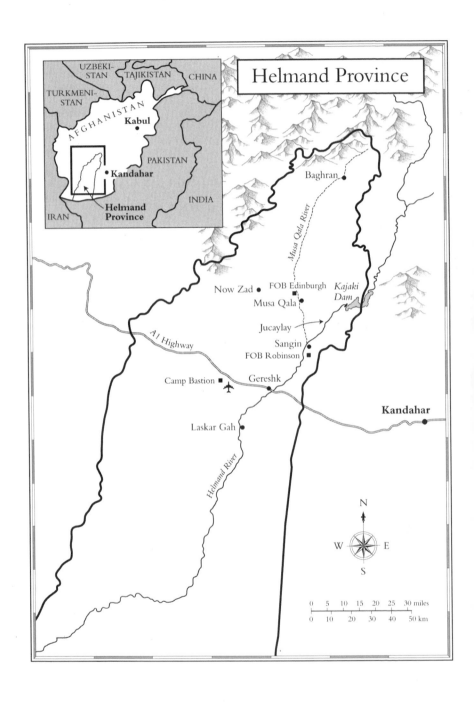

CONTENTS

PROLOGUE

August 2007. The British base in Sangin, Helmand Province.

I've only recently returned to Afghanistan, I'm still acclimatizing and, not to put too fine a point on it, nature is calling. Not for me, however, the quiet comfort of my home lavatory, with perhaps a newspaper to keep me company as I do what needs to be done; nor even the relatively clean facilities of Camp Bastion.

Not out here. Nothing like.

I pad down to the thunderboxes, wet wipes in hand. They're a rickety line of cheaply cobbled-together cubicles, positioned well away from those parts of the base where soldiers congregate. And with good reason. As I approach, I hear a buzzing sound, then a familiar and unloved smell becomes gradually more intense. It is the unmistakable aroma of human turds.

There are two things that make this aroma more stinky than it might otherwise be. Firstly, they represent the accumulated waste product of three companies of soldiers. Secondly, the turds have been festering and maturing nicely in the midday sun. You can imagine what that does for them. I try to stop myself from gagging.

Inside the thunderboxes I know that whole families of flies will be feasting upon the soldiers' rancid deposits. More than once I've had a swarm of these insects fly out of the pan, up between my legs and onto the edge of my mouth. From one area of moisture to another. My lips clamp involuntarily shut as I suppress a shudder at the thought. It's not the only embarrassment I've had to undergo while sitting on the throne: there's clearly something very funny about a guy off the telly in an army thunderbox. Sometimes I wonder if there's a single soldier in Helmand Province that doesn't have a picture on their digital camera of Grant Mitchell taking a dump.

I take a breath. Not too deep, because I don't want to inhale the smell too much. Before I venture into one of the cubicles, I mutter under my breath, 'God, I've missed you.'

As if in reply to my sarcastic comment, I get a slightly more putrid whiff.

'My God!' I shout. 'That stinks!'

It's at just that moment that one of the doors opens.

I blink.

Out of the cubicle walks a woman. An intelligence officer. Like me, she's carrying wet wipes and she's still rubbing alcohol gel into her hands—a precaution against D and V, the all-too-common diarrhoea and vomiting. She raises an eyebrow in my direction.

'Thank you very much,' she replies.

I open my mouth to try and explain that I meant the thunderboxes in general, not what she just left behind. But the moment has passed and so has any chance I might have had of a candlelit dinner for two at Sangin DC.

I shrug. It's 40 degrees in the shade. I'm hot, sweaty, dirty and more than a bit fragrant. Hardly what you'd call a catch, even without the disadvantage of my big mouth. Still, I wish I'd kept quiet.

I turn back to face the thunderbox. Come on, Ross, I tell myself. Worse things happen at war. You've been ambushed, RPG'd and shot at. Stop being such a pansy. I take another breath, walk towards these delightf''h-air facilities, open the door and wn inside.

And not for the first time I wond st what the hell it is I think I'm doing here, miles from home and in the middle of a war zone.

*   *   *

This book will not tell you what it's like to be a soldier in Afghanistan. No book will. Nor will any TV show, film or documentary. It won't fully describe the blind fear you feel the first time you know an enemy marksman has you in his sights and is doing whatever he can to kill you. It won't fully relate the thrill and excitement of battle. Words are inadequate to convey the intense, brutal, burning heat of the Afghanistan summer; the vicious whipping of the coarse sand against your skin; the blunt shock of knowing that someone with whom you had joked and laughed only that day, is now dead; or the stark, unexpected beauty of flying along the Helmand river. These are things that can be understood only by experiencing them.

What I hope this book does give you is some small idea of what it's like for a young soldier fighting today on the front line of Britain's war on terror. I hope it gives you some insight into what it is we demand of our armed forces, and what sort of war it is they are fighting. There is a myth, I think, among the public at large that modern wars are fought from a distance, with smart bombs and technical wizardry, that the days of infantrymen fighting *mano-a-mano*, risking their lives, are at an end. If I've learned one thing during my time in Afghanistan, it's that this couldn't be further from the truth. Wars are still fought by men with spears. The spears might be more advanced than once they were; but our safety and liberty is still being defended by young men living and dying in the field.

This is not a political book; nor is it meant to be. The whys and wherefores of the war in Afghanistan are for more experienced political minds than mine. I'm interested in the soldiers. How they live, how they fight and how they cope with the intense and incredibly difficult situations they find themselves in. I've experienced in some small measure what it is that they go through, and if this book and the films that I've made on the subject have captured a small portion of that then I'm content. Because I feel very strongly that it's a subject that deserves to be explored.

Unlike the thunderboxes. I miss many things about Afghanistan, but I don't miss them. And if the female intelligence officer I so gravely insulted happens to be reading this, all I can do is offer my most sincere and heartfelt apologies . . .

Ross Kemp
London, 2009

PART ONE
Herrick 6

1. ALL QUIET ON THE WESTERN FRONT

When I was a kid I had a dog and an airgun, and I used to take them both for walks. Why I felt I needed an airgun in the quiet fields of the Essex countryside I don't quite know. I suppose I was just that kind of child. One day, though, my mum gave me something else to take on my walk. Something a bit less macho. It was a book.

Reading wasn't really my thing at the time. My brother Darren was a regular bookworm, but not me. Clearly my mum had decided to do something about it, so she had hunted out a book that she thought would capture my imagination. Like most young boys, I had an interest in things military—nothing out of the ordinary, just the regular fascination kids of a certain age have. The book my mother had bought me was a war book. It was called *All Quiet on the Western Front* by Erich Maria Remarque, a veteran of the First World War, and I still remember lying down in the field, the dog snuffling away under a hedge somewhere and my airgun by my side, and starting to read it.

It tells the story of a young man of nineteen who is deployed to the Western Front, the zone in France and Belgium, characterised by the horrors of trench warfare, where the German forces engaged their western enemies. Here he witnesses the terrible effects—both physical and psychological—of intense combat. It is a harrowing read. I was transfixed by the description of war. I was just a child, of course, who had never seen any real fighting apart from the usual playground aggro, but even so I was struck by how authentic those words appeared to be. To this day I remember the description of a young man under fire, hugging the ground and wanting the earth to swallow him up.

It was not until a good thirty years later, however, that I finally understood just how real that emotion was. And it was not in the damp fields of East Anglia with a dog and an airgun at my side but on the parched earth of a country I had probably not even heard of back then, surrounded by young men carrying SA80s who hadn't been born at the time I was reading that book, and with AK-47 rounds zipping inches above my head. The events depicted in *All Quiet on the Western Front* happened nearly a century ago. Warfare has changed—not as much as some people think, but it has changed. What has not changed is the way a soldier feels when they know someone is trying to kill them.

I always wanted to be an actor, never a soldier, and for years the world of the military was about as far removed from my own life as it's possible to be. When I started making documentary films, however, it struck me that there was very little out there that gave anyone a real idea of what it was like to be a soldier at war in the modern day. There were news reports, of course, by established and insightful journalists who argued the rights and wrongs of our recent military escapades. There were great war films that claimed to be authentic but were nevertheless brushed with the gloss of Hollywood. But nothing I had seen or read seemed to me to shed much light on the life of an ordinary infantryman on deployment in the dangerous parts of the world in which the British Army finds itself in the twenty-first century. I started to feel strongly that this should change.

At the time Iraq was the focus of everyone's attention; Afghanistan was somehow below the radar. My original thought had been to go to Iraq, not to comment on the politics or the whys and wherefores of that controversial war, but just to see what life was like for the soldiers out there. It never happened. I went back to making films about gangs; the political events in the Middle East evolved and moved on. But the idea in my head refused to go away. It was resurrected when I learned that a group of soldiers with whom I felt a certain connection—the First Battalion the Royal Anglian Regiment—were soon to be deployed to Afghanistan as part of Herrick 6.

(Operation Herrick is the codename under which British operations in Afghanistan are conducted.)

Recruiting from East Anglia and the East Midlands, the Royal Anglian Regiment has a long history and is a result of a series of amalgamations of regiments from the east of England. I knew something about them because as a young man my father served for several years in the Royal Norfolk Regiment, one of the regiments that eventually became part of the Royal Anglians, and had seen active service with them in Cyprus. In addition, I was born and brought up in Essex and all my family come from Norfolk. Had I ever been tempted to join up, it is more than likely that the Royal Anglians would have been my first port of call.

Theirs is a name from my childhood. My brother and I used to watch British troops being transported along the old A12, which ran alongside our house. One day, when I was about ten, a Bedford truck full of troops passed us and one of the soldiers grabbed a beret from his mate and threw it towards us. Lose your beret in the army and you face having to pay a fine, so it was obviously just a bit of horseplay for the soldiers in question. I was intrigued by it and wanted to find out where it came from. It transpired that the cap bore one of the insignias of the Royal Anglians.

So it was that when I heard that this regiment was to be deployed to a major war zone, the flame of the idea I'd had of spending time with the British Army was reignited. And if I was to join the First Battalion the Royal Anglian Regiment, it was to Afghanistan— Britain's front line—that I would have to travel.

*   *   *

If history has taught us anything, it is that Afghanistan is a deeply dangerous place for British troops. Or, indeed, *any* foreign troops.

In the first half of the nineteenth century the political geography of the area looked very different to the way it is now. Afghanistan's southern border was with British India; to the north were the lands of the mighty Russian Empire. The Russians feared the northward expansion of the British Empire; the British viewed Russia's southward expansion as a threat to their interests in the Indian subcontinent. The rivalry between Russia and Britain became known as the Great Game and Afghanistan, sandwiched between the two, became the playing board.

In 1838 the British in India became worried that the Afghan ruler, Dost Mohammed, had started to ally himself with the Russians to the north. Claiming the need for a trustworthy ally on the Indian border, they sent a large force of

7

20,000 British and Indian troops over the treacherous mountain passes into Kabul, where, in 1839, they toppled the leader and installed Shah Shujah—the country's former leader—as ruler of Afghanistan, claiming that they were merely reinstating him to the throne that was rightly his. Nobody was fooled, however: this was regime change, pure and simple.

Shah Shujah had a tenuous grip on power, so two brigades of British troops remained in Kabul, along with two British politicians, William McNaghten and Sir Alexander Burnes, to advise the new ruler. He was entirely reliant on British arms to quell insurgencies and British money to buy the loyalty of the Afghan tribal chiefs. There were approximately 4,500 British soldiers in the country at that time. In addition, 12,000 British and Indian civilians had followed the army to Kabul and for two years they lived in a British encampment just outside the capital.

The British troops, however, were not popular guests among the Afghan people. In November 1841 an insurrection broke out in Kabul. Sir Alexander Burnes was viciously murdered. The British Army was vastly outnumbered and its base surrounded. A truce was agreed and the Afghans made it clear that they wanted the British to leave. And that's what might have happened, had the son of the ousted leader Dost Mohammed not arrived in

Kabul and, reportedly, murdered Sir William McNaghten.

The British and Indians—more than 16,000 of them—began their withdrawal in January 1842, intending to march the 90 miles to Jalalabad. They didn't have much choice: to have stayed in Kabul would have been to have signed their own death warrants. Afghan winters can be harsh, especially in the north where temperatures can drop to –10 or below, and many died from exposure to the biting weather in the first few days of the withdrawal. And when the British reached a mountain pass called the Khurd Kabul, they came under attack.

What was at best an ignominious retreat became a disastrous, bloody massacre. The Afghans knew the territory and they had hate on their side. The British—men, women and children—were massacred in one of the bloodiest scenes that part of the world has ever known. Many were cut down by the Afghans; others continued to perish in the harsh mountain snows. One man, a British Army surgeon by the name of Dr William Brydon, escaped the carnage and successfully reached the British garrison at Jalalabad. He explained what had happened. Fires were lit and bugles sounded in order to guide any survivors to safety.

None came. After a few days it became clear that of the 16,500 who had left Kabul,

Dr William Brydon was the only survivor.

The First Anglo-Afghan War had been a grisly disaster for the British and that one episode revealed Afghanistan to the British for what it was: a country of great strategic importance, filled with a brutal, inhospitable terrain and inhabited by a fiercely proud, warrior-like people.

A place where invading armies were likely to come a cropper.

*   *   *

There were plenty of reasons for the British Army *not* to let me take a documentary team to Afghanistan: reasons of safety, tactical reasons, PR reasons. When we first approached the Ministry of Defence (MoD), half of me expected them to reject our suggestion out of hand. They didn't. Quite rightly, however, they wanted to vet us, to make sure that our reasons for taking a camera crew into a war zone were the right ones. The last thing they wanted was a journalist with an agenda who would turn them over and misrepresent them; and nobody wanted a team out there with the wrong attitude who would endanger their own lives and those of the soldiers.

So it was that I found myself travelling to Warminster in Wiltshire with my co-executive producer Clive Tulloh to visit Brigadier John

Lorimer, formerly of the Parachute Regiment and who at the time was in charge of 12 (Mechanised) Brigade, one of the army's seven deployable brigades, of which the First Battalion the Royal Anglian Regiment—also known as the Vikings—is a part. If my plan to travel to Afghanistan were to go anywhere, we would need the thumbs-up from the Brigadier. As it happened, he and Clive had been at school together (it's not *what* you know!), so we got off on the right foot and Lorimer seemed to understand and approve of our reasons and motives. It seemed a bit strange that the old-boy network should help grease the wheels for this Essex boy to head off to Afghanistan, but it did. And with that first hurdle passed, the Brigadier gave his blessing for us to meet the Anglians' Commanding Officer, Lieutenant Colonel Stuart Carver.

We travelled to Elizabeth Barracks in Pirbright, Surrey, for the meeting. This is where the Anglians are based. Pirbright is a strange place, a massive training depot for new recruits nestled in the relatively quaint environs of Surrey, not far from London. It's an unlovely place, desolate when the soldiers are away, and the Anglians' families live here, cheek by jowl with the unglamorous army training facilities. It's drab and utilitarian—especially the living quarters—but then I guess it's not supposed to be a holiday camp.

Stuart Carver seemed a bit distant at first, a

11

bit hard to know, but once we'd slipped outside for a crafty cigarette, the ice was broken and I found him witty and intelligent in a deadpan way. He appeared to understand where we were coming from as I explained that we didn't want to make a political film, or a training manual for the Taliban. We wanted to see what life was like for the soldiers, plain and simple. I bigged up my family connection with the regiment, explaining that I was from the area from which the Anglians recruit. Stuart took all this on board before telling us that the success or failure of our venture relied on one thing: whether the RSM—the Regimental Sergeant Major—said it was OK.

Images of the stereotypical RSM flashed through my mind—I was half expecting to be presented with Windsor Davies from *It Ain't Half Hot Mum*. I couldn't have been more wrong. The RSM, Ian 'Robbo' Robertson, was a quietly spoken, no-nonsense individual whose first concern was for the safety and wellbeing of his men. He explained to me that his major concern was not that we would compromise the safety of his troops on the ground. Instead, he worried that if we concentrated on *his* men, would that engender jealousy in other parts of the army? Would the attention put his boys off their job and consequently cause lives to be lost? It was something I hadn't even considered, but as he voiced his concern I realized he was absolutely right to be thinking in that way. It was an eye-opener for me, and perhaps the first time I realized that the army's duty towards its soldiers does not stop at making sure they have the right tools to do their job; they also need to make sure that they are psychologically prepared to perform the dangerous work that they carry out. It is the RSM's role to maintain standards and discipline in the regiment, but also to ensure the troops' welfare. He's a first among equals, the best soldier in the regiment. Within minutes of meeting Robbo it was clear that he was amply cut out for the job.

We went well and let the Anglians' command structure think about it. A few days later word came back. We could attach ourselves to B Company under the command of Major Mick Aston. They were being deployed to Helmand Province, the lawless region of Afghanistan where the Taliban insurgency was at its strongest, the enemy at its most fanatical and persistent. Why B Company? Because, like everything else in the army, you get what you're given. And we were being given everything we had asked for. We could film B Company at work. We could film B Company at play. And, most importantly, we could follow B Company into battle.

*   *   *

In the Afghan National Army, when you have finished your training, you're put in an aircraft hangar so that the authorities can inform the new recruits whereabouts in the country they are to be deployed. The soldiers headed for Kabul are led out of the hangar; the soldiers headed for Kandahar Province are led out of the hangar; and so it continues, until only one final group of recruits is left. The hangar doors are shut and the bad news is broken: these are the ones that are going to Helmand Province.

When the thumbs-up came through for our venture, the truth finally hit home. I started to live with a creeping sense of unease. We really were going to that dangerous, lawless war zone. One of the most inhospitable places on earth. A place many people return from in a box.

It was a situation of my own making, of course, but all of a sudden I felt as if the hangar doors had been shut on me too.

2. 'SAS, MY ARSE'

Up until this point it had just been an idea.

I wasn't in any way blasé about going to Afghanistan, but now what had seemed like a wild, exciting plan had turned into a stark reality. It was like joining up, and I don't feel at all shy about admitting that I felt cold fear at what I had let myself in for. Half of me wanted to run away from the whole thing, to hide and pretend I'd never even suggested it. But after all the strings we had pulled and all the meetings we'd had, after Stuart Carver and Ian Robertson had taken the brave decision to let us accompany them on their six-month tour, there was no way we could back out. And my pride wouldn't have let me do that anyway.

Looking back, I think my reaction was a natural one. A normal one. Probably not much different to the feeling any soldier gets when they learn they are about to be deployed. There's a sense of excitement, certainly, but if anyone tells you they're not scared before going somewhere as dangerous as Helmand Province, either they've got a synapse missing or they're lying.

The only thing you can do is make sure you're well prepared for the challenges to come. So it was that eight weeks before the Anglians were to be deployed, we found ourselves heading to the Army Training Estate on Salisbury Plain. Our motives were twofold. We wanted to get to know some of the soldiers and officers we were to spend time with out in Helmand Province; and we wanted to take part in their training. After all, the intention had never been for us to observe events from the sidelines. We were going to be in the thick of it, on ops side by side with the infantrymen as they engaged their fanatical Taliban enemy. It was essential that we knew how to stay safe—and to defend ourselves if necessary.

The army have not always had a happy relationship with the media, so perhaps it wasn't surprising that when we turned up for training exercises on Salisbury Plain we sensed a feeling of edginess, a feeling that we weren't entirely trusted by the regular soldiers, or indeed by the officers. This didn't stop the guys opening up to us, however, and it was clear from the off that morale was high, and that while the Royal Anglians were in no doubt about the gravity of the situation they would face in Helmand Province, they had confidence in the fact that they would be well prepared for whatever the Taliban could throw at them. Company Sergeant Major Tim Newton—a man who would become a good friend of mine—spoke in no uncertain terms about the attitude he felt was prevalent among B Company.

'They're going to do a job they've been

trained to do. And we've been training long enough for it now; they're excited at the prospect of going.'

Tim was right: this was no example of a senior NCO being out of touch with the real feelings of the men, though it should be added that the guys did not have a gung-ho attitude. When I spoke to nineteen-year-old Private Dan Smith and twenty-one-year-old Corporal Aaron Coolidge, they qualified their enthusiasm with an admission that this was going to be no tea party. 'I don't think we're going to know quite how we feel till we get out there and start taking the flak . . . You're going to have rounds landing beside you, you're going to be, oh, crap, you know, fucking move out the way, keep moving, keep moving . . .' Their expectations didn't do much for my own nervousness at the prospect of what we had taken on.

Any military commander will tell you that the morale of the troops is a decisive factor in the success of any campaign. Lose morale and you lose the fight. Major Mick Aston clearly understood that as he briefed B Company in a chilly barn in the middle of Salisbury Plain. The mood was serious, but not sombre; the guys listened quietly and attentively as Mick told them what they could expect in a few weeks' time. Having already been out to Afghanistan, he didn't pull any punches about the enemy they would be facing. He explained

17

that in parts of Helmand Province there were places where troops could literally point to the location of the Taliban: that was how close the lines of engagement were. But if he was realistic about the nature of the threat, he was equally uncompromising in his assessment of the British Army's abilities.

'We hear a lot,' he announced, 'about what good fighters the Taliban are, how strong they are, that they've been fighting for hundreds and hundreds of years and they're going to kick our arse and all that sort of stuff. Well, I don't fucking believe that for one minute. Although they are quite motivated, let's not be under any illusions: we're pretty fucking motivated as well.'

Nicely put, Mick. Not exactly *Henry V*, but you could just sense the guys agreeing with what their OC was telling them.

Motivation is essential; but training is even more important if the soldiers' standard operating procedures are going to become second nature. It's nearly impossible, of course, to replicate the sort of environment they could expect on deployment, but Salisbury Plain is about as far removed from the hot, arid deserts of Afghanistan as it's possible to be. It was freezing cold, and there was snow on the ground and a biting wind that seemed to cut through to the bone. It was wretched and miserable, but one thing's for sure: it toughens you up.

18

For me and the crew the training sessions were indispensable. Basic skills such as alighting from a helicopter, carrying our kit and—crucially—hitting the ground at a moment's notice would be important when we got to the front line. One of my greatest worries about going to Afghanistan was that the team and I would get in someone's way and in so doing endanger our lives or theirs. It was crucial, therefore, that we spent some time accompanying the guys during their mock battle situations.

On Salisbury Plain there is a replica village. It was built during the Cold War, when the threats to national security were very different and the army would be called upon to fight in very different situations. Designed to look like a small Eastern European village, it bears no resemblance to the compounds B Company could be expected to storm in Helmand Province; nevertheless, it gave them the critically important opportunity to practise a key task in Afghanistan: FIBUA, or Fighting In a Built-Up Area. Or, as the soldiers have nicknamed it, FISH: Fighting In Somebody's House.

There are plenty of other differences between fighting on Salisbury Plain and fighting in Helmand Province. The most obvious, of course, is that in Wiltshire you don't have anyone shooting AK-47s or RPGs at you. In order to make the training more realistic, the army have developed a system called Tesex—Tactical Effects Simulation Exercise. It's like a complicated version of paintball. The soldiers wear a special vest and helmet that sense infrared light; the weapons they carry fire a laser. If you get shot, your equipment registers the hit. They can also drop artillery shells and mortar rounds that will take out a whole area and light the soldiers fighting in it. Anyone who gets lit has to stop fighting, because in a real-life combat situation, it would mean they are at best wounded, more likely dead. You can carry on fighting when the game is reset, but it's not lost on anyone taking part in the training exercises that when it comes to the real thing, a well-placed sniper shot means game over. There's no one there to press the restart button. Dying a few times on Salisbury Plain is a pretty sobering experience.

Even more sobering are the amputees who are brought in to add authenticity to the battlefield and to desensitize the soldiers to the horrors that they can expect to encounter. These amputees are people who have lost limbs, often in combat situations. They are convincingly made up with fake blood and gore, so that they genuinely appear to have been gravely wounded. They scream not like actors but with the howling desperation that only a man who has lost a limb and truly feared for his life can know. This is role play taken to its most extreme, an attempt to accustom the troops to the grim reality of warfare, as well as teach them how to perform triage—the process of categorizing the injured according to the severity of their wounds. It's a brutal process, but crucial. When a soldier is down, they would be given a triage category. T1: on the verge of death; T2 wounded; T3 walking wounded; T4 dead. Everyone was fully aware that the likelihood of B Company taking casualties was high, and that T4s were not only a possibility but a probability. As for the amputees, the statistics spoke for themselves. Between April 2006 and September 2007, sixteen soldiers lost limbs in Helmand Province. What these soldiers were seeing on Salisbury Plain was very close to what they could expect in Afghanistan.

B Company consists of three platoons: 5, 6 and 7. During the FIBUA exercise, I was attached to 7 Platoon under the command of Lieutenant George Seal-Coon. The platoon is known as 'Lucky 7' and George was to have more than his fair share of luck when we finally made it to Afghanistan. The camera team and I were given our orders: tag along behind the assault section. Mindful of our desire not to get in the way, we were happy to obey.

The purpose of the training exercise was to clear the enemy from the village. In order to make it more realistic, the soldiers were instructed to ignore the first floor of the houses, as all the buildings they were likely to storm in Helmand Province would be single storey. They needed to concentrate on room clearance and methods of entry, all the while ensuring that their actions were appropriate and in accordance with the British Army's rules of engagement.

The rules of engagement, laid down in a document called Guidance Card Alpha, are, in the words of the MoD, 'directives issued by a competent military authority which delineate the circumstances and limitations under which UK forces will initiate and/or continue combat engagement with other forces encountered'. To you and me, that means how, when, where and against whom military force can be used. The rules of engagement can change according to the nature of the conflict—indeed they did change during the time I was in Afghanistan in 2007—but the first rule of engagement for the British armed forces is always this: a soldier has the right to use force in self-defence. The rules are important: make them too loose and a conflict can escalate. But make them too tight and they restrict the soldiers' ability to perform their role effectively. And as I would find out, the Taliban often used these rules of engagement to their own advantage.

One of the lads involved in the training exercise on Salisbury Plain was Private Josh

Hill. He had joined the army at the age of sixteen because it was a steady job that would give him the opportunity to see the world. As a kid he had always enjoyed running through the woods with a stick as a gun, so he decided he might as well sign up for the real thing. I couldn't help but wonder how much different his experiences in Afghanistan would be from those childhood games. Josh was a friendly young man with a face that made him look even younger than he actually was. Now that he had reached eighteen—an age when some lads are still at school—he was officially allowed to take a combat role. To my eyes, he looked too young to be facing the Taliban—in fact, he looked too young to be watching a scary episode of *Doctor Who*—but there was no way he was to be treated any differently from the other soldiers preparing to go to war. Not that he would have wanted to be. It was made perfectly clear to me what the regiment's attitude towards young men like Josh was: he had joined the army now, to kill if need be. He wasn't Mummy's little boy any more and even if some people didn't think of him as a grown man yet, that would soon change within a couple of months of being out in Helmand Province.

The training exercise was noisy and chaotic. The soldiers' SA80s, as well as firing lasers, were shooting blanks. Men were screaming orders which, more often than not, became confused as they were passed from man to man down the chain of command; enemy combatants dressed in *dishdash*—the Afghan robes we could expect the Taliban as well as regular Afghan villagers to be wearing—were shouting at each other. Smoke was rising from the ground and a sense of urgency filled the air. If the intention was to recreate the confusion of a battle situation, it seemed to me at the time that they were doing a very good job; in fact, I would soon learn that the real thing is several degrees more intense.

I watched from the sidelines as young Josh Hill clambered out of the ground-floor window of one house with a ladder and crossed a few metres of rubble to the window of a second enemy house. It was a painfully slow process: he struggled with the ladder, dropped it and tripped; as he leaned the ladder against the window of the house he was trying to enter, one of his mates climbed it and stepped on his fingers; he then spent far too long attempting to climb it himself. If he'd been under genuine fire at the time, the results of this clumsy attempt at FIBUA could have been disastrous. If this was the dress rehearsal before the opening night, I think anybody there would have been hard pressed to say it went without a hitch.

The camera team and I would not be carrying weapons in Afghanistan. However, as British citizens, we had the right to defend

24

ourselves should we be the last men standing. Colonel Carver made it a condition that we were familiar with all weapons systems used by the British Army before we left for Afghanistan. For that reason, it was essential that we should be proficient with the SA80 A2, the standard rifle of the British Army. Corporal Stuart Parker gave us the low-down. The SA80 A2 is well liked by the troops, unlike its predecessor, the A1. SA80 stands for Small Arms for the 1980s, but in fact the weapon is based on a design from the 1940s, developed as a result of the army's experience of combat in the Second World War. The A1 was unreliable and much maligned during the First Gulf War; in 2000 it was overhauled by Heckler and Koch. This was the military equivalent of having your Mondeo looked at by BMW. The resulting A2 is far more reliable and able to mount a 40mm grenade launcher. The SA80 has been used in all the conflicts in which the British Army have been involved since the mid-1980s: Northern Ireland, the two Gulf Wars, Bosnia, Sierra Leone and now, of course, Afghanistan.

Before I even fired the weapon, Stuart Parker gave me a quick tour of its capabilities. For close-quarters battle, he explained, a bayonet was fitted on to the end. These bayonets have been carefully designed to be thrust into the body and to give what Stuart described, in a delightfully military term, as 'rib-parting capability'. One edge is kept permanently blunt to help it split bone and a long indentation along its length—the 'blood drain'—is there to allow the air to get in and prevent a suction effect.

Stuart then took me to the firing range, where I was to see just how well I could handle the weapon. It was difficult at first to hit the mark, as the rifle I had been given had not been zeroed to my eye, but that only made the exercise more authentic because if I were to pick up an SA80 on the battlefield, that wouldn't be set up for me either. I'd had some experience with guns on the range before but this was different because it involved running, kneeling and then shooting. It's one thing taking time to aim at your target; it's quite another going from moving to being very still, and my first few shots went wide of the mark. I began to get the hang of it, however; I even started to enjoy it—even though I knew I was going to have to put up with a bit of ribbing from the lads if I failed to make the grade. The fact that I had portrayed an SAS soldier on screen made it too irresistible for them not to take the mick. In the end I passed the exercise, though hardly with special forces-like accuracy. 'SAS, my arse,' commented the guy reading out the scores. Everyone laughed. At me or with me? I wasn't sure, but I knew I had to take their teasing in good heart if they were ever going to accept me into their confidence.

I was pleased that I had done reasonably well, but I also knew it would be a different kettle of fish if someone was actually firing back at you. If that's the case you often need more than a rifle and the SA80 is just one part of the infantry's arsenal. Over the days that followed I was introduced to a whole range of weaponry that would be used in the fight against the Taliban in Helmand Province. The .50 calibre machine gun—or fifty-cal—would be one of the infantry's most valued weapons. It's not new—the same weapon was used during the Second World War, as well as in Korea and Vietnam. I was soon to learn, though, that along with the GPMG—the General Purpose Machine Gun—it's the most effective weapon in Afghanistan. The fifty-cal is too heavy to carry, so it's generally mounted on a tripod and fixed to the top of a vehicle or on top of a building and it's often used by Fire Support Groups—teams that deliver artillery fire from separate locations to help infantry on the ground—from tactically superior situations. From these locations it fires its destructive rounds at a ferocious rate. The Taliban don't like it. When they see fifty-cal rounds, they run like hell.

The 81mm mortar is another powerful weapon. It fires shells at low velocities and high-arced trajectories. The rounds can be fired so high in the air that they can hit aircraft—a problem if you have air support,

27

but the teams that run these weapons are incredibly efficient and good at their jobs, and mortar fire is an essential part of the infantry's weaponry.

The grenade machine gun fires 40mm grenades at a rate of 340 per minute. It's accurate and deadly. Not as destructive, though, as the Javelin anti-tank missile. A single shot from this machine costs approximately £60,000, but you get a lot for your money. It's a fire-and-forget missile that comes with a reusable Command Launch Unit, or CLU. The operator can look through the CLU and lock on to a target. Then, even if the target moves, the missile will follow it. It's an amazing weapon to watch. The missile is ejected relatively slowly from the launcher. It appears to hover for a few seconds while, like a dog after a bone, it sniffs out its target. Then it powers up and when it hits its mark, its destructive capabilities are astonishing. Of course, a weapon like this isn't much good in close contact, but for long-range, moving targets it can be invaluable. And although it's called an anti-tank missile and is not designed to take out infantry, I've seen it used in that way. In fact, I've seen it used to take out one person. Sixty grand to kill a single Taliban— it's no wonder war is an expensive business. One of the company told me he wanted to be a Javelin millionaire by the time his tour was over. I don't know if he managed it, but he probably wasn't far off.

The need for the troops to train properly with these weapons was brought home to me pretty sharply that first day. I was standing by the Javelin during the training session, wind blowing through me and snow on the ground. I watched as the weapon was fired. Instead of reaching its target, it fizzed and dropped about 30 metres away from us like a firework that had failed to explode—a very big firework with the capability of taking out half a football pitch when it went bang.

I stared at it in horror for a few seconds, then turned to the range master. 'What do we do?' I screamed at him over the howling wind. 'Run?'

'It's a bit fucking late for that now!' he roared at me.

I started backing off, edging away from the weapon that was sizzling on the ground in front of me. If it had gone off, there was no way I'd have made it to Afghanistan. In fact, there was no way I'd have made it off Salisbury Plain. Thankfully, the technology of the weaponry is such that the missiles don't arm themselves until they've travelled about 100 metres in case such things happen. It brought home to me, though, what a dangerous environment soldiers work in even when they're not on the front line.

Some bits of our training went better than others. During a mock contact, the platoon to which the camera team and I had been assigned found themselves stuck in the crossfire between the rest of B Company and the 'enemy'. If live rounds were being fired, we'd have been dead. Subsequent to that, during the night exercises, similar mistakes were made; the platoon seemed to be confused, not knowing what to do as orders were shouted and rounds cracked overhead. It was a quiet group of soldiers that received a no-holds-barred bollocking from Sergeant Ben Browning. The lads assembled under canvas. They did their best to hold their heads high, but they couldn't hide their sheepishness and disappointment in themselves as they sat around with the embarrassed grimaces of pupils being told off by their teacher. This was no schoolmasterly ticking off: it was a robust reminder that this was more than just a game of soldiers. 'It just wasn't fucking acceptable tonight. Just because you don't know what's going on, it's no excuse to stand around walking up and down the line. Who sent the schmooly out?'

There are two kinds of schmooly—a type of flare—both of them generally sent up by mortars. One of them lights up the sky, the other sends out an infrared light. If you're wearing infrared goggles it means your enemy is displayed without being able to take advantage of the light. But it's essential that the schmooly lands in the right place, as

30

otherwise the advantage is given to the enemy—and that's just what had happened that night.

A sheepish private raised his hand when Sergeant Browning asked the question. 'Fucking hell, buddy,' Browning told him, his voice at once comradely and chiding, 'it's got to go over their side. All you done was fucking light us up.'

Nobody was under any illusion that if these battle situations had been replicated in Helmand Province, there would have been casualties. As for the camera team and me, we could only hope that the training we had received on Salisbury Plain would be enough to keep us safe if and when we finally came under enemy fire.

3. THE ROAD TO KANDAHAR

They say that when somebody goes away, it's always more difficult for the people left behind. It seemed to me that this might be especially true in the army. Many of these men had wives and children; those who didn't had parents. All were to be subjected to the agony of waiting for their boys to be sent to one of the most dangerous places in the world. I wanted to know how they would cope with this; while the lads were in Afghanistan fighting the Taliban, I wondered how they would deal with the uncertainty and the fear.

Josh Hill, the eighteen-year-old private who'd had difficulty with the ladder during the FIBUA training, had a markedly resolute attitude to the prospect of the tour. When I asked him how he felt about the fact that he might be called upon to kill someone, he answered without hesitation. 'At the end of the day it's either I get shot, or my muckers get shot, or the enemy gets shot. I'd rather kill them than they kill me or my muckers, so it'll have to be done.'

Fair enough. But speaking to his parents Lesley and Graham a few weeks before the Anglians departed, I got a different perspective. They sat together on their sofa in the comfortable front room of their house, clearly bristling with pride at what their young man was about to achieve—and rightly so. There were other emotions than pride, however. Josh had just told them that their departure had been brought forward a day. 'You look at his face,' Lesley told me quietly. 'You see worry on his face and then he's gone, because he doesn't want to talk about it.'

They were full of parental anxiety but, as Graham explained, they didn't want to show Josh how worried they were. Their son was looking forward to the thrill, the excitement of doing what he had trained to do, and I sensed that they did not want to stamp on that excitement by making their own worries too obvious. But worried they were. Desperately. I could only imagine how difficult it must be, spending your life ensuring the safety of your child and then standing helpless as they are sent to perhaps the least safe place in the world. I admired them for dealing with it so calmly, albeit only on the surface.

Many of the Anglians had been soldiers for a lot longer than Josh Hill and not all of them had yet come in contact with the enemy. Sergeant Keith Nieves had been waiting thirteen years for this moment and he was looking forward to it. 'It puts a glint in your eye,' he told me. 'You know the cliché: we're trained to do it. It's like a dream come true for me . . . hopefully I'll get the chance to actually do my job and fight an enemy.'

Keith didn't know it yet, but his first experience of enemy contact was going to take a toll. He was clearly looking forward to getting out to Helmand, which is more than could be said for his wife, Angie, who would be left at home with their two sons, four-year-old Harry and two-year-old Peter. Angie became tearful when Keith described his preferred method of leaving for a tour of duty: early in the morning while everyone was still in bed. That way all the goodbyes could be done the night before and he could just give his family a farewell kiss while they were still sleeping. 'That's the easiest way,' he told me. I wasn't quite sure that Angie agreed.

I wondered how she dealt with the sudden absence of her husband. 'That's the hardest bit,' she wept, 'when Keith goes. There's lots of tears for the first couple of weeks and then you just let the weeks go past until they come home. That's all you can do.'

Angie apologized for crying, but really she had nothing to apologize for. As she stood there in the kitchen of their army accommodation, I was struck by how different her life was going to be to her husband's while he was away. It made me painfully aware that it's not only the fighting soldiers who are affected by this war. Girlfriends and wives like Angie wouldn't be facing the enemy on the front line, but they would have their own battles to fight, bringing up children by themselves, not knowing whether a grim-faced representative of the MoD would be knocking on their door the next day to give them the news that every armed forces family dreads hearing.

Away from home, the lads lack many of the comforts that the average civilian takes for granted: hot food, a table to sit at, porcelain toilets. They are allowed to take a comfort box—a stash of personal items intended to make their lives out there a bit more bearable. Obviously, when they were on operations at the outstations they would only be able to take the bare necessities with them; but at Camp Bastion, the main British base in Afghanistan, where there would be a bit more room, simple comforts such as quilts, footballs and rugby balls might put a smile on their faces and make all the difference to them. Keith Nieves supervised the packing of some of these comfort boxes as I looked on. He performed this task with a quiet sensitivity—he knew how much some of these items meant to the troops.

If only the same could have been said for me. When I saw one of the lads packing a small cuddly toy, I started jeering. 'Who's taking a teddy bear?'

The lad looked a bit crestfallen. 'It's mine,' he said.

'What, are you going to want cuddles from your teddy?'

He shook his head. 'No,' he replied. 'My

girlfriend gave it to me when our child died.'

I felt about two inches tall, clumsy and foolish. Not for the first time I wondered what right I had to be holding a spotlight up to these people's lives; and it was a reminder that the infantry troops I was to be spending time with were not just fighting machines. They were ordinary people, with ordinary concerns and ordinary lives. They just happened to be doing an extraordinary job.

On 5 April 2007, the First Battalion the Royal Anglian Regiment left Pirbright Barracks for their six-month tour of Afghanistan. Many of them left wives and children behind them. None of them really knew what would be waiting for them. Some of the soldiers would come back wounded, their lives irreparably changed.

In a sad kind of way they would be among the lucky ones, because others would never return.

*   *   *

Britain's disastrous retreat from Kabul, which ended the First Anglo-Afghan War, did not make Afghanistan any less tactically important. And though it took a while for the British to lick their wounds, it wasn't long before they started trying to exert their influence once more in that country, which had become a buffer between the British and

Russian Empires.

Dost Mohammed, the Afghan leader whom the British had toppled, regained power in 1843. A decade later, realizing the need to have some kind of influence in the area, the British resumed relations with him and in 1855 signed the Treaty of Peshawar, which pledged that Britain and Afghanistan were friends of each other's friends, and enemies of each other's enemies. It even permitted the British to establish a military presence in Kandahar, the main city of the province adjoining Helmand, from which to wage their conflict with the Persians to the west. This promising political situation deteriorated over the next twenty years.

On 22 July 1878, an uninvited Russian diplomatic mission arrived in Kabul. The British demanded that the current leader, Sher Ali, receive a British mission too, but he declined. Not only that: he would hinder such a mission by force if it were despatched. In September, the Viceroy of India, Lord Lytton, ignored this warning and sent a diplomatic delegation to Kabul. They were turned back at the eastern entrance to the Khyber Pass. This diplomatic rebuke sparked what would become the Second Anglo-Afghan War.

The British deployed 40,000 troops and proceeded to occupy huge swathes of the country. In order to prevent the full occupation of Afghanistan by the British, the new leader, Mohammad Yaqub Khan, signed the Treaty of Gandamak. This treaty ceded control of Afghan foreign affairs to the British, who withdrew their army, having installed representatives in Kabul.

Perhaps the British had forgotten what a treacherous place Afghanistan could be for those not welcomed by its people. On 3 September 1879, the British representative in Kabul, Sir Pierre Cavagnari, was murdered along with his guards and staff as a result of an uprising. It was suspected that the Afghan leader, Yaqub Khan, was complicit in the assassination. Khan was forced by the British to abdicate in the aftermath of this bloody event. The British considered placing his brother, Ayub Khan, on the throne, but instead opted for his cousin, Abdur Rahman Khan. As a result, Ayub Khan started a rebellion and in July 1880 he clashed with British forces at the Battle of Maiwand.

Maiwand saw 25,000 Afghan warriors fight against a combined force of 2,500 British and Indian troops. Nearly 1,000 of these British troops were killed and although the Afghans lost almost 3,000 of their men in some particularly vicious fighting, the battle represented a decisive victory for them.

Ayub Khan was later defeated in the Battle of Kandahar and it is generally accepted that the Second Anglo-Afghan War eventually resulted in a victory for the British. But not before they had sustained unacceptably heavy casualties and a bloody nose. They withdrew from Afghanistan once more, the determined, warlike nature of its inhabitants having been displayed to them yet again.

*　　*　　*

Six weeks after the Royal Anglians left for Helmand Province I prepared to join them. The night before my departure my documentary series *Gangs* was awarded a BAFTA. The award did not go uncelebrated so, truth to tell, I could have arrived at RAF Brize Norton in better shape. Maybe that wasn't such a bad thing. A fuzzy head isn't the worst accompaniment to your first trip to a war zone. It helps keep your mind off the reality of what you're doing. In the few short weeks they had been away, the Royal Anglian Regiment had already lost two men. A tragedy for their families and colleagues; a bitter reminder for us that this was going to be a long way from the world of awards ceremonies and parties.

Checking in at Brize Norton is not quite like checking in at Gatwick. There's something a bit unusual about the soldier behind the check-in desk asking you in one breath whether you've got any sharps on your person and in the next if you have your body armour and helmet with you. We were to fly to Kandahar

39

Airport before transferring to Camp Bastion. Kandahar Airport was constructed by the Americans between 1956 and 1962. Ostensibly it was built as a refuelling station for aircraft travelling between the Middle East and South-East Asia; the fact that it was designed along the lines of a military base, however, suggests a bit of forward planning on behalf of the Americans in the case of a military confrontation between the US and the USSR. During the Soviet occupation it served a military function and it is now maintained by ISAF—the International Security Assistance Force, part of the United Nations. It's the second biggest airbase in Afghanistan and home to more than 12,000 personnel. It functioned as a staging post for the 7,000 British troops serving out there at the time.

Our transport was one of the TriStar aircraft that ferry troops to and from Afghanistan. Some of them are suitable for carrying personnel only; others can also carry equipment; there aren't enough of them and they are all a good deal older than most of the men they fly to war. They are regularly delayed because of mechanical failure—on one of my trips we had to wait an extra twelve hours because our plane had suffered an oil leak on to the brakes. The RAF do an amazing job with the materials they have, but the honest truth is that these five TriStars are not suitable for what's being asked of them. I met a high-ranking officer whose role was to coordinate the movement of troops to and from the war zone. He told me that he would much prefer it if the men on the ground were not given their two weeks' rest and recuperation leave in the middle of their tour because it puts such a strain on his limited resources and screws up his schedule for getting essential supplies and ammunition out on to the ground. Try telling that to a squaddie who hasn't seen his wife and child in three months; but it didn't seem right to me that the RAF and the army shouldn't have the capability to perform their job efficiently. Nor would it be the first time that I was struck at how stretched we are as a land army.

The flight time from Brize Norton to Kandahar is seven hours—a long haul when you're going on holiday, but it's amazing how the time flies when you're en route to a war zone, and it's impossible to forget that's what you're doing. Along one side of the aircraft were a number of beds. There are no first-class bunks on a military transport, however: these are for wounded soldiers being repatriated back to the UK. It's hard, on that solemn flight out, not to wonder whether you might be making use of one of these beds on the way back home. To take my mind off thoughts such as these, I joined the pilot in the cockpit. We had been told to ensure that we had our body armour and helmets with us in the cabin and I

41

wanted to know what the dangers of landing at Kandahar actually were.

Our pilot had the composed, reassuring intonation pilots seem to have the world over. I asked him—a bit nervously, I suppose— whether there had been incidences of his aircraft receiving enemy fire as it came into land in Kandahar. He shook his head. So far there had been no firing on the aircraft while it had actually been airborne. The most dangerous time, he said, was when the plane was on the ground. He'd had experiences both in Afghanistan and in Iraq when the aircraft had come under fire from rockets and mortars while troops were alighting and the aircraft was being refuelled.

And I thought getting off an EasyJet flight was a scramble.

The mood on the plane was sombre. The troops I was travelling with caught up on their sleep, listened to music or read their books. I tried to calm myself. There was a stillness in the atmosphere. A seriousness. I looked out of the aircraft window to watch the arrival of the magnificent, snow-capped peaks below us. From this height you could only be awestruck by such a sight, by the amazing vision of these mountains which have stood sentry over the turmoil with which this part of the world has become almost synonymous. Unaware of the history that has led so many of our young men and women to make the same journey I was now making. Had all those soldiers felt the same sense of unquiet apprehension as they looked out over those snowy peaks? I think they probably had. It was some comfort, I thought to myself as evening started to fall and Kandahar grew inexorably nearer. Some comfort, but not much.

*   *   *

Historically, the British were not the only nation to sustain heavy losses as a result of their interest in Afghanistan. They handed back control of Afghan foreign affairs in 1919 as a result of the Third Anglo-Afghan War. For the next sixty years, Afghan politics were a picture of internal turmoil. In 1978 the Democratic Republic of Afghanistan was formed. The new government—the PDPA—assassinated the deposed leader and was communist in its outlook. It discouraged men from wearing beards and women from wearing the burqa; and it was allied to the communist Soviet regime.

These new policies were popular with some and unpopular with others. In the cities the new liberalism was welcomed, but conservative Afghans, who objected in particular to the eroding of traditional Islamic restrictions on the rights of women, formed anti-government groups. Some of these, who came to be known as the Mujahideen—a word meaning 'those

43

who fight in a jihad, or holy war'—started a guerrilla insurgency against the new regime.

The Afghan government was unable to control the violent Mujahideen rebellion. And so, on Christmas Eve 1979, the Russian tanks rolled in. The Soviet occupation of Afghanistan had begun. Happy effing Christmas. For nearly a decade, the Russians waged war on the Mujahideen. But in those days of the Cold War, the world of international politics was complicated and murky. The Americans were keen to see the Russians fail in Afghanistan and so they— along with the Pakistanis and the Saudi Arabians—started bankrolling the Mujahideen, helping them in their anti-Soviet crusade.

The Soviets were well armed and determined. They were soon to find out, however, that taking on the Afghan people on their own turf is not a straightforward operation. Huge swathes of the country remained out of the control of the government; and although the Soviets inflicted a great deal of damage on the insurgent fighters, it was well reciprocated. Backed by American arms and CIA intelligence, the Mujahideen were a fragmented but effective fighting force and the Soviets sustained heavy losses.

Afghanistan in the 1980s was a violent, dangerous place. As such, it attracted violent, dangerous people. And because of their pro-

Islamic, anti-Soviet stance, the Mujahideen attracted help not only from the Americans but from other foreigners. One of these allies was a devout young Sunni Muslim, a Saudi-born man from a family of immense wealth. He started an organization called Maktab al-Khidamat, which existed to channel funds to the Afghan Mujahideen, to help train them and to aid their fight against the Soviets. In 1988 this young Saudi man split from the organization he had founded in order to form a new group that he wanted to have a more military role: he wanted to expand his fight against the Soviets into a bigger, more worldwide Islamic fundamentalist struggle.

This new organization was called al-Qaida and the young man's name was Osama bin Laden. Afghanistan's hostilities were about to morph into a sequence of events that no one in the West could ever have predicted.

*   *   *

Night fell. The sound of the plane's engines changed and the nervous lurch of my stomach was compounded by the sensation of the aircraft starting to lose height. A voice came over the loudspeaker. 'Ladies and gentlemen, we are just beginning our descent into Kandahar. To comply with the current procedures for this operational theatre, you are required to don your body armour and

45

your helmet now. Those passengers seated next to a window must ensure that the blind is firmly closed. The cabin will remain in this blackout state until the aircraft is safely parked in a dispersal area.'

Along with everyone else in the cabin, I started to follow my instructions.

The body armour is like a heavy, sleeveless jacket. There is a pouch in the front that holds a thick, ceramic plate. This covers the area around your heart. Take a bullet there and you'll most surely know about it; but you might not die. The first time you don the body armour it feels impossibly heavy. It soon becomes like a second skin and you forget you're wearing it, but as I pulled it over my head on the approach to Kandahar before attaching my helmet, it felt alien. I strapped myself into my seat and waited for the lights to be switched off.

Darkness surrounded us.

The captain had told me that he had never been fired upon while coming into land and I kept that thought in my head to reassure myself. But I knew that there was a risk of small ground fire coming through the aircraft. If that happened, we were in for an unpleasant time. And if any large ground fire hit us, we'd drop from the sky like a stone.

It was the longest landing of my life, but when I felt the wheels hit the ground I didn't know whether to be relieved or more scared, because I knew what that sound meant. It meant that we had arrived in Afghanistan. And if there was no going back before, there was certainly no going back now.

4. CAMP BASTION

The exit lights flickered on. My eyes readjusted. The voice came over the loudspeaker once more. 'Please leave the window blinds closed and remain in your seat with your seatbelt fastened until the aircraft comes to a halt in a dispersal area.' The words were almost what you'd expect to hear at the end of a package flight to Spain. Almost, but not quite. They don't have 'dispersal areas' in Palma.

We left the plane and were loaded on to an old-fashioned bus. This happened quickly—they wanted us off the aircraft so that it could get moving again, away from its position on the ground, where it was vulnerable to attack. The lights of Kandahar Airport glowed in the night. It was some comfort to have my body armour and helmet on, but I was relieved to get out of the dispersal area and into a place of greater safety. Quite unexpectedly, as we were arriving, we bumped into a group of the lads from B Company who were on their way back to England for their much-needed—and much anticipated—two-week rest and recuperation. It was a shock to see just how much they had changed after only six weeks in Afghanistan— none more so than Josh Hill, the eighteen-year-old private. Josh looked as if he had grown five years older. His skin was tanned and he had the air of an adult; but it was his eyes that had changed most of all. They had some quality that I could not put my finger on, but there was no doubt that whatever he had experienced in Helmand Province had aged him.

The lads told me just what some of those experiences were, but not before they had given me some grave news about Sergeant Keith Nieves. Their platoon had been in contact with the enemy and needed to be extracted. A Royal Marine crew arrived in Viking personnel carriers. The Viking is an all-terrain, amphibious vehicle designed to be deployed in jungle, desert or arctic conditions. The lads told me what an amazing job the armoured Marines—who were performing gruelling tours of six months on and six months off because there was nobody else to drive the much-needed Vikings—did in Helmand Province, how vital they were to the infantry troops on the ground. 'We were all pinned down,' one of them explained, 'and the Vikings rocked up. The Marines started malleting them for us and then we all jumped in the Vikings and bugged out. You haven't seen a smile on a bloke's face till you hear the powering of these Vikings and the Marines coming through to you.'

The smiles didn't last long. Keith Nieves's Viking hit a landmine. The passenger door to the vehicle—Keith's only escape route—was dented and buckled by the force of the explosion and the interior was filled with flames. He tried to push the door open, but without success. He mustered the strength for one more push. The door inched open and he screamed for help.

Three soldiers ran to his rescue. They pulled him from the burning Viking. As he was tugged from the vehicle, the skin peeled away from his arms on account of the blistering heat inside. But that wasn't the worst of his injuries. He took two steps, and then fell to the ground. It transpired that, in addition to terrible burns on his hands and face, his heel had been shattered by the explosion. He was airlifted back to Camp Bastion, where the medics set to work on him straight away, removing the shrapnel and tending to his awful burns. The following day he was repatriated. His heel needed rebuilding with the aid of nine pins and a metal plate. One of the tendons in his elbow needed to be reattached. He later admitted that for a desolate moment he had resigned himself to the fact that he was going to die in that burning oven of a vehicle.

I thought of his wife Angie and the two children. I remembered how she had cried at the prospect of Keith going to Afghanistan. No doubt there would be a lot more tears in the future. Perhaps, in a weird kind of way, she would be pleased to have him back; and no doubt they would both realize how lucky Keith was not to have died in the landmine strike. But their lives would be very different from now on. Keith's eagerness to get out to Afghanistan and do the job for which he had been trained took on a very different hue now.

I wanted to know how the lads at Kandahar had reacted in a contact situation like this, not least because I knew it wouldn't be too long before I would be in their shoes. Josh Hill spoke his mind. 'I didn't even have to think. You don't get scared—well, I personally didn't get scared . . . I knew my job. I knew what I had to do.'

As I say, a big difference from the kid who had had trouble climbing a ladder back on Salisbury Plain. The others appeared to agree with him; indeed they went further. Their first contact, one told me, was 'the most exciting moment of any of our lives. On my section we sat there and we looked at each other and we giggled.'

I guess in somewhere as unwelcoming as Afghanistan, you take your laughs wherever you can get them.

These lads were on their way home, but just for two weeks. When the R and R was over, they'd be on a plane back to Kandahar and then on to Helmand Province. How did they think they would manage the transition, going from Disneyland back to hell? The answer surprised me.

51

'I'm going to find it much easier. I don't think it can get much worse than this—we've had casualties and losses, and we've been in some very serious contacts. I need to make sure I've left everything at home squared. I wish I'd not tried to be such a big man about coming out here. Now I can go back and have a nice teary one with my mum and say, "Let's get it all off our chest now." Then I can come out here and fight for the last four months, rather than always being worried about back home.'

Not for the first time, I was struck by the very adult sentiments coming from the lips of these young men. Some of them weren't even twenty years old and yet already they'd had friends injured, colleagues killed. They'd been involved in numerous contacts and each one of them had a look in their eyes to prove it. I'd been in Afghanistan for less than fifteen minutes, but already I'd heard stories that both scared me and made me proud of the way our boys were handling themselves.

B Company quite freely referred to this place as 'hell'. If that's what it was, then I was only at the gates. The following day, after a night at Kandahar air base, we were to be taken by Hercules transporter to Camp Bastion, the British Army base in the heart of Helmand Province. And it was there that our story would really begin.

The Soviets withdrew from Afghanistan in February 1989. As a result of their occupation, 14,500 Soviet soldiers had been killed. A substantial number, but nothing compared to the havoc wreaked on the Afghan population, of whom 1 million were killed and 5 million fled across the border to Pakistan.

Despite the fact that they had left, the Soviets continued to lend support to the government, while the Americans continued to bankroll the Mujahideen. With the collapse of the Soviet Union, however, the political landscape altered dramatically. The Afghan government fell and the Mujahideen entered Kabul to seize power. But now that their common enemy had disappeared, the differences among the various Mujahideen factions came bubbling to the surface. The civil war that had rocked Afghanistan for years continued.

The Province of Kandahar was home to one of these Mujahideen factions. They considered themselves to be religious scholars and their vision was to revert Afghanistan to a fundamentalist Islamic society. This group called itself the Taliban—a word meaning 'students' or 'seekers of truth'—and in the years that followed they were to take control of most of Afghanistan.

The Taliban's aim was to implement the

strictest interpretation of sharia law the Muslim world had ever known. With their rise to power, life for ordinary Afghan citizens became brutal and unrelenting. Many of the luxuries that you or I would take for granted were banned: one list of prohibited items included 'anything made from human hair, satellite dishes, equipment that makes music, pool tables, chess, masks, alcohol, tapes, computers, television, anything that propagates sex, wine, lobster, nail polish, firecrackers, statues, sewing catalogues . . .' The list goes on—you name it, the Taliban probably banned it. Men were obliged to have a beard longer than the length of their fist and anyone who broke this—or any of the many other rules—was hunted down by the Taliban's religious police and beaten with long sticks. Those convicted of stealing could expect punishments ranging from having one hand cut off to public execution; adulterers were stoned to death.

Men living under the Taliban regime had it bad; but women had it worse. They were expected to wear the burqa, of course, but that was just the start. Women were banned from having an education; and because they were also banned from working, many of the schools in the country were shut down because such a large number of the teachers were female. More abhorrently, they were banned from attending hospitals, with the exception of one all-women hospital in Kabul. For women under the Taliban, childbirth became a kind of medieval health risk. And any woman suspected of breaking the Taliban's laws risked at the very least being beaten in the street by the religious police.

The full extent of the atrocities that the Taliban carried out on the people of Afghanistan belongs to another book. Suffice to say that they were barbarous and extreme. Western governments refused to give the Taliban diplomatic recognition and it is perhaps to their shame that, aside from providing funds to a small resistance movement in northern Afghanistan, they did nothing more to stop the Taliban's treatment of its people.

But then, in 2001, the world changed. The September 11 attacks on the World Trade Center and the Pentagon by al-Qaida changed things for ever.

Osama bin Laden and al-Qaida had had an alliance with the Taliban ever since they came to power. There were even rumours that bin Laden had financed the Taliban; and shortly before the attack on the World Trade Center, an al-Qaida suicide bomber had assassinated one of the Taliban's most troublesome opponents. In return, the Taliban had allowed bin Laden to use Afghan territory to set up some of his notorious al-Qaida training camps. It was hardly surprising, then, that in the wake of the September 11 bombings, when bin Laden became the most wanted man in the world, it was in Afghanistan that he hid.

The United States issued an ultimatum to the Taliban. Deliver the leaders of al-Qaida, close their training camps and hand over any terrorists in those camps. The Taliban refused. And so, on 7 October 2001, a coalition of forces from America, Britain, Canada and other NATO countries started military action. The Taliban government fell. Their supporters were forced to retreat from Kabul and then Jalalabad; by the end of the year they had fled their last stronghold of Kandahar city.

The Taliban were dispersed and a new government installed. In 2004 Hamid Karzai, a former Mujahideen, became Afghanistan's first democratically elected president. Coalition forces stayed on in the country in a peace-keeping role. By this time the attention of the world was focused on a more controversial struggle: that of the ongoing war in Iraq.

But the deposed Taliban were not to be so easily defeated. Away from the big cities of Afghanistan and in the smaller, more traditional villages—especially in the south—they started to recruit from the local population and in some areas there was strong support for them. They were not, by any means, universally popular; but they were armed and determined, and as time passed, the threat that they posed to peace in

Afghanistan increased. The coalition forces started to prepare offensives to root out the Taliban insurgency and the battle between the two escalated sharply in 2006.

The British government's policy against the Taliban was determined and robust. They could not be allowed to regain power because if that happened Afghanistan would once more become an easy hiding place for al-Qaida and other terrorist groups. Thousands of British troops were maintained in that country where so many lives had been lost in military conflict over the past 200 years. They were concentrated in the area of southern Afghanistan where the Taliban was strongest, Helmand Province, and there they became engaged in what military commanders described as the most ferocious and relentless ground combat British soldiers had seen since the Korean War.

Rumours of the Taliban's brutality became widespread. It was said that when four French special forces soldiers were captured near the northern ISAF base of Kajaki, the insurgents made them beg for death. The men were hung by their feet, then emasculated. They were blinded, then flayed. Once their skin had been stripped off, they were rubbed in salt. Only then were they left to perish. An old wives' tale, or an accurate description of a vicious enemy? It's difficult to say. What is sure is that back home in England, Helmand Province became a byword for violence and danger. And for the troops posted there, it became the scene of a bloody conflict against an unflagging enemy who didn't fear death because they believed they were fighting a holy war.

*   *   *

At Kandahar air base I shared a room with our assistant director, John Conroy. I slept badly and woke early, and we headed off to eat. We had a good breakfast—typical American fare of eggs, sausages, waffles, brownies and juice. It was perfectly adequate—not the best food I'd ever eaten, but Shangri-La compared to what the troops can expect when they're away from the base. We were surrounded by soldiers from all sorts of countries—primarily Canada, but also guys from our allies in the Middle East. A real mixture of faces—including a relatively large number of women in uniform.

After breakfast we went to the PX—the Post Exchange, a kind of shopping mall that exists on American military installations. You can buy all sorts here. To start with it stocked virtually every kind of knife under the sun—ones to gouge someone's eyes out, ones to cut someone's bollocks off. John Conroy took a healthy interest in these knives, earning himself the nickname Rambo; I bought one too, so I guess this pot was calling the kettle black. There were more benign items on sale, of course. We had been told that in the desert sweets would be an important provision: the dust is so dry and caustic that you need something to help lubricate your mouth. We stocked up on American candy. Had we wanted to, we could have bought cheap American boots, stereos, iPods. Less conventionally there were Operation Enduring Freedom mugs—souvenirs of the US government's operation in Afghanistan—and T-shirts emblazoned with slogans such as 'Kill the Taliban before He Kills You'. The people running the Post Exchange have to do so on a commercial basis, so they stock only the stuff that sells. Hence the fact that it feels a bit like a Midwestern shopping mall with a military twist.

Our shopping spree over, we were transported—along with our twenty flight cases worth of camera equipment—to the airport section of the base, where we awaited the departure of our four-engine turboprop Hercules to Camp Bastion, Helmand Province.

The Hercules flew high, well out of the range of any missiles that some enterprising Taliban might otherwise decide to fire in our direction. From the window of the aircraft during the forty-minute flight all I could see for miles around was desert. There was perhaps one conurbation and certainly no water. This was a hostile, featureless place. We kept our height until we were very close to our destination for reasons of safety, then began a sharp descent.

Camp Bastion came into view.

From the air it looks like some futuristic encampment on the moon. It's massive— 8 square kilometres and at the time of writing home to 4,000 troops. Amazingly it was built in only four months by the Royal Engineers and on this, my first visit, there were areas that were still under construction. From the air you realize just how isolated it is—it's built 20 kilometres from the nearest town. This can be a blessing and a curse. The perimeter of the camp is surrounded by radar, meaning it's impossible to approach Bastion without being seen; but equally it's difficult for the huge quantities of supplies that have to be brought in by truck to get to the base.

The moment we disembarked from the Hercules the heat hit us. Dry, overpowering, the sort of oppressive heat you don't experience anywhere else. I knew this was the one thing the camera could never adequately capture and as I tramped through the dusty earth off the Bastion runway, I wondered how well the crew and I would be able to deal with it. And we'd only been in the open air for a few minutes—already we were covered with sweat—when we came face to face with the brutal reality of warfare.

Lance Corporal George Davey was twenty-three years old and had been in the army for three years. He was a section second of B Company's 5 platoon and had been on operations in the Helmand town of Sangin when he was killed as a result of a firearms accident. His repatriation ceremony took place just after we arrived. Soldiers from different regiments posted to Bastion lined up, quietly and respectfully, on the airstrip. We joined them. The sun beat down on our heads and I noticed quite a few of the lads around us fainting in the heat. A khaki military ambulance waited by the aircraft that would take George's body back to Kandahar and then return it home to his family. It was difficult to keep my eyes off that ambulance because I knew it contained a coffin. There wasn't a sound from the troops as a chaplain spoke in clear, solemn tones; I looked about and saw that the faces all around me were stern and pensive. There were tears. It didn't take much imagination to deduce what was going round their heads and I couldn't stop my mind from wondering who had been waiting back home for this young soldier to return. I later learned that he had a wife and two young daughters. The pain they must have been feeling was something I knew I could never fully understand.

'The Last Post' was played as George's coffin, draped in a Union Jack, was lifted from the ambulance and slowly carried by his mates on to the waiting aircraft. We watched as, blurred in the haze of the intense sun, the plane took off. As it passed us it dipped one wing, a final gesture of respect and an acknowledgement of the sacrifice the soldier it carried had made for his country.

As the plane disappeared into the distance, the solemn crowd dispersed. I could sense that I was not the only one there who was having thoughts about their own mortality and I started to feel even more uncomfortable than before about the fact that in just four days' time I would be heading out to the front line.

In the meantime, though, I had to get used to my new home.

The running of Camp Bastion is an amazing logistical feat. Every soldier, every drop of water and every ammo belt used in combat in Helmand Province passes through these 8 square kilometres of desert. That's a lot of soldiers, a lot of water and a hell of a lot of ammo. But it's not just a processing centre: this was home to 3,000 troops, mostly British but also Danes, Estonians and a handful of Americans. And keeping soldiers safe and well in the unrelenting heat of this dangerous desert is no picnic.

The soldiers at Bastion are housed in air-conditioned pods, a bit like enormous tents perhaps 10 metres long, that can comfortably sleep about twelve men, or more if necessary. The air conditioning is better than nothing, but it is still immensely hot in the pods. Each soldier has an aluminium-framed camping bed, famously impossible to put together. I made the mistake at first of putting a roll-mat over the canvas mattress, but that way no air comes up from underneath, so you cook as you're lying there; once I had figured out to remove the roll-mat I actually found the bed quite comfortable. Come the small hours of the morning, though, the temperature in the desert drops; when this happens the presence of the air conditioning units is more of a hindrance than a help and you're glad of your sleeping bag.

Some of the pods are interconnected. Those that aren't are separated by lines of Hesco barriers. These are collapsible wire mesh boxes with a heavy fabric inlay. They concertina out and are filled with local sand and earth. The resulting fortifications are very effective against enemy fire and although Bastion itself is principally constructed out of concrete, many of the army's Forward Operating Bases in Helmand Province are largely constructed from Hesco. There are ditches all around—a nightmare in the dark, but if the base should come under fire you need somewhere to take cover.

As this was our first trip to Afghanistan we were told we needed to have three or four days' adjustment. This was a very new environment for all of us and it was essential that we acclimatized to it before we went up country. It took some getting used to. The desert air is constantly filled with mini dust whirlwinds. Sometimes they're as big as a truck, sometimes they're as big as a ten-pence piece. The sharp dust gets everywhere, inducing a complaint known as Bastion throat; if you clamp your mouth shut to reduce the effect, you find yourself bleeding from your nose as the dust scrapes abrasively against the skin. Later the authorities at Bastion introduced large trucks to douse the ground and stop the dust from becoming airborne, but when I arrived there in 2007 that particular luxury was some months away.

The affectionately named 'desert bogey' was another complaint we would have to get used to. The dry dust that you're breathing in creates massive stalactites that hang down from your nose. They reminded me of being a kid and decorating sandcastles with fistfuls of watery sand. If you pick them, you pull away the surface of your skin. The flies love that and they're always flying round to try to get at your bleeding nostrils. The temptation to rip out your desert bogeys is immense—a bit like trying to eat a doughnut without licking your lips—but it's best to leave them there. It just means you snore a bit more. Or in my case, a *lot* more.

One way of keeping the dust down is to cover the ground with a kind of interlocking plastic flooring. This is everywhere—in the pods, on the way to the mess, on the way to the shitters. The sanitary facilities are pretty good: clean and comfortable, if unbearably hot. You don't want to go and powder your nose at midday in Camp Bastion because you come out feeling as if you've just had a sauna. The showers are equally acceptable, but again the water is boiling hot because the tanks in which it's kept have been baked by the sun. Cold water for washing is hard to come by.

We quickly became accustomed to life as what the troops on the ground would jokingly refer to as REMFs—rear-echelon motherfuckers. I went running each day, and made use of the gym with some bulky Royal Anglians and a few Estonians who were built like brick shithouses. Everyone was welcoming and friendly, although I had to put up with the inevitable piss-taking from the soldiers encamped there as I had on Salisbury Plain. It was schoolboy stuff, mostly. If you respond to something that's intended to be obvious and a wind-up, that's a laugh. If someone shouts out 'Ross!' and you turn round, that's a great joke. If someone shouts out 'Grant!' and you turn round, it's an even better one.

'What have you got stuck on your heels, Ross?' You raise your foot and turn round—it's an effeminate posture. You look like a girl with a handbag, it means you're gay and the jokers fall about laughing. No one could say

65

it's sophisticated comedy, but I got my fair share of it and it was mostly pretty good-natured, designed to test if the new boy, the pampered bloke off the TV, was cut out for life in Camp Bastion. I took it in my stride, responding with what I hoped was good humour, and after a while the ribbing started to die away.

Most of B Company were out on an operation, but we'd go to the Anglian mess tent and chat with those who were there. The mess is about the size of three tennis courts and is just by the laundry where the troops can take their washing—or 'dobie'—to be cleaned. In the mess hall you need to wash your hands with an alcohol gel before joining the queue for food. The food was adequate if not great. I would never have a go at the caterers because they do an amazing job with what they're given. Not only that, but being stuck in a kitchen full of ovens when it's 50 degrees outside suggests to me that even though they're not on the front line they're hardly living a cushty existence. However, out in the desert there isn't much opportunity to supply the troops with fresh food. There are always baked beans on the menu, and maybe some pie. What you really want in that kind of heat is something lighter. If you were lucky there would be some salad with tuna out of a tin. And pigs might fly.

Compared to what anyone is used to back in

66

England, nobody could say that Camp Bastion was the lap of luxury. But in military terms it was fine. And it wouldn't be long before I would find out just why soldiers out on the ground would be desperate to return to the relative security and comfort of their base.

5. T4

My introduction to hostilities in Helmand Province was as part of Operation Lastay Kulang. *Lastay kulang* is Pashtun for pickaxe handle. I suppose the name should have been indication enough that this would be no gentle stroll through the sand. It was with a certain amount of apprehension that I attended, as instructed by Lieutenant Colonel Stuart Carver, a briefing with the rest of B Company so that we could learn what the operational intentions of Lastay Kulang were.

When I had met him back at Pirbright Barracks—a place that seemed a million miles from where I was now—Stuart Carver had seemed, as I said before, a little detached. Now that I saw him performing the nitty-gritty of his job, the qualities that had propelled him to CO of the Anglians became perfectly clear. He was a career soldier with a good sense of humour but who largely kept himself to himself. There were no airs and graces about him, no snobbery. He was a family man, and I had the impression that that sense of family extended to the soldiers under his command. I found that I liked him very much.

We met during the unbearable heat of the afternoon. Some of B Company had only just returned from another operation and the difference between them and the guys who'd had a few days relaxing in the relative tranquillity of Bastion was astonishing. Major Mick Aston, OC of B Company, looked as if he'd had a punishing time of it. He'd dropped a load of weight, his skin was raw and his face was covered with scraggly stubble. As with Josh Hill, most noticeable were his eyes: he had a dark, serious expression, no doubt the result of several days of intense stress. It was an expression I would see any number of times during my time in Afghanistan. If you'd seen him on civvy street you might have thought he'd had a few heavy nights. And so he had—but this was a Taliban hangover.

Mick was not the only one who looked like he'd had a hard time, and it truly brought home to me how demanding the next few days were going to be, as did Stuart Carver's matter-of-fact briefing. 'What you are about to receive,' he announced to the assembled company, 'is orders for Op Lastay Kulang. It's an offensive operation in the area north-east of Sangin and the wider aspiration is to keep the Taliban on the back foot. The reason we want to do that is to allow reconstruction and development to get underway and there hasn't really been much of that so far. There's been a lot of talk about it, but no actual physical tangible results to display to the local people that we're going to provide them with something. All these people in Sangin are wavering about whether to fully support us or whether to go back to the Taliban.'

They call it the battle for hearts and minds, but in the fight against the Taliban, it's a battle that can often be forgotten about. From our Western standpoint it is easy to assume that the ordinary Afghan villagers in Helmand Province see the war in black-and-white terms, as you or I do: Taliban bad, British Army good. They don't. For years—centuries, in fact—Afghanistan played host to many invading forces. None of these forces were there for entirely selfless reasons. The Soviet occupation occurred within living memory; it is hardly surprising, then, that many Afghans view the current occupying force with suspicion, even though they might not wish a return to the brutalities of the Taliban era.

The British Army understand this and there is a genuine desire up the chain of command both to engage in projects of reconstruction and to win over the respect, if not the affection, of the Afghan people. The issue adds an extra layer of difficulty to the struggle in Helmand Province, not to mention an extra layer of ambiguity. Nowhere is this better demonstrated than in the military's policy towards the poppy harvest of Afghanistan.

Poppies mean heroin and 93 per cent of the drug on Britain's streets can be traced directly to Afghanistan, of which 66 per cent comes from Helmand Province. The poppies are farmed by ordinary Afghans. The process involves slicing into the head of the poppy with a razor-type implement. The poppy is then left for several days while a milky sap accumulates; this is then harvested and sold on to the drug lords of the area. In a good year an Afghan farmer could expect to make a sum of £1,000 from an area of less than 100 square metres. And in Helmand Province £1,000 goes a very long way.

The raw opium, however, gets sold on and refined, increasing in value at every stage until it arrives on the streets of Britain—and elsewhere—as the insidious powder that causes so much damage to those who develop an addiction to it. On the face of it, it would seem that the eradication of the poppy fields of Helmand Province is a reasonable objective for the troops in the region; indeed, one of the stated aims of the British deployment in Helmand Province is the elimination of the opium trade. It's more complicated than that, however. Destroy the poppy fields and you would destroy the livelihood of the very people whose hearts and minds you are trying to win. At a stroke, you would send them running into the arms of the Taliban who, despite the fact that the use of any kind of drug is banned under their ideology, tolerate the production of opium because it is intended for export to the infidel drug users of the West.

In the long term, the plan is to educate the

poppy farmers in the cultivation of other crops, but as we prepared for Operation Lastay Kulang, that was a long way off. In the meantime, the hope of the British forces was that other kinds of help could be offered to the Afghan people. Hospitals and schools could be built, bringing much-needed healthcare and education to the region; running water could be introduced to areas that had none. There were any number of positive, constructive projects the British Army could bring to Helmand Province to show the local population that, as well as achieving their principal aim of quelling the Taliban insurgency, they intended to bring practical benefits as a result of their occupation.

Operations such as Lastay Kulang were intended to disperse the Taliban from the area so that reconstruction could begin, the local people would accept that the British troops were a Good Thing and the Taliban would therefore find it increasingly difficult to gain support among the local population. As with all these things, however, it was more easily said than done while the Taliban remained such an active presence in the province.

Lastay Kulang was going to be a perilous operation by anyone's standards. The plan was this. B Company—along with myself and the camera crew—would travel north from Camp Bastion in a convoy of Viking, Pinzgauer and Mastiff armoured vehicles driven by the

Royal Marines to Forward Operating Base Robinson, or FOB Rob, as it's commonly called. From FOB Rob we would continue to Sangin. The journey to Sangin would be incredibly dangerous. Landmines would be a constant threat and B Company had already been ambushed twice by the Taliban taking that very same route. From Sangin, we were to travel north-east to an area known simply as Jupiter.

Jupiter is in the green zone. This is a strip of moist, fertile land that borders the Helmand river and which plays host to most of the compounds, fields and irrigation ditches that form Afghan settlements in the region. For obvious reasons, the Taliban avoid fighting in the wide, open spaces of the desert; they prefer these mazes of compounds and ditches where they know the territory, have arms stashed and can rely on a tactical advantage—if not an advantage of numbers and weaponry. For a British soldier, entering the green zone means being prepared for a fight.

The part of the green zone to which we were headed was, according to the intelligence reports that had been received, where a Taliban leader by the name of Haginika was located. There was every reason to expect that when we advanced upon him, he would dig in and make a fight of it. And when that happened, the camera team and I would be in the line of fire.

The moment Stuart Carver issued the order, Bastion became a hive of activity. Getting the Vikings, Mastiffs and Pinzgauers—the latter would become my least favourite vehicles on the planet—ready for the journey to FOB Rob was a big deal and one that made it clear what sort of dangers we could expect. The vehicles are surrounded by a kind of metal caging designed to explode RPGs should they hit. It's not failsafe—it all depends on what sort of warhead the RPG is fitted with—but most of the time it works. Our rucksacks, full of the equipment we would need out in the field, were attached to the outside of the vehicles, and boxes of water were loaded inside. Water, of course, is a precious and essential commodity in the desert and while we were out there I, along with everyone else, would be expected to carry and drink 6 litres a day. Equally important were the extra fuel and, of course, ammunition that were being stashed on to the trucks. Nobody watching the loading process could be under any doubt that the convoy about to leave Bastion meant business.

It took two days to prepare the vehicles. Personally, I found the process extremely nerve-racking. It didn't seem to worry the Anglians in the same way—when they weren't making preparations they played football in the sun, cracked jokes and seemed quite at ease. Unlike me. I spent those painful final

74

hours before the off speaking to the lads and trying to determine what the camera crew and I should do if the convoy came under attack. Corporal Stefan Martin explained that should this happen, we were to stay in the vehicle until we received orders to the contrary from our section commander, Corporal Kennedy. The inside of these vehicles is cramped and claustrophobic. Most of them are air-conditioned, but if you're unlucky enough to be in a vehicle where the air conditioning is broken, you cook. It's better to be hot and uncomfortable than full of holes, of course; but what became clear during the course of our conversation was that even strict instructions such as the ones Corporal Martin was giving me were subject to change on account of the unpredictable nature of enemy contact; and vehicles—even well-armoured ones like the Viking—were not always the safest place to be. He explained that only a week before a Viking had been involved in an ambush. An RPG had hit a fuel canister that was being stored on top of the vehicle. It exploded, causing burning fuel to drip through the top-gunner's position into the main cabin of the Viking and on to the troops inside. The soldiers had to escape the flaming vehicle under fire from the Taliban.

Bastion was full of such stories and it was important that we heard them so that we were fully aware of the dangers that could await us, but they did nothing for my nerves. It was difficult to imagine how I would react if I came under fire, but should the worst happen I needed to know how to save my life and, potentially, the lives of those around me. With this in mind, I went to pick up my army trauma kit. This includes a self-pressurizing dressing that can be wrapped around a wound to stem the bleeding as well as a 10mg ampoule of morphine.

The morphine injection is a crucial piece of kit. Morbidly or aptly—I couldn't decide which—it is housed in a little plastic box called a coffin. The coffin is ripped open to reveal a tube with a red cap at one end and a yellow cap at the other. The red cap is removed to reveal a button; the yellow cap is placed against the skin and when the button is pressed the needle shoots through the yellow plastic and injects the morphine into the skin—although I did hear stories of soldiers getting it the wrong way round in the heat of battle and having the needle shoot straight through their thumb taking their nail off (Billy—you know who you are). The placing of the injection is important: it needs to be located at a distance from the area of trauma. So, if someone has an injury to their lower left leg, the morphine needs to be injected into their upper right thigh. The reason for this is simple: inject the morphine too close to a bleeding wound and the drug will simply seep out with the blood, making it practically useless. Two of these shots should be enough to numb most kinds of pain. If you need any more than that, you're probably not going to make it. And perversely, if an injured man is shouting for morphine it is, relatively speaking, a good sign: it means, at the very least, that he's aware.

Another important task I had to complete before the off was to apply my blood group— A+—to all my clothes, including my body armour and helmet, with a thick black marker pen. That way, should I get wounded, the medics would know what kind of blood to pump back into my body. It's a weird feeling doing this, another of those things that brings it home to you what you're about to embark upon.

The night before we were due to depart for Operation Lastay Kulang you could almost taste the apprehension in the air. To pass the time I visited the NAAFI, where the soldiers could while away the time drinking cups of tea, smoking and taking the piss out of each other. It was going to be an early start and I knew I should at least try to sleep, so it wasn't all that late when I decided to get my head down for the night. I had started wandering back to my pod when I bumped into a guy I knew by the name OH. He was a member of the Grenadier Guards, who were part of the battle group, and our paths had crossed a couple of times. The moment he saw me, he fixed me with a steely stare.

'You,' he said. 'Come with me.'

It wasn't an invitation. It was an instruction. And OH being six foot four and brawny enough to pick me up and throw me, I did as I was told.

He led me silently to the hospital. Once we were there, he showed me four lads who were under his command. They'd been on a night-time patrol down south when they had stumbled upon an IED—an improvised explosive device. The results were horrific. One of them had lost part of his leg and was in a coma; another appeared to be blind in one eye. The two others had taken a lot of shrapnel but hadn't lost limbs. They were awake, but high on morphine. They were covered in pockmarks where the metal and sand from the explosion had burned into them; their skin was stained with black, congealed blood. One of them, his eyes rolling on account of the drugs, started babbling incoherently.

'All right, Grant!' And then, 'I haven't got enough points. I haven't got enough points.'

I turned to OH. 'What does he mean?' I whispered. 'What's he talking about?'

'I'll tell you later,' OH breathed.

As we left the hospital, he explained. Because the army payout for injured troops was so poor at the time—and especially so if

78

your injuries were considered 'minor'—soldiers are encouraged to pay for 'points' from private insurance companies. The more points you have, the bigger your payout should you get wounded. This poor kid, his mind muddled by injury and morphine, was panicking that he didn't have enough points to get anything approaching reasonable compensation for what he had just endured. I learned too that stitches needed to be of a certain length in order for the wounded soldier to receive a payout, so it isn't uncommon for the guys to ask for more stitches. More often than not, the doctors are happy to oblige.

I walked away from the hospital with a slightly empty feeling. It left a bad taste in the mouth to know that soldiers who risk their lives to protect my liberty—soldiers who earn very little money indeed—are encouraged to pay cash they can ill afford into an insurance scheme to cover an eventuality that is, after all, not unlikely. OH was as moved as I was. We both walked round a corner, sat down and had a brew and a cigarette. I think we both had a slight tear in our eyes.

And it would be wrong for me to say that this was the only thought that went through my mind as I sought my bed that night. Over the past couple of days I had been forced to confront certain realities about what we were about to do. But those wounded men lying in a hospital bed, they were the bitter truth of war.

It was with that uncomfortable thought in my head that I went to bed that night, and waited for Operation Lastay Kulang to begin.

*   *   *

Camp Bastion. 04.00.

It gets light very early in Helmand Province. The sky was bright as I emerged from my sleeping pod in full gear and with my heavy bergen on my back. The camp was already bustling with activity as the final preparations were made to the convoy of Vikings and Pinzgauers, led by three Mastiffs. The convoy was to travel north, up to the main A1 highway, which travels west to east across the middle of Helmand Province and over the Helmand river. We would head east, through the town of Gereshk, before leaving the road and heading north through the desert to FOB Rob, where we would meet up with the rest of B Company. We would then continue north through Sangin, where the previous year 3 Para had been involved in some of the heaviest fighting of the conflict, before heading out into the desert again to lay up for the attack on our target: a reported Taliban stronghold in the village of Jucaylay.

I was travelling in a Pinzgauer with our director John Conroy, cameraman Andy Thompson and sound man James Snowdon. Inside the Pinzgauer was hard and uncomfortable and I grew to loathe it. There are other reasons not to like this vehicle, too. Mastiffs are protected by top-gunners with fifty-cals or grenade machine guns; Vikings have GPMGs; Pinzgauers, if you're lucky, have a bloke with an SA80. If I felt vulnerable, imagine what he felt. The only plus side was that the air-conditioning pipe was broken and I was seated right by the outlet, so I had some respite from the incessant heat, which was scorching even from an early hour. Already soaked in sweat and covered in dust that came in from the top cover, I gazed through the window and out into the unforgiving desert landscape with something approaching numbness. As I did so, I tried to rationalize the danger of what we were doing. I guess we've all sat on a plane before take-off and worried that this might be one of the few planes to be involved in a crash. We persuade ourselves, of course, that it's not going to be. We remind ourselves of the statistics. Deep down we know that the plane *could* go down, but it probably won't. I grappled with the same thought processes as the convoy trundled along the A1 highway. This was a perilous situation, no doubt. But most trucks in Afghanistan *don't* hit a landmine. Most soldiers *don't* die. And anyway, landmines are much more likely when you turn off the road. In a situation like that, you persuade yourself that you're not going to be one of the unlucky ones. It's all you can do;

otherwise you'll go mad.

So far my time in this country had been spent in military bases or at 12,000 feet in the air. Gereshk was my first experience of the real Afghanistan. I surveyed it from the—I hoped—safety of the vehicle. The sides of the road were crowded with children watching the troops roll through. Many of them were missing limbs because of the mines littered all over the country, left over from the Soviet occupation. The Russians covered Afghanistan with mines. In the mountainous parts of the country they can slip downhill or be dislodged by snow or rain, which makes it difficult to map them because they are constantly moving. As a result, amputees are a common sight and I defy anyone to remain unmoved by the sight of young children without arms or legs as a result of wars that happened before they were born or that they are too young to understand.

Along the side of the road were plenty of little booths—cafés for the lorry drivers travelling on the A1. From the relative safety of the Pinzgauer I saw the locals stopping at these booths for chai, or tea. They wore traditional Afghan garb—*dishdash* and headdresses. I saw many older men with dark skin, white beards and heavily lined faces. They eyed the military convoy curiously as they sipped their drinks and it was impossible to tell from this distance what they thought of our presence.

Gereshk is on the Helmand river. It's part of the green zone and is an area heavily favoured by the Taliban. As we were leaving the town, our top-gunner, David, announced that he thought we were being 'dicked'— military terminology for being observed. The worry was that Taliban sympathizers were taking note of our direction and numbers, then speeding ahead on their motorbikes or calling their friends with their mobile phones so that an ambush could be laid up ahead. It did nothing to make our journey any more comfortable.

The going was slow. Our driver did his best to make sure the Pinzgauer travelled in the tracks of the vehicle in front of us so that we could avoid hitting an IED or a landmine. The Mastiffs at the front of the convoy were mine-protected trucks that have a V-shaped hull that is designed to deflect the blast of a landmine or IED away from under the vehicle. You wouldn't particularly want to be in one if it hit a mine: the wheels would come off, the chassis would be devastated, but you would probably survive the encounter. With the Mastiffs out in front, the remaining convoy could be a little more confident of not hitting an explosive device—but only if the subsequent vehicles stayed in their tracks. And over a fifteen-hour journey, that's not an easy thing to do, especially with the trucks ahead billowing up clouds of dust. There were also rumours doing the rounds that the Taliban were wise to the army's anti-landmine techniques and had developed a system to foil them. They would find a genuine vehicle track and take a plaster of Paris cast of it, which they would paint the colour of the sand. They would then set a landmine or an IED before laying the cast over it. The device would be hidden and at a cursory glance you wouldn't notice that the track had been tampered with.

As we trundled out of Gereshk and into the desert, I tried not to think about the implications of being outwitted by the Taliban in that way. Everyone in our Pinzgauer realized how much we were relying on our driver to follow the tracks accurately. If we hit a mine, it would have been like shaking an egg around in a can: we wouldn't have stood a chance. On either side of us were two ranges of mountains that met at a point up ahead. The mountains gave the Taliban cover, which meant that this was a particularly good place for an ambush.

The heat was intolerable—almost 50 degrees outside the Pinzgauer and like an oven inside. And then suddenly we ground to a halt.

The convoy stood still in the middle of the dusty, stony earth. Troops exited the vehicles and tried to find out why we had been ordered to stop. Rumours started to circulate. We were being followed by A Company and before long we started to hear garbled, unconfirmed reports that there had been casualties. We knew something serious had happened because we became aware of air support in the skies above us.

For three hours we stayed there. Three long, hot, nervous hours. Eventually we saw the dust clouds in the distance that meant A Company were catching us up. The convoy came to a halt and the Regimental Sergeant Major, Ian Robinson, approached us. He wore a serious expression: the kind of face that instantly told us he had bad news.

In fact the news was more than bad. It was the worst. The operation had claimed its first T4.

One of the Vikings had been involved in a mine strike. Corporal Darren Bonner, A Company's lead signaller, was dead.

Darren Bonner—'Big Daz' to his mates— was thirty-one years old. He had been in the army for fourteen years and was engaged to be married. I was later to see footage filmed by the soldiers of A Company of the damage that had been done to Corporal Bonner's vehicle. It was genuinely shocking, a bleak scene of devastation.

As soon as I heard the dreadful news, a riot of emotions passed through my mind. Sorrow, obviously, for the death of this young man I didn't know but with whom everyone in the regiment felt an attachment not only because he was one of them but also because he was a

85

popular guy. Sorrow for his family. And the sense of unreality there is whenever someone dies: it didn't seem possible that one of the lads setting out from Camp Bastion that morning had seen his last sunrise, that his life had been brought to such an abrupt halt. There were more selfish reactions too, if I'm honest. Reactions like: A Company's convoy were travelling over the same ground that we had just covered. We must have just missed the mine. But for the indiscriminate hand of fate, that could just as easily have been us. And then there's the anger. I could sense it in everyone. The enemy had killed one of our men and every member of that convoy wanted to make them pay for what they had just done.

Ian Robinson, as the NCO in charge of battlefield casualties, was clearly affected by what had happened. But as I spoke to him I could tell that the events of that morning had not weakened his resolve or distracted him from his duty. 'We're going to push on as normal,' he told me. 'We've still got a job to do, we've got all these boys to get to their assembly areas, their lines of departure, and that's what we're going to do. It's difficult for those blokes that were there but unfortunately it's the reality of what we're here doing.'

There was not a cloud in the piercing blue sky, but there was a metaphorical one hanging over the convoy as we started moving again. Quite by chance, the remnants of Darren

Bonner's Viking were towed by the vehicle in front of us: a very obvious and poignant reminder that this was a most dangerous journey.

It felt less like a military convoy and more like a funeral procession as, three hours later, we approached our destination for that day: Forward Operating Base Robinson. It had taken us fourteen hours to travel the 75 kilometres from Camp Bastion to here and we were emotionally and physically exhausted. This was just the beginning of the operation, however. The following day we were to push north into enemy territory. So far Lastay Kulang had been tiring enough, and for myself and the crew the operation hadn't even begun.

We needed some sleep. Putting the camera away, we tried to get our heads down and not contemplate too much what the following days would bring.

6. TETHERED GOATS

Morning took a long time to come in that godforsaken place. FOB Rob is like a shit sandwich without the bread. It's a piece of mud with a load of shit in the middle and a piece of mud on top. It stinks of diesel and is surrounded by Hesco and barbed wire. It derives its name from an American soldier, Staff Sergeant Christopher Robinson, who was killed nearby in 2006. It regularly comes under attack by the Taliban and in truth it is little more than a small area that ISAF forces are able to defend in order for troops in the region to be restocked with supplies.

We weren't allowed to make any fires that night because of the large amount of diesel that had been spilled over the ground. We ate cold rations—some kind of unappetizing lamb stew that did little to cheer us after the strains of the day. I tried to spend a bit of time by myself. I needed it. One person dead already, and the dread certainty that this unwelcoming place in the middle of the Helmand desert really wasn't for me. What the fuck, I wondered as the stars started to emerge, had I got myself into?

And of course I thought about Darren Bonner. If the rest of us had had a bad day, what sort of day had he had? That put things into perspective somewhat.

I couldn't sleep. We rose early and by 06.00 FOB Rob was hot, dusty and full of activity as the soldiers of A and B Companies prepared to make the journey to the town of Sangin. It wasn't far, but the route had been the scene of some of the company's fiercest fighting to date. And Sangin itself had seen more than its fair share of fighting. In the summer of 2006, 3 Para had responded to a distress call from Afghan officials and were Chinooked into Sangin to deal with the Taliban who had overrun the town. They took up positions in a compound which became their home during a prolonged siege. Outnumbered and on the verge of being overrun, the soldiers had to call in repeated air strikes at great risk to themselves to keep the enemy at bay. They renamed this siege 'The Alamo'.

It was here that Keith Nieves's Viking had hit a landmine—indeed as we slowly made our way towards the outskirts of Sangin, we passed the scarred remains of that vehicle. After the mine strike an Apache attack helicopter had launched a Hellfire missile into the Viking to deny it to the enemy. It's very important that none of our military kit falls into the hands of the Taliban: they can't be allowed to parade it in front of the locals and make it seem as if they are winning the war; nor can they be allowed to gain intelligence about the weaponry and other equipment. There was no chance of that happening now: the Viking was little more than a metal casing, the sort of thing you'd see at a scrap yard. It looked to me like some kind of voodoo sign, warning us to keep the hell away. Unfortunately keeping away simply wasn't an option.

The outskirts of Sangin were like a ghost town. We were told by Tim Newton that the previous day when we arrived at FOB Rob the streets had been full of locals. Our appearance had encouraged them to leave. It looked as if they had just dropped everything and scarpered. Clearly they knew our advance was a prelude to something and I couldn't help wondering what that augured for the battle for hearts and minds. Certainly, if the ISAF troops were in Helmand Province to aid reconstruction, one look at Sangin would suggest they weren't having much success. For a kilometre around Sangin DC—the military base there where we were to lay up for the remainder of the day before preparing for a dawn attack—the town appeared to be totally destroyed. It was apocalyptic, nothing but an expanse of rubble, on account of the many thousands of pounds of explosives that had been dropped on the area. Buildings had collapsed in on each other; concrete reinforcing rods pointed dramatically up to the sky. It looked as if the whole town had been bulldozed. We might not be able to see any actual people, but just one glance at the devastation around us made it quite clear that this was a very, very dangerous place.

We came to a halt at Sangin DC, a grim fortification surrounded by Hesco and huge, winding tunnels of barbed wire. The air temperature had risen back up to its usual 50 degrees. Even though the journey from FOB Rob had been a relatively short one, we were all hot and tired. Near our base there was a section of river where the lads and I were able to strip off and cool down—the first wash some of them had had for four weeks. A very kind soldier lent me a pair of his desert shorts (sorry, mate, I've still got them—don't lend me anything . . .) so that my modesty was preserved and any unseen Taliban snipers were denied the temptation of playing target practice with a different kind of privates on parade. I strode gratefully into the cool river with the rest of the guys.

We had to be careful: the water was fast moving and if you allowed the current to wash you downstream you would very soon end up in the heartland of Taliban territory. And if that happened, you could bet your boots that they wouldn't throw you a rubber ring. No doubt it was not the cleanest, most hygienic stretch of river in the world; no doubt there are safer places to go for a dip, and more picturesque ones too; but in that scorching midday heat I relished every minute.

The water was refreshing but there was

nevertheless a pervasive smell in the air. It didn't take the lads long to find out where it came from. Not far from the river there was a pit of sorts that had been dug for some reason—probably to bury rubbish. Don't ask me why or how, but it seemed to have been filled instead with human piss. You can only imagine what the smell in that burning heat was like when you got up close. Astonishingly there were frogs living in that malodorous lake of urine—how they managed to survive there I simply do not know. The afternoon's sport, once the guys had had a dip and a bit of a scoff, was to collect rocks and hurl them at the frogs swimming around in the pond of piss. Ribbit, ribbit. Splash. Simple pleasures. There was an unpleasant foam of scum over the top of the pond and of course there were certain lads among our number who couldn't resist throwing the rocks in such a way that they splashed their mates with this foamy soup. Not the most sophisticated of pastimes; but then I guess they couldn't just kick back and watch the telly. It was the sort of thing bored kids might do, and of course a lot of the regiment still *were* kids.

Their orders were as follows. A and B Company would separate. A Company would lay up above the village of Putay; B Company would head east and lay up in the hills above Jucaylay for the night. There was no doubt that the Taliban knew we were coming, and even roughly where we were, but we didn't want to reveal our exact location—which was about 5 klicks, or kilometres, outside Sangin—so, as we pitched camp in the darkness of the desert, all lights and fires were forbidden and we were ordered to keep noise to a minimum. Our vehicles formed a protective circle, while the Fire Support Group used night vision from their vantage point at a distance from us to make sure we weren't attacked or mortared. Mick Aston came and gave us a brief outline of what would happen the next day. He was calm and reassuring.

The silence of the desert closed in on us. There was a low hum of voices all around as last-minute preparations were made for our dawn attack. But after a while there was nothing anyone could do but wait.

And wait.

As I sat there in the desert it occurred to me that what we were doing was something that had happened from time immemorial: men, sitting round their wagons, waiting to go to war the next day. The Greeks had done this at the walls of Troy; the English and the French had done this on the eve of the Battle of Agincourt. It wouldn't do for me to compare myself with those soldiers, but in one way, at least, I now knew something of what they had gone through. I understood something of the unnerving sensation a man feels the night before he's going to come under fire.

The lads sat around in little groups. I could hear some of them cracking jokes and I could tell that for others there was a sense of false bonhomie. Of nervousness. And of excitement. I understood how they might feel that. Half of me wished dawn was upon us; half of me wished it would never come. It's a weird feeling, knowing that you are willingly going to war, that in the morning you're going to be shot at and possibly killed. I knew, as I waited for the time to pass, that this was a night I would never forget for the rest of my days.

I tried to distract myself from the prospect of morning's inevitable arrival by lying on the stony earth, resting my head on my backpack and gazing up at the spectacular canopy of the stars. It was breathtakingly beautiful: in the absence of any ambient light the constellations shone like beacons and it looked almost as if there was less darkness than there were stars. It was a rare moment of stillness. Of peace.

It was the quiet before the storm.

*   *   *

In Africa, if you want to catch a lion that has been killing all your animals, this is what you do. You hammer a stake into the ground and to the stake you tie a goat. Around the goat you make a ring out of whatever bush happens to be available, making sure that there is only one way in. Then you hide. The lion will hear the goat in distress and come to investigate. It will attack. And while it's feasting on its prey, if you're brave enough, you spear and kill the lion.

It's called the tethered goat strategy but its usage is not limited to Africa. It's not limited to goats either. It's a common military tactic and it was this strategy we were about to embark upon. In this case, however, the lion was the Taliban; the bush ring was the green zone of Jucaylay; and B Company were the goat. The hope was that by engaging the Taliban we could bring them out into the open so that our 'assets'—heavy artillery, attack helicopters and fast air—could act like the African's spear and hopefully kill the enemy. It sounded to me like a dangerous way to pass the time, so it was little wonder that I woke nervously just before dawn on day three of Operation Lastay Kulang. I had been woken by the 'pre-barrage'—the whistle of artillery shells being fired from FOB Rob into Putay before A Company's attack on the village. It set the tone for the rest of the day.

We got dressed in the dark, packed our kit away in the dark, put our body armour away in the dark. As the sun rose we were allowed to boil a brew and cook some beans and sausages on a Hexi stove and then I felt the urge for a pre-battle crap. I padded down into a nearby ravine and started to do my business. Of course, that meant it was time for everybody in

95

B Company to come and take a photo of me squatting. I started throwing stones at them but to no avail: my posterior was recorded for posterity.

It was just after dawn that we entered our vehicles and started to approach the outskirts of Jucaylay. The convoy kicked up a massive dust cloud, so we knew there was no way the Taliban would not realize where we were or that British soldiers were on their way. They knew we were coming. And they knew, too, that we hadn't arrived to shake their hands and make them a cup of tea. All around us were poppy fields and as we made our approach I caught glimpses of the green zone, the fertile area around the river where the Taliban would be congregating in force. We wouldn't be able to use our vehicles, however. The green zone was too boggy and soft for that. It meant leaving the relative safety of my Pinzgauer and, along with everyone else, walking to the green zone.

Major Mick Aston was in command of the attack. As our convoy came to a halt and we prepared to continue on foot, he ordered the camera team to join him as we moved down into Jucaylay. We were instructed to walk 6 metres from each other. This was important: bunch up and we would present an easy and obvious target for the Taliban.

It was still early, but already hot. We walked for about a kilometre until we hit the edge of

96

the green zone. It's amazing how sharply this area of irrigated land is delineated from the surrounding desert: you go from stony sand to lush, verdant vegetation in a matter of a few paces. Or, to put it another way, from safety to danger in the blinking of an eye.

Ordinarily, the green zone would be bustling with activity. There would be adults working in the fields, children playing. But as I stood there, sheltered by a high mud wall, it became clear that the area was almost deserted. This led us to believe that the Taliban had ordered everyone to get out. They understood that there was going to be a contact; hence the unnatural, spooky silence.

The silence wouldn't last long.

Lieutenant George Seal-Coon interviewed an old boy we passed with a dog. He said he hadn't seen or heard anything. I couldn't help feeling he might not be telling the truth. His dog started barking, along with all the other dogs tethered in the nearby compounds. If the dust storm we'd kicked up hadn't given away our position, these barking dogs certainly had.

We knew the Taliban would be hiding in the trenches and irrigation ditches of the green zone. We knew, as we walked in, that this was the perfect place for an ambush.

We followed the line of soldiers across poppy fields and other wide expanses that made me feel uncomfortably vulnerable. We walked past a compound in the cover of an irrigation ditch. From the ditch we had to step out into a raised cornfield that had been harvested and was now simply an expanse of stubble. Ahead of me was a soldier called Cookie; in front of him was the forward observation officer (FOO). Behind me was sound man James and cameraman Andrew. Though we knew the Taliban were close, we didn't know just *how* close: in fact they were crouched on the opposite side of the cornfield and it was from here that the first RPG was launched. It went straight over my head.

I'd never been shot at before, so I didn't know what to expect. I heard the sudden whoosh of the air pressure—imagine a football the size of a garage flying in your direction. I felt it too. Instinctively I hit the ground, allowing my feet to kick backwards before falling into a kind of face-down crucifix pose. That reflex movement saved my life: if I had fallen too far forwards, I would have nutted the round. My first contact would have been over before it had even begun.

The opening salvo of an ambush had been launched directly at us. It was almost as if that one RPG had been a signal. All of a sudden the air was filled with five or six of them. Some of them were starbursting—exploding in mid-air—and shrapnel rained all around me as I pretended to be dead. Whether the Taliban thought that the camera was some sort of weapon system, or whether we were simply the most exposed, the RPGs seemed to be aimed in our direction. It was more by luck than judgement that we avoided them: they skimmed over my head and exploded against the wall of the compound behind us. All around me there was shouting as everyone hit the dirt and AK-47 rounds started coming.

When I had hit the ground, corn stalks had perforated my skin and I was bleeding. I felt a moistness round the top of my trousers. The jury's still out on whether it was because I had burst my water pouch or pissed myself. You know what? I don't really care. The smell of cordite was everywhere. I kept my eyes tightly shut but managed to call to James, 'Are you recording this?'

A castrato voice replied, 'Yes!'

I prayed that the Taliban couldn't see me, but in fact I knew they could simply because their rounds were hissing over my shoulder. You can hear the bullet cutting its way through the air—lead in a steel jacket. It's on its trajectory and there's nothing you can do about it except try and get the ground to suck you up. The rounds were so close they felt as if they were burning the backs of my legs. I knew at that point that somebody had definitely V'd me out: they had me in their sights and were doing their level best to put a bullet in me. It's a strange moment in your life, when you first realize someone is looking down the barrel of a gun and trying to kill you, like I used to do with an airgun and a tin can; when you realize it's only the other guy's inability with his gun that's making him miss. It's not a feeling of which I would grow particularly fond.

I tried to hold it together for the camera, which was facing me at a skew-whiff angle and somehow still being operated by John Conroy, who was also clutching the earth; privately I was offering up another desperate prayer. Please, God. Don't let me die.

A round fell past my arm, just between my shoulder and elbow. It deafened me in one ear and I honestly thought the next round would split me down the middle.

It didn't come.

A voice. Urgent. It was Cookie. 'Ross? Are you alive?'

'Yes,' I replied, and we both started to laugh.

Return fire had started. I lifted my head up for the first time. Immediately there was more incoming.

'*Ross! Keep your fucking head down!*'

I buried my head again.

It was a proper two-way range now. The air was filled with the deafening sound of rounds—theirs and ours—as SA80s, AK-47s, GMGs, mortars and RPGs were discharged with a brutal ferocity. But we weren't out of the woods yet. The Taliban started to flank our position.

'They're getting closer!'

100

Frankly, I thought they were close enough already. But there was now enough covering fire to let us crawl back to the ditch we had left. The ground began to shake—artillery was being brought in to hit their positions. We listened with grim satisfaction as the chugging sound of fifty-cals suddenly silenced the sound of our ambushers. We ran for cover.

Having reached the safety of the ditch, Sergeant Ben Browning ordered his men to protect the flanks. But that wasn't going to be enough to protect us from the advancing Taliban. They were only 100 metres away from us and the artillery shells that had been launched in their direction hadn't stopped the firing. We crawled to a ditch further back; meanwhile B Company still had an ace up their sleeve. They called in air support, the hope being that some attack helicopters or fast air could drop something big on the men trying to kill us. Waiting for the airstrike, I attempted to salve my parched throat with some water from my pouch but it had split. There was another water pouch on my back but the tube was in my bergen and no one's going to help you out at a time like that. I was going to have to stay thirsty for a while longer. I realized my perforated face was bleeding. Not as bad as the cameraman, who had a corn stalk stuck into his eyeball. Not good in his line of work and with everything that was going on around us we had to find some tweezers to pull it out.

If I'd expected to feel ambivalent about the air strike, I was wrong. The battle lines had been drawn and it was them or us. One of the Taliban we were facing had been specifically trying to kill me; now I was rooting for the fast air to pick him and his mates out. We all wanted the enemy dead and an airstrike was the best way to achieve that aim. I could almost taste the relief in my parched mouth as I heard the sound of the fast air approaching. Their bombs or missiles would be accurate and deadly. They would get us out of this.

The sound of the planes grew louder. Louder. But then it faded away. There was no sound of a bomb strike.

It transpired that the Taliban had sought refuge in a mosque. The rules of engagement were such that the army would not bomb them while they were in there, if only because the battle for hearts and minds would take a severe hit if we started destroying the Afghans' religious buildings and monuments. Now I've no more desire to bomb a mosque than I have to bomb a church, but I couldn't help feeling the Taliban were using the rules of engagement to their own advantage. The tethered goat had brought the lion out into the open; the men had advanced with their spears; but at the last minute the wild animal had earned itself a temporary reprieve.

In order to draw the enemy out further into

the open, B Company needed to go on the offensive. But before they could do that, they had to face a new threat. A lone sniper was trying to pick us off.

The Taliban do not have superior firepower or machinery. They do have certain other advantages, however. They know the terrain; and most of them wear little more than a *dishdash* and carry only a bottle of water and a bandolier of ammo. So unencumbered by the weight of a full pack, body armour and communications system, they can move a lot quicker. As a result they are very skilled at flanking manoeuvres and at making it seem that there are more of them than in fact there are. As the sniper moved from position to position, he certainly gave the impression of there being more than one of him. Moreover, he made it much more difficult for us to move from our defensive position to somewhere where we could go on the offensive and draw out the remainder of the Taliban. B Company pushed forward anyway.

The sniper's shots rang through the air. It was impossible to know where the next one was coming from, but we were exposed and we needed cover. We had no option but to travel across open ground and break into some compounds up ahead. When my turn came to run, I sprinted faster than I had in a long time, all the while cursing the camera batteries I was carrying that weighed heavily on my body and slowed me down. As I ran, shots cracked in the air; I almost expected to be plugged halfway across the open ground, but in the end I reached the objective—out of breath, exhausted, but in one piece.

There was to be no let-up, however. I heard Mick Aston bark an order. 'Two packs, get forward. See if you can identify that sniper.' For myself and the crew, there was another nerve-racking run across open ground as we approached the compound Mick had identified. He ordered his men to break in so that they could use the roof as a firing position. I stuck as close to them as possible and, once Stu Parker and another soldier had kicked the wooden doors in, entered the compound. It felt good to be within the safety of the compound walls, but there was continuous fire all around. The air was full of smoke, radios were crackling. I could hear chopper blades in the air—a good sound, because the Taliban don't have helicopters. Then the sound of an attack helicopter firing thirty-cal rounds on to enemy positions in a different part of Jucaylay. An Apache circled threateningly overhead. I think everyone was relieved to see it—it's a terrifying piece of kit that the Taliban have to respect.

Mick Aston and his men had set up a firing position on the roof of the compound. The radio operator—or JTAC—was communicating with the Apache's commander; there was a

104

heavy machine gunner and Lance Corporal Teddy Ruecker acted as a sniper. I approached Mick and asked if he had located the enemy. He had, and from his position of advantage he was using his communications system to direct 6 Platoon towards the Taliban. He invited me up on to the roof to take a look. I clambered up the steps that led to the roof and joined the soldiers who were firing across at a compound about 100 metres away.

I lay next to Mick, facing towards 3 o'clock. From the corner of my eye I saw something moving. I looked up. *'What the fuck's that?'*

By that time, the RPG had gone past us. It had been travelling slowly because it had been launched so close to us and hadn't been charged properly. If it had hit us, no one on that roof would have survived. Mick and his lads used the incident to their advantage. The RPG had given away the Taliban's exact position. The guys opened fire on them while the Apache above us hit the Taliban compound. It despatched a Hellfire missile and thirty-cal rounds which thundered in our ears as they hit their target. A cheer arose from the lads—a cheer of relief and satisfaction that was doubled when Teddy Ruecker announced that he had just shot the RPG gunner dead.

At first, with the ambush, it had seemed the Taliban had the upper hand. Now the tide was turning. Mick was eager to capitalize on this

105

new advantage and he ordered his men to take ground closer to the enemy's position. We prepared to leave the safety of the compound and advance once more. As we were about to move off, however, we gained further information about the Taliban's movements, not because of our superior tactical advantage or because we had expert intelligence techniques, but because of our director's swollen bladder. John Conroy had nipped round the corner of the compound for a leak when he observed the Taliban moving across the field to our right. B Company opened fire. Soon the air was once more filled with 556s and the enemy were on the back foot.

So far the contact had lasted two hours: the longest, most exhausting, most nerve-shredding two hours of my life. We pushed on and approached the compound the Hellfire missile had hit. Its high mud walls bore the scars of conflict: enormous marks in the wall inflicted by the thirty-cal rounds also from the Apache. It astonished me that these rounds—easily big enough to demolish a house in the UK—were unable to pierce the walls of the compound. It was a testament to the strength of those walls, created from little more than mud, straw and water and baked hard by the fierce Afghan sun. I wasn't able to marvel at it too much, however. As we approached the compound there was the sound of more gunfire: we hit the earth as we waited for it to subside, and then gingerly headed for the protection of our destination.

The Taliban had been forced north. B Company had been on their feet for hours in the blistering sun, carrying full pack and rifle. Everyone needed a rest; what was more, I wanted to talk to some of the lads without the constant threat of enemy fire. I had just survived my first contact, I'd been scared and exhilarated in equal measure and I wanted to hear other people's thoughts and feelings.

Private Monks was eighteen years old. He had arrived in Afghanistan at the same time as me; as for me, this had been his first contact. We swapped notes. Monks admitted that he had found it a bit scary.

'Same for me, mate,' I told him. Understatement of the century.

Monks told me that one of his friends had been running across a field and an RPG had come over his head and knocked his helmet off. Monks himself had seen rounds landing inches from his feet.

As we were speaking, there was a huge explosion beyond the compound. It rocked the earth beneath us and we nearly jumped out our skin. It was the sound of a Taliban bunker being blown up. Having had my first taste of war, I knew it was a noise I was going to have to get used to.

It had been quite a morning. And it wasn't over yet.

7. SPLASH

We rested for an hour.

The compound we were in was typical of the region. The tough external walls formed a square, inside which covered buildings had been built around a central courtyard. Often these courtyards would have vegetable gardens for the inhabitants of the compound; this one had flowers. You quickly get used to the colour of sand and to see these beautiful colours was transfixing, particularly after what I'd been through. The compound was deserted, of course: the inhabitants had fled because they knew what was coming. Now it was full of exhausted soldiers, buzzing from the thrill and the fear of the contact and glad still to be in one piece. I ate some 'tails and eyes' (fish paste) on biscuits brown washed down with well water tasting of chlorine.

The contact may have lasted for two hours, but we'd been on our feet for six. We needed that rest. When the hour was up, however, the order came through that we were to continue our foray into Jucaylay.

It was as at least 45 degrees. The sun was at its height as we trudged for a further four hours without seeing any sign of the enemy. I was so tired that if we stopped for more than a minute I'd find myself falling asleep where I lay. We drank our water sparingly, wary that it might run out if we gulped it too quickly.

The green zone itself was full of mulberry trees. Often these trees are used as firing positions by the Taliban as they offer a certain amount of camouflage. They also serve another purpose. The Taliban dig a hole in the ground, then tunnel and groove mulberry trunks as a roof which they cover with mud and camouflage. Once inside, they dig deeper down and that's where they go to shelter from the artillery shells. You might be deaf for the rest of your life, but you'll probably survive.

As we patrolled this deserted town, however, there was no sign of any hidden Taliban in the mulberry trees and I tried to use them to shelter myself from the intense sun. They didn't do much good: for some reason it was just as hot and humid in the shade of the trees as it was in direct sunlight.

Even though there was no sign of the Taliban, it didn't necessarily mean they weren't there. So it was that we patrolled to the constant accompaniment of artillery shells overhead; and as we secured the area, some of the lads were ordered to clear compounds using fragmentation grenades—a dangerous process which led to one of the guys putting a piece of shrapnel into his own thigh. At one point we came across an enemy position that had been recently—and hurriedly—deserted. The Taliban had left the head of an RPG, a box of snuff that had been mixed with something, maybe poppy, as well as his sandals. Clearly we'd just missed him. More poignantly, in that same compound, we found a pile of children's books. It brought home to me that these places weren't just enemy positions. They were people's houses. At least, they had been.

Once it was clear that the area had been secured, that the Taliban truly had left, we started to retrace our footsteps back to the compounds that we had cleared earlier in the day, where the intention was to lay up for the night. I was so tired I could barely put one foot in front of the other. I'd ripped my trousers from the groin to the boot, and was practically hanging out of my pants. We came across a Viking on a resupply and a few of us—myself included—managed to hop on board back up the hill to our destination. I've never been so happy to hitch a lift in my life. It wasn't all roses, however. When our cameraman, Andy, was getting out of the vehicle, he fell over and split his hand open. That night he had to be given twelve stitches, in the dark and without the benefit of a local anaesthetic. It must have been agony, but he was adamant that he would carry on filming the next day.

And it promised to be another long one.

The following day—day four of Operation Lastay Kulang—I joined the Fire Support Group. The FSG were located on a ridge above Jucaylay. From this vantage point they could cover the troops on the ground with artillery, as well as keep a lookout around the wider countryside. They also acted as a main mobile base with Vikings, armoured Marines and doctors. It was from the FSG's position that morning that the Taliban were spotted.

There was movement about 3 klicks away, in a cave system on the other side of the valley. The Fire Support Group believed that the Taliban had retreated to these caves as a result of being forced out of Jucaylay by B Company's operations the previous day. It certainly sounded likely, but David Robinson, Mick Aston's second in command and the ranking officer on the high ground, needed to be sure that it was enemy combatants who had been spotted and not simply locals who had retreated to escape the battle in their village. The caves were carefully surveyed through binoculars and it was eventually decided that this was indeed a Taliban refuge.

An airstrike was ordered.

Over the radio I heard the request for 'some sort of ordnance . . . or a delayed fuse down in and around that grid'. It was military terminology and I wasn't sure quite how it would translate. What was being requested, I realized a few minutes later, was a big bomb. A thousand pounder. That was going to do a lot of damage.

The hum of the aircraft seemed to come

from nowhere and to disappear as soon as it had arrived. Not before it had delivered its package, though. The 1,000lb bomb found its mark with unerring accuracy. It had a fuse delay so it could penetrate the ground before it went off and create more subterranean damage. It exploded in the distance. There was a devastating flash of orange, like something from a movie, and then a huge cloud of sand and dust mushroomed hundreds of feet into the air. The radio operator confirmed the direct hit with a single word.

'Splash.'

There was no way anyone who had been in the range of that explosion could have survived it. But the Taliban must have been more widely spaced out than had previously been believed as more movement was spotted. Without hesitation, the JTAC called in a second strike. 'You are clear for a re-attack on similar bunk system, same nature with a 10-millisecond delay.'

The hum of an approaching aircraft. And then the second bomb, as awe-inspiring as the first.

'Splash.'

This time the observers spotted no movement. At least, no movement from human beings. The only survivors, it appeared, from those two 1,000lb bombs were a herd of goats scarpering terrified down the valley.

*   *   *

As far as we could tell, the immediate Taliban threat had been neutralized. That didn't mean B Company's job was over. Far from it. As the morning turned to afternoon, it started to become clear that the Taliban were not the only people to have been hurt as a result of the fighting in Jucaylay. Bit by bit, a stream of villagers approached. Their children had been hurt on the outskirts of the battle and they were seeking help from the army doctors.

The help was given, of course. Unconditionally. The children barely made a sound as B Company's doctor removed shrapnel from their bodies and bandaged their wounds. After the exhilaration of watching the bombs being dropped on the Taliban positions, seeing these injured children was a solemn, sobering reality check. Those whom the company doctor could not adequately treat out here in the field were taken back to Camp Bastion in a Chinook for more advanced medical care.

We kept the cameras rolling as these children's undeserved wounds were patched up. At this time we knew that we would never responsibly be able to show their faces on TV, however. The Taliban insurgents would inevitable return to Jucaylay, and if they were to learn that these people had sought help from the British troops, the repercussions

113

would be severe. The children were given sweets and biscuits; but before they left the care of B Company they took pains to remove the wrappings so that the treats could not be identified as coming from the soldiers.

As the afternoon wore on, more villagers approached, this time without children. They were village elders, with their white head dresses, long white beards and dark, leathery skin, and they sat in a circle on the dusty ground at a respectful distance from our position, having asked for a *shura*, or meeting. None of us knew what they wanted, and as Mick Aston was still in the green zone it fell to Captain David Robinson—second in command, or 2ic—to conduct the meeting and listen to their concerns. He walked down to them, taking bottles of cool water with him. The rest of us sat and watched from the hill.

David returned after a tense hour. The villagers were concerned, he explained, about the bombs that had been dropped on the caves. They knew that there had been Taliban in the area, but equally they were worried that there had been ordinary villagers taking refuge in the same cave system. They wanted to go and have a look, to check that there had been no innocent civilian casualties and, if necessary, bring back any dead bodies for burial, without B Company mistaking them for Taliban.

The 2ic was convinced that everyone we had

engaged had been carrying weapons; nevertheless, the idea that we might have killed civilians in the bomb strike was an uncomfortable one. The Afghan villagers—who had been friendly and unswervingly practical about the situation—could not be denied the right to go and check, so David gave his permission for them to head towards the caves. It was a great relief when word came back that the villagers had failed to find any civilian casualties.

The Taliban had either fled or been killed. Now the villagers were starting to reclaim their homes. A counter-attack by the enemy was possible at any moment, of course, so everyone needed to stay vigilant; but this seemed as good a time as any to head back down into the green zone and talk to some of the locals. It would be the first time I had actually had a chance to meet ordinary Afghan folk: I was eager to know—and apprehensive about—what they thought of our presence and the events of the past twenty-four hours.

It was good to see the village returned to some semblance of normality. Sure, there were British troops everywhere; sure, there were Vikings with fifty-cals mounted on top. But there were also children, dressed in traditional, richly coloured garb. Some of the young boys wore charcoal mascara and had painted nails. They were very happy for the sweets handed out by the soldiers. These

115

children had returned with their parents, who were clearly satisfied that the Taliban would not be coming back imminently. That's not to say, however, that we were unconditionally welcomed.

I approached a group of men. They all wore beards, though they were shorter than the length of a fist once ordered by the Taliban when they controlled the country. I asked a translator what it was these people would like to see done; but my question was answered with another question, and a confrontational one at that. 'Our question is: what have you done for us since you've come here? You have destroyed our homeland, you have killed our people and you have demolished our houses. We have supported you, but what have you done for us?'

I was being drawn into a political conversation. I asked the man if he thought one of the reasons for the army's actions was that the Taliban had been allowed free rein to come in and out of this village. He ignored the question.

'We haven't got irrigation channels,' he declared. 'The ones we have are in a bad way. They need repairs. The other problem for us is the river. When it floods it washes away the houses and the fields. Also we don't have a hospital. We've got sick people in our houses but no medicine.'

What this Afghan man was saying was

116

undoubtedly true; yet the more I found myself drawn into the conversation, the more I found myself arguing. Did he not realize, I asked, that before you can have doctors and teachers, you had to get rid of the people who *didn't* want them? If there were no forces around, teachers would be killed by the Taliban and that was why the Taliban had to be dealt with before reconstruction could begin in earnest.

My conversation partner, of course, had an answer. 'That's down to you. You've got power, you've got tanks, you've got planes. Bringing security is also down to you. It's your responsibility, not ours. Why do you ask me these questions? It's all up to you.'

I found the interchange a frustrating one. I had great sympathy for the way these Afghan villagers were being forced to live their lives; I had sympathy for their wounded children and for the adults who, not for the first time, found their homeland turned into a war zone. But equally I had seen the sacrifices that the Royal Anglians had made to try to bring peace to Jucaylay. I had seen the reality of their job and the ferocity of their enemy. It was galling that the locals were not as welcoming to the troops as they might have been, even if it was understandable.

I was beginning to see just what a struggle the battle for hearts and minds was in this difficult, morally ambiguous territory. With one breath the Afghan man had condemned the destruction of his homeland; with the next he had stated that it was up to the forces to use their tanks, planes and power to bring peace. In the face of such a contradictory demand, it was impossible to know how successful we could ever hope to be in winning the support of the Afghan population. I also realised that the locals knew they couldn't be that friendly. There could well have been Taliban collaborators in the village.

What was clear, however, was that chasing the Taliban from Jucaylay had been a good thing, no matter that the Royal Anglians were not being praised left, right and centre by the Afghans. I sensed a determination in the air, a resolution that whatever the reception, the lads were not going to be deterred from carrying out their orders.

*   *   *

Even though the Taliban had been fought back, Jucaylay remained a dangerous place. None of us knew when or even if a counter-attack would happen, so we took the opportunity to rest for the remainder of the day. I fell asleep in a ditch and woke with the radio operator's socks under my chin. Trust me, his socks were nearly as bad as his tuna breath.

At 04.00 the following morning—the fifth day of Operation Lastay Kulang—we attached

118

ourselves once more to the Fire Support Group and headed back up to the ridge. In Afghanistan, as I had found out, most fighting is done in the morning, before the midday sun has had a chance to sap the energy of the combatants. The FSG were scrupulous in keeping up their observation of the surrounding territory, and the first thing I saw as I arrived on the ridge was a group of Afghans being escorted by soldiers. They were placed inside a Viking vehicle and driven up the hillside to where we were positioned.

There were five detainees. They had been captured during the course of the operation and interviewed by Company Sergeant Major Tim Newton. There was a suspicion that they might not be the innocent villagers they claimed to be but were in fact Taliban. Despite their denials, Tim clearly still had his doubts, so he had called in the Regimental Sergeant Major, Ian Robinson. The detainees were treated firmly but with respect. They were allowed to sit in the shade of a tree and were given water, but when Ian completed his questioning of them, he found their responses vague and unsatisfactory. He made the decision that the Afghans should be taken to a position further back from the village in an attempt to make it clear that this was not a game and that if the Anglians believed them to be Taliban, the consequences could be severe.

For me, the incident highlighted one of the

most difficult things about the war in Afghanistan. The enemy don't wear T-shirts with the word 'Taliban' emblazoned upon them; the moment they put down their AK-47 or their RPG launcher, there's really nothing to distinguish them from innocent civilians. Of course, they use this to their advantage, which means that the British troops need constantly to be on alert. They can never quite trust anybody. And in the battle for hearts and minds, a lack of trust is a difficult hurdle to jump over.

In the end, it was decided that the detainees were not in fact Taliban. They were released, taken back to their village and given compensation. What effect their experiences had in terms of the relationship between the locals and the occupying force it was impossible to say.

The remainder of the day passed slowly as I started to learn one unchangeable fact about war: it's made up of long periods of extreme boredom punctuated by moments of abject terror. When the boredom comes, you don't complain. It gave me a chance to recover to some small extent, and to try to make sense of the events of the past few days. Operation Lastay Kulang was almost at an end. So far, it had lasted five days. As far as I was concerned, they had been the toughest five days of my life. The camera crew agreed. No question. I was totally exhausted; my feet were cracked, infected and blistered, with pus running between the toes. I had scratched the inside of my ear and the flies had been attracted to the blood. Blocked with pus, scab and sand, it had become infected.

Even the rest of B Company, who were infinitely more used to the realities of warfare than us, agreed that it had been the most arduous operation they had yet undertaken. Even so, it wasn't lost on me that while I had been on the ground for less than a week, the rest of them were out here for a relentless six-month tour of duty.

But I was alive, which was more than could be said for one young man who had set out with us from Camp Bastion five days previously. Despite Darren Bonner's death, Lastay Kulang had, in operational terms, been judged a success. The Taliban had been forced from the area and ISAF forces were in a better position now to start some measure of reconstruction.

Whether that would happen or not was a different question.

8. STAND-OFF

The excursion into the green zone around Jucaylay was not over for B Company, who were going to continue to patrol for a few more days; but it had come to an end for the camera team and myself. Our high-definition camera, which was never designed for the job it was doing, needed attention after so much heavy use; our power packs were dead and we were running out of film stock. There was no point in our being there if we couldn't film— we'd just be in the way. The soldiers were resupplied with ammo and provisions and continued to patrol the area. We, on the other hand, caught a Chinook back to Camp Bastion.

If our camera equipment was suffering, so, frankly, were we. From exhaustion. We weren't sorry to be returning to base so that we could be reinvigorated too. The troops on the ground have grown to love Chinooks more than anything else on the planet. When I saw the chopper arriving to take us back to Bastion, I understood why. It's like Christmas morning every time you see one; knowing I was about to be taken back from the front line made me feel as if I was about to open all my presents.

Christmas morning was going to have to

wait a bit longer for B Company. Operation Lastay Kulang was supposed to last for only four days. In the event, they ended up being away from Bastion for the best part of three weeks in total. We hung around Bastion licking our wounds while B Company carried on the fight. When the day finally came for them to return, they trundled out of FOB Rob in convoy, just as they had arrived. Almost immediately they suffered two mine strikes, both within thirty minutes and 200 metres of each other. No one was killed, but having witnessed at first hand the kind of damage a mine strike can do to a Viking armoured vehicle, I knew how very lucky they had been. It was a great relief when B Company arrived safely back at Bastion with the same number of men as they had had when they left Jucaylay.

The guys also knew how differently their return journey could have turned out. When I spoke to Mick Aston his voice oozed relief. 'Fuck,' he told me. 'It's good to be back in one piece. I was shitting myself with those mine strikes, but I think everyone was. We're lucky not to have casualties.' He smiled as he spoke, the nervous, elated smile of a man who knew that he and the men under his command had just faced great danger and come away unscathed.

As the soldiers limped wearily back into Bastion I was interested to know how their

123

morale was after such a gruelling operation. After all, I had only spent five days on operations with them and that had been enough to sap all the energy from me; and for obvious reasons there hadn't been a lot of opportunity for chinwagging. As I chatted with Teddy Ruecker I was not completely astonished to learn that it wasn't the constant threat of contact with the enemy that undermined his enthusiasm for the operation; it was the lack of basic comforts that any of us would expect as our due.

'It was the rations that got to me,' he explained. 'By the third week I had to physically force myself to eat the food because I just couldn't stand it any more. It was just the same shit every day, having to wear the same dirty socks, the same dirty clothes. It fucking gets to you. And the blokes are just fucking exhausted, especially having to carry all the fucking extra ammo.'

I'd noticed a lot of the guys using the word 'fuck' on their return. I wasn't surprised. They'd had a fucking hard time of it. It's easy to forget, amid all the other dangers they face, that soldiers' morale can be severely compromised by the conditions they have to live in on the front line. Napoleon said that 'an army marches on its stomach' and it's true. I had become increasingly aware of the poor quality of the ration packs issued to the troops. Not only are they substantially less inviting than those issued to the American and Canadian armies; they show evidence of a severe lack of forethought. What is the point, I couldn't help wondering more than once, of issuing chocolate bars to troops fighting in 50-degree heat? It turns into chocolate sludge and the best thing you can do with it is squeeze it over your biscuits brown or your biscuits fruit. And there's a reason why the soldiers renamed their corned beef hash 'corned beef gash' . . .

While I was out on Operation Lastay Kulang, Colour Sergeant Ivan Snow—Snowy, as everyone called him—had thrown me a Canadian MRE (Meal, Ready-to-Eat). The difference between that and the British ration pack was stark. I found a sachet of pineapple chunks in syrup—it was like nectar in the arid heat of the desert. I was like Homer Simpson as I tried to squeeze every last drop of that fruity syrup down my parched throat. In addition, there was a Sloppy Giuseppe pizza. It sounds like a small thing, but the morale boost of a bit of half-decent food—a taste of home— was unquantifiable. It changes your outlook for the day. It's a sad truth that the care the Americans and Canadians put into the MREs is replicated in other facets of their soldiers' lives. They're looked after better than British soldiers, of whom we claim to be so proud.

Camp Bastion is hardly luxurious, but it sure as hell must have felt like it to the soldiers returning from Operation Lastay Kulang. The first thing they did on their return was square away their kit and clean their rifles—just in case they needed them again straight away. They soaked up the relative luxuries their desert home afforded like a dry sponge absorbing water. Fresh food, a decent bed, washing facilities, lots and lots to drink. Having been away for so long in the dust and the heat it took all of them a number of good, hot meals to rid themselves of the memory of all those relentlessly undelicious ration packs and several showers to wash away the accumulated grime. I knew from experience that there was no greater relief than getting back to camp and bathing your sandy eyes in Optrex. The dust gets ingrained in your pores. I have a watch that I wore out there, the leather strap of which is peppered with specks of dust that I can't get out, no matter how much I scrub it. Similarly it takes a good few scrubs even to start getting it out of your skin, and you bleed for a few days after that.

Like wilted plants that had been given water, you could see their spirits rise dramatically. That process was immeasurably helped by some morale-boosting contact with the people they had left back home. It's impossible to overstate how important it is to the troops to have letters and news from loved ones in England. The smiles on their faces as three weeks' worth of accumulated mail was handed out was testament to that. While they were out on the ground, one of the lads—Corporal Pete Toynton—had become a godfather. He was clearly chuffed to bits by the news, and by receiving a picture of his new godchild. There were not only letters but also parcels containing food and other bits and bobs to make the lads' life a little easier and to remind them of what was going on back home.

These letters and treats came not only from friends and family. Good-natured members of the public write postcards and send food to the troops, which are dished out equally. It does the soldiers no end of good to realize that what they are doing is remembered and appreciated by the folks back home. It doesn't even really matter what's in the package—it could be a pair of socks that you're never going to wear, or a slice of cake so hard and stale that you could use it as armour plating—but it means so much to have that little bit of contact with the outside world. A taste of home.

We filmed one such postcard being read out by Private Robert Foster. 'We just thought we would drop you a line to let you know we are thinking of you all. We're so proud of you.' This message of support was accompanied by a food parcel. By complete coincidence, several months later I was walking with my parents along a beach in Norfolk when a couple came up to me. It turned out that they were the people who had sent that very package. It felt good to be able to tell them how much their gesture was appreciated by the lads of B Company. It felt less good to know that Private Foster, at the time he read that message, had only months to live . . .

The brief respite at Bastion gave the lads time to relax, relaxation being a commodity in short supply when you're facing the Taliban. Alcohol was banned, of course, although I could tell that a certain amount of booze was smuggled in via food packages and it was hard to disapprove of that entirely. (I never, *ever* saw booze anywhere near the front line, however, and despite the fact that marijuana grows like a weed in Afghanistan, I never saw anyone partake.) Reading matter of a predictably laddish nature was passed around. I seem to remember *Nuts* magazine featuring highly, and various centrefolds being pinned up on the wall. Women's breasts were allowed to be on display, but there was a strict pussy embargo. The rule seemed to be pretty well adhered to. It surprised me that a lot of them would unwind by playing war-based video games on their Nintendos. Maybe it was a generational thing; maybe it just felt good that Game Over meant you could start again with all your lives intact.

Despite the fact that everyone appeared to be recuperating nicely, there was an unspoken acknowledgement that the death of A

Company's Darren Bonner had affected everyone in the regiment deeply. When Darren had been repatriated, the remainder of A Company had been in the field, unable to pay their last respects. So it was that a memorial service was held at Bastion for their fallen colleague. It was a subdued group of soldiers who congregated to honour Darren's memory, and it was humbling to see the looks of solemn reverence they had on their faces as they watched a montage of images from his repatriation ceremony. Tears fell as his friends gazed at photographs of his coffin, draped in the Union Jack, being loaded on to a plane to be returned to his grieving family. All this accompanied by the strains of 'Wake Me Up When September Ends' by Green Day. An emotional tune. Emotional lyrics. I had to struggle to hold back the tears myself; and I couldn't help but wonder how many more Royal Anglians would have to make that same return journey. After all, they weren't even halfway through their time in Afghanistan.

I'm sure I wasn't the only person entertaining such thoughts.

*   *   *

There wasn't a lot of time for the regiment to mourn their lost colleague. Nor was there a great deal of time for B Company to continue resting their battle-weary bones. Very soon after their return to Bastion, the lads were briefed for their next task.

The town of Now Zad lies some 70 kilometres north of Camp Bastion. It had been the site of some severe fighting in the past and parts of the town were still rife with Taliban. As a result, many of the local people had been driven away. A Company had already been stationed there, with the intention of driving the Taliban away from Now Zad so that the locals could return; B Company were to replace them and continue that task. Easier said than done, although as we were being briefed in the heat of the Bastion day by A Company's 2ic, Captain Paul Steele, it was made clear to us that headway had already been made. A projector beamed a detailed satellite map of Now Zad on to a screen in front of us; a green dotted line appeared, bisecting the town. When the Anglians had taken over, the Royal Marines would not cross this line. This meant that the Taliban were calling the shots—literally. When the Anglians arrived, they started to push northwards into Taliban-occupied territory. This put the enemy on the back foot and gave A Company the opportunity to start to decide where and when contacts would happen. Progress, of a sort.

Now Zad, though, presented certain difficulties for which Jucaylay had not prepared the lads. For a start, the town was out of the range of our artillery. This meant that the Fire Support Group—located on a hill on the outskirts of the town—would shoulder much more of the responsibility for keeping the troops stationed in the town itself safe. Perhaps more worryingly, the Taliban in Now Zad seemed to be of a different calibre to those we had encountered during Operation Lastay Kulang. In Jucaylay, the enemy had fled as soon as the troops started to get the upper hand. In Now Zad they had a track record of digging in and making a fight of it. Despite the fact that A Company had undertaken an offensive role, they were still there. Their mortar fire was extremely accurate, as was their small-arms fire. It was also clear that they had a sentry point that enabled them to identify British troops whenever they pushed east, but so far the soldiers had been unable to pinpoint its location.

B Company were to be stationed in Now Zad for six weeks. It was a long time to be away from the comforts of Bastion and we would be joining them to see how they coped in this unfriendly outpost of Helmand Province. An advance party of thirty or forty men would be going on ahead to get the lie of the land; the rest of us would be following on when the order came through. We didn't know how we'd be getting there. There were two options. By road, which I knew from past experience was incredibly dangerous. Or by helicopter, which wasn't much better, as the landing area at Now Zad had come under regular attack by the Taliban. While the 140 men of B Company waited to find out how they would be deployed to Now Zad, they kept busy. All their additional weapons systems needed cleaning, as they had fired a lot of ammo during their time in Jucaylay; equally their vehicles needed to be thoroughly checked over by the armoured Marines. When you rely so heavily on your machinery, you want to make sure it's not going to let you down at the crucial moment. Morale had been boosted by the brief period of rest at Camp Bastion and I noticed that B Company seemed to have a renewed appetite for a fight. Tim Newton articulated it well. Although our location in Now Zad would be a relatively secure one, that didn't mean we would simply be sitting back and taking it easy. 'We've got to take a fight to the enemy. We're not there to mince around.'

Quite.

Finally the word came through: we would be travelling to Now Zad the following morning by Viking, crewed by the Royal Marines.

Having already gone out on one operation, I felt a little more sanguine about our deployment to Now Zad. Not complacent, but at least I knew something of what to expect. I didn't have the fear of the unknown to contend with: just the fear of battle.

The Viking vehicles were prepared that evening. There wasn't a chance for much sleep, as preparations were completed in the pitch black of the small hours the following morning. It was amazing that everyone could prepare their gear with such ease in the darkness; but I guess they knew the vehicles and their kit so well by now that they could almost have done it blindfolded.

We set off in the dark, not knowing how long the journey would take us. We expected to be in Now Zad in somewhere between six and twelve hours; but I knew only too well from the trek to Jucaylay how such estimates could turn out to be wildly wrong. I knew, too, just what dangers we faced as we rolled through the desert at a crucifyingly slow 15 kilometres per hour. Just as before, there was a constant threat of landmines and ambushes. We relied heavily on the skill of our drivers to keep us safe and whole. I watched the sun rising magnificently over the desert in an attempt to keep my mind off the dangers.

The terrain was hard, the Viking hot and uncomfortable. And it wasn't just explosive devices that we had to watch out for. The desert earth was filled with deep indentations or wadis, which in the winter are wide streams of water but in the summer are baked hard into treacherous trenches. It's almost impossible for the drivers to see where these indentations occur because of the massive dust

133

clouds kicked up by the vehicles churning over the sand. We were miles from anywhere when our Viking suddenly juddered and fell into one of these wadis. Our driver kept his speed up to try to force us up out of the other side, but without success. We came to a sudden, jolting stop, the Viking cocked at an angle, its tracks spinning uselessly in the sandy ground, the only thing keeping the two parts of the vehicle together being the hydraulics in the middle.

We were stuck.

It was a tense, risky moment. I was virtually hanging upside down and felt like an egg in a tin can. We were sitting ducks, a prime target for any passing Taliban. Our only option was to be towed out of the wadi by another Viking. As that happened, our gunner shot covering fire into the desert to make sure that we were not the object of any opportunistic enemy bombardment. It was a great relief to feel the Viking being hauled out of that ditch, ready to continue the slow journey to Now Zad.

Thankfully we approached the town in one piece. Well, almost. As a result of that choppy, juddering journey I lost a tooth—a fascia, in fact, the result of an old rugby injury. An unimportant event in the scheme of things, of course. We were all acutely aware that injuries of a much graver nature were more than possible and as we neared the end of our journey we were happy at least that it had not been blighted by tragedy as my last trip in similar circumstances had been. It had taken us nearly six hours to come into range of a strategically crucial land formation on the outskirts of Now Zad called ANP Hill.

So called because the Afghan National Police were once posted there, ANP Hill is a key location in the struggle for superiority in Now Zad. Located to the south-west of the town, it offers a view, and the possibility of making an arc of fire, over all the surrounding area, and most importantly over the military base in Now Zad District Centre as well as the rest of the town. The District Centre, or DC, is actually located in the western part of Now Zad, approximately 900 metres from ANP Hill. To its south-west is a patch of desert. This is used as a landing zone for incoming helicopters and is under constant surveillance by the Fire Support Groups on ANP Hill.

It felt good to come into range of the hill. It didn't mean that we were safe from incoming fire, but it did mean that if the enemy were foolish enough to give it a go, the fifty-cals and mortars up on the hill would soon give them the good news that we were under their protection. Under the watchful eye of the Fire Support Group we moved into Now Zad towards the safety of the British base. There was something slightly spooky about the deserted streets of this war-ravaged town. The sturdy metal gates that marked the entrance to the District Centre opened to let our convoy in; then they closed firmly and, I hoped, safely behind us. We had arrived at our new home.

*   *   *

Now Zad DC had seen its share of action. The Gurkhas and the Paras had been holed up here while ANP Hill was still under the control of the Afghan National Police and Now Zad itself was fully inhabited. Things were different now. The area around the DC was deserted, for a start. Most of the residents of the compounds that made up the town had fled to surrounding villages or sought safety in the mountains that hulked in the distance. One of these mountain ranges was known as the Crocodile's Back because of its resemblance to the reptile; the name seemed appropriate, somehow. Towards the north-east of the town was a wide dried-out wadi that marked the heart of the green zone and it was here that the Taliban were congregated in force. The DC itself was a square compound surrounded by wicked-looking barbed wire and with lookout posts at each corner. It was once home to the Afghan National Police, and other buildings inside its walls included a prison and a mosque. At least, that's what they used to be. Although the Afghan national flag flew from the top of the DC, the compound was now completely controlled and occupied by the British and was the base from which they kept

136

the Taliban at bay.

As soon as B Company arrived, it fell to Mick Aston to introduce them to their new surroundings. He was characteristically direct. 'I'll be straight with you,' he announced to the assembled company. 'The tempo here is a lot lower than what we've had up until now.' That, at least, was good news. It meant that we didn't have to expect the same level of contact with the enemy that we had experienced during Operation Lastay Kulang. But Mick immediately qualified his statement. 'That doesn't mean we need to take it easy or become complacent. And to tell you the truth, that is my biggest fear. When you look out there and you go up to ANP Hill and you look out into the green zone over there, that's where the Taliban are. And they're there in force, in well-defended positions. You only have to look out 400 metres from the front gate and that's where A Company got themselves into a fair bit of trouble.'

What Mick was saying was this: Now Zad DC might seem like an oasis of safety, but it was an oasis surrounded by a desert of danger. 'There's a lot of Taliban activity over there,' he continued. 'There's a big wadi and that's like a Taliban highway between the north and further down to the south-east to Musa Qala and Sangin. We need to pick our fight. And when we do, we'll go out in strength. Pick the time and the place, and we choose that, not

137

them. We'll fucking put them in the hurt locker.'

Put them in the hurt locker. A favourite saying of Mick's and one that caused a ripple of laughter through the troops. They seemed motivated by his speech, and ready to do what he was asking of them: to take the fight to the Taliban.

In order to get more of a sense of the British base and the surrounding area, I joined Private Thomas Cox in one of the four fortified lookout posts, also known as sangars. These sangars are cramped, low-ceilinged little places, reinforced with sandbags and surrounded by the same caging that encased the armoured vehicles that had moved us through the desert. The caging is there to diffuse the force of any RPGs that are fired towards the sangar. How much good it would do I wasn't sure and I hoped I wouldn't have to find out. At eye level there was an observation gap through which Thomas could aim his GPMG. It looked out over the deserted area of Now Zad and into the green zone. On the wall in front of him there was a photographic map with a grid superimposed and each of the compounds numbered, an exact replica of the view from the sangar. This map is an important tool: in the event of a contact, it means a spotter can join the gunner in the lookout post and point to the exact area on the map where he thinks there is enemy

138

movement, rather than try to explain it, which would be cumbersome and far from effective. The way in which the compounds on the maps are numbered is changed on a regular basis in case one of these maps should fall into enemy hands.

From these observation posts, the green zone was easy to see. The difference between our location and the enemy's was stark. We had the dry, arid desert where nothing grows and there is no water; they had irrigated land with all that comes with it—water, fruit trees, fresh food. I knew where I'd rather have been, if it weren't for the fact that walking unprotected into the green zone would have been less good for your life expectancy than it would for your appetite. The area intervening the British and Taliban troops was the deserted part of Now Zad. I couldn't help thinking that the situation bore all the hallmarks of a classic stand-off.

Private Cox had been working shifts in the sangar of two hours on and two hours off. I asked him if he managed to get much sleep in those two hours. He tried, he said, but I had the impression that sleep came with difficulty. From the sangar, you got a real sense of the true situation in Now Zad. The British troops had been forced into a static position whereas the Taliban had the run of the green zone and were also able to make use of the many compounds surrounding the DC. The streets

139

between compounds provided cover and access and meant that the enemy could get within 20 or 30 metres of the British base without running the risk of being observed. Indeed, when the Paras and the Gurkhas had been there they had found that the Taliban were able to come close enough to hurl grenades over the wall into the DC. There was also a long, straight street approaching the base that had become known as RPG alley because it was easy for the Taliban to jump into the road, fire an RPG at the DC and then jump immediately back out of range before the lookouts had had time to counter-attack.

All this made me realize that having the base in the middle of the town presented a distinct strategic disadvantage. As Private Cox philosophically put it, however, you play the hand you're dealt. And it wasn't as if the positioning of the base was ideal for the ordinary inhabitants of Now Zad, either. Although the compounds were deserted, they occasionally needed to return to their houses and before they could even consider doing that they had to approach the British base and ask permission. They knew what would happen if they walked unannounced through the streets and were mistaken for Taliban; and I was left in no doubt that if whoever was manning the sangar saw any kind of unauthorized movement ahead of him, he'd open fire. Card Alpha, of course, would dictate that he would

140

need to identify the target as a threat—the rules of engagement were such that he couldn't have shot someone simply for being a 'dicker'. But it was pretty obvious to everyone concerned that if movement was spotted from the sangar, it probably wasn't someone coming to fix the roof. Private Cox told me that their hope was to get as many civilians to move back into the town as possible; but it was perfectly clear that with this kind of stand-off, that wasn't going to happen any time soon.

'It's quite beautiful,' I observed as I looked out of the sangar at the surrounding mountains. Private Cox didn't reply. I suppose, in his position, the beauty of the Afghan landscape was the last thing on his mind.

Leaving Private Cox with the distinct impression I was a bit of a luvvie, I tried to imagine what Now Zad might have looked like before the ISAF forces invaded. The nearby bazaar was lined with relatively newly built garage-type buildings with sliding metal doors. These would once have been shops selling the standard wares of an Afghan town: motorcycle parts, Calor gas, clothes, shoes, more motorcycle parts, more Calor gas. Even under Taliban rule, the bazaar would have been buzzing with life and activity; but not now. Now the shops were closed down, their metal frontages firmly shut. There was no activity here, and there wouldn't be for a long time.

My sleeping quarters were below the sangar.

141

After a couple of days in Now Zad DC I made the decision not to sleep inside—it was just too hot and claustrophobic and I would wake with my eyes and throat clogged up with dust—so instead I would bunk down outside against the exterior wall of the compound. It probably wasn't the safest place to sleep, especially given that I knew it was theoretically possible for the Taliban simply to lob a grenade over the wall. But I decided not to think about that. The Afghans often spend the night outdoors when the weather is very hot and with the company of the astonishing canopy of stars overhead, I slept much better outside than in.

Just outside the sleeping quarters was the area where we would wash and eat. This outside space was covered with camouflage netting. Normally this is draped over vehicles to stop them being spotted, but in this instance it was there to dissipate the sun and provide us with some level of protection from the fierce heat of the day. As always, that heat started early. When the time came for me to perform my morning ablutions, the big plastic canister of water with which I would wash was already hot. The water at Now Zad DC came up from a well and there were two types. The stuff used for washing was untreated; the stuff for drinking was purified, using chlorine or iodine tablets, and came in bottles with a white seal so that you didn't mistake one for the other.

Keeping yourself and your gear clean when

you're out in the desert is difficult, and important. It's vital that you keep clean and dry those parts of your body that are inclined to sweat, especially—look away now, ladies—the area around your groin. Ignore the basics of personal hygiene round there where your clothes are rubbing against the sweaty skin and you'll end up with a nasty case of 'dobi itch', a kind of thrush on the inside of your legs. You can also get it up the crack of your arse, and around your bollocks, so it's a good idea to use powder or Vaseline. Thank God I was spared a bout of embarrassing and uncomfortable scrot rot, but there were soldiers who suffered from it.

One of the biggest difficulties I had in Afghanistan was with my feet. I first started having problems with them during Operation Lastay Kulang and I wasn't the only one. When you're going in and out of the green zone, your feet get wet in the irrigation trenches. They also get very hot because of the climate and when you're on a long patrol or operation, they get no chance to breathe. Essentially, they boil. When you finally remove your boots and your feet dry out, the skin splits. My feet would crack on the underside where the toe meets the foot itself. Because they've been in hot, wet conditions, the feet start to get mildew and the fungus eats away at the split skin, making it even sorer. Flies love the raw, gooey skin, so it's a struggle to keep

143

them away and once all this starts it's a vicious circle. Soldiers in Afghanistan are forever trying to dry their feet out; but if it's a choice between getting shot and having sore feet, you'll take the sore feet any time. On my first trip out there, I would try to dry my feet out with foot powder, but this was a mistake: the fungus can become attached to the powder and work its way deeper into your cracked feet, causing infection. In an environment where people's lives are at risk, it might sound a bit pathetic to complain about your feet, but it could be very, very painful. Soldiers become very pernickety about looking after their extremities.

When I went back home for the first time, I visited a chiropodist. Even she found the state of my feet disgusting. She said the dead skin she had spent 20 minutes scraping away looked like a bowl of pasta (Bolognese, anyone?) and she gave me plenty of advice on how to look after them when I returned. I learned to spray the skin with an alcohol spray to kill the fungus and to rub them with a fungicidal cream to keep the infection at bay. It made me reflect on the fact that certain aspects of being an infantryman at war have probably not changed all that much over the years. No doubt the invading forces in Afghanistan during the First Anglo-Afghan War had trouble with their feet; no doubt they too had dobi itch. It's one of the difficulties of fighting in such an inhospitable place and I couldn't help wondering if having to endure everything that goes with living in such an extreme climate is what has made the Afghans such tough people.

Whatever the truth, I had the impression that B Company's stay in Now Zad was going to present them with different challenges to those they had so far had to deal with.

9. MR NOW ZAD

B Company were given only twenty-four hours to acclimatize to their new surroundings. The day after we arrived, they started to prepare for their first patrol, which would take them into the main town of Now Zad and up to the Fire Support Group's location on the top of ANP Hill. This was no walk in the park: A Company had been attacked by the Taliban just outside the compound of Now Zad DC on a number of occasions, so it was with a certain amount of foreboding that I prepared to accompany them.

We stepped warily out of the main gates to the DC and headed east, past RPG alley and into the town itself. B Company aside, there was not a soul to be seen—sort of a relief, but then it was unlikely that a Taliban sniper would be dancing in the streets in front of us. The soldiers around me gripped their weapons firmly; there was a sense of genuine apprehension, a sense that danger could be around any corner.

It was as we were climbing the exposed slope of ANP Hill that we heard the first rounds. They were fifty-cals from the FSG at the top of the hill, loud enough and unexpected enough to send a frightening shock through my body. I stopped walking and looked around to see if they were firing at anything in particular, but all I could see was a herd of nervy sheep scurrying away from the noise. The test firing of the fifty-cal carried on as we continued up the hill in the baking heat. I stopped to admire the view, which drew a few sharp words about not hanging around from James the sound man.

The original fortification at the top of ANP Hill was built by the Russians during their occupation of Afghanistan in the 1980s—a testament to the location's tactical importance. Corporal Pete Toynton told me that when he had arrived there, he had scraped away part of the wall to find some vintage examples of high-quality Soviet porn—not exactly cash in the attic, but the nearest you'd get out there. He'd also found an old Soviet General Purpose Machine Gun. It had clearly been used by the Taliban at some point in history because it had little bits of coloured tape and tassels on it which they use to decorate their weapons. For some reason the gun had been buried in the wall. Pete had dug it out and cleaned it up, a monument to a time when ANP Hill was home to a very different force of soldiers.

Now, though, ANP Hill was home to B Company's Fire Support Group. The FSG generally occupies the high ground. It means they can shoot down on enemy positions, but it also means that they attract a lot of fire themselves. Hence the fact that the location was well protected with high walls of sandbags. From the top of this hill, though, with its spectacular 360-degree views, you can appreciate why it's such an important location, and also why it is that forts have been built on hilltops since time immemorial.

Colour Sergeant Ivan Snow was in charge of the FSG. He was uncompromising, fearless and one of the best soldiers I've ever met. He hailed from Wisbech, one of the toughest parts of East Anglia, and his aim when he finished the army was to return there and become a social worker. I couldn't think of anybody better suited to do so. Nor could I think of anybody better to run the FSG from ANP Hill. He had the most unbelievable eyesight: he was able to spot Taliban movement in the distance that most people would need a pair of binoculars to view.

Snowy gave the patrol a quick briefing, pointing out the various areas of Now Zad that could be seen from this vantage point and explaining which bits of the sprawling town tended to be frequented by Taliban. The areas had mostly Afghan-sounding names—Changulak, Hojamal—with the exception of one that had been dubbed 'Plymouth' by previous incumbents of the hill. Snowy wasn't impressed. 'Fuck that,' he announced. 'That will now be known as Wisbech.'

The FSG would be living on ANP Hill for the next six weeks and I was given a tour of their living quarters by Corporal Pete Toynton. I felt almost as if I were being taken around a museum exhibition of First World War trenches. Almost, but not quite, because these trenches were very obviously lived in. Originally constructed by the Russians, they're dug deep into the ground for safety, but space is very tight indeed—you have to crouch down extremely low if you want to move around, and the fact that all the lads' ammo and weapons systems have to be stashed down here as well makes it even more cramped. It's hot, of course, and the air is incredibly muggy. This is better than the alternative, however. It's easy to forget in the blistering heat of an Afghan summer that during the winter ANP Hill could well be covered in snow. At the very least it will be rained upon and these trenches will turn into underground rivers of mud. They still have to be occupied, though, and under those conditions I'm sure the First World War analogy becomes a bit more pertinent. Now, the air was full of dust that fell away from the clay walls every time someone brushed against it.

The lads sleep in metal bunks set into the walls, but they also have lookout posts surveying the surrounding area with weapons permanently set up and pointing out. So these bunkers are not just living quarters: they are firing points too. For the FSG on ANP Hill, there isn't much scope for relaxing and their quarters make Pirbright Barracks look like the Connaught.

It was as I was being ushered around this cramped warren that the guys on guard outside raised the alarm. One of them was looking out towards the green zone through a military telescope. This is a crucial piece of kit. It has a great lens, but also a range-finder that will tell you exactly how far away an object on which you are focusing is. This distance can then be programmed into a weapons system to give you very accurate fire. Ivan Snow announced what was going on. Movement had been spotted down on the ground and intelligence had come through that twelve Taliban had left the area of Changulak and were heading towards what had been identified as Taliban HQ. Snowy's orders came thick and fast: within seconds various members of the FSG knew which part of the town they were keeping watch over. A sniper took charge of a General Purpose Machine Gun and waited for orders while the spotters kept track of what was happening on the ground.

There was more movement: a motorcyclist dressed in a black headdress and white *dishdash* heading into the green zone towards Taliban HQ. The FSG kept their eyes peeled, attempting to identify the remainder of the twelve Taliban whose presence had been reported. It was difficult to see what was going on in the thick vegetation of the green zone, even with all their technology. A positive ID was crucial, though, before they started to launch an attack. Nobody wanted to drop a fifty-cal round on an innocent father heading home for his dinner.

In the absence of a definite, identifiable target, Mick Aston ordered a test fire of the guns. This would let the Taliban know that B Company's FSG were now up and running; it would also establish that the weapons systems were in place and properly zeroed; and it might even tempt them into a contact. At the time I compared it to thrusting a stick into a hornet's nest and seeing what came out. Very poetic, Ross—but not far from the truth. The fifty-cals and mortars thundered out across Now Zad and to start with there was increased movement in the green zone. It was an impressive display that kicked up huge dust explosions at the edge of the tree line towards which they were aiming. Less successfully, B Company managed to set fire to a cornfield. I wasn't sure that this would signal a great advance in the battle for hearts and minds.

In the end, it was little more than a show of force, a flexing of muscles. The Taliban movement stopped and the lads with whom I had walked up the hill returned down to the town to continue their patrol. The FSG were ordered to stand by their weapons and be ready to supply covering support to the patrol should they need it.

I continued my guided tour of ANP Hill. Cleanliness is as important up here as it is down in Now Zad DC; it's just a little harder to achieve. There's no well, for a start, which means water is that bit more scarce. Pete showed me the shower area. It was little more than a makeshift enclosure with a big blue water tank on one side. Unfortunately, however, the water tank was bone dry. Nobody in the FSG was going to be having a shower any time soon. A little further down the hill were the toilets.

'Obviously,' Pete told me, 'they're nothing glamorous.'

I'd say that was the understatement of the year, Pete.

The desert urinals—known as 'desert roses'—were simply tubes that burrowed down into the ground to drain the piss away. If the urge took you to perform a number two, then you needed to stroll over to what is referred to as the thunderbox. I was to see my fair share of these during my various stays in Afghanistan. Generally speaking, the thunderbox is a small cubicle made of plywood, sandbags and canvas. Inside there is a hole in the plywood with a plastic loo seat on the top. It opens up into a removable metal drum. Perched next to the toilet seat is the essential tube of alcohol cleaning gel used in an attempt to stop outbreaks of D and V—diarrhoea and vomiting. As Pete explained, once one person

152

gets that, everyone else will most likely succumb. And trust me, the top of ANP Hill is not a great place to have the runs.

You shit into the drum. It's rancid beyond belief and the process of evacuating one's bowels in an army thunderbox is something I'd happily never undergo again. When the drum gets full, it is removed and the contents are dealt with by whoever's on 'shit detail'. Petrol is poured into the drum and then set alight. Once the turds have been burned, the remaining residue is buried. The lucky squaddie who gets to do all this is awarded an extra few pounds a day. Frankly, having smelled what those things turn into in the heat of the Afghan sun, I think I'd rather go without the dosh. Sometimes the air is so thick with the stench of burning shit that you can't escape it: it's in your throat, in your eyes, everywhere.

The Afghans, of course, have a similar problem. There's no infrastructure for sewage in the middle of the desert. As I would find out in a later trip to Afghanistan, they don't burn theirs, but rather pile it up into large pyramids, allow it to rot down and then use it as compost for their crops. Makes sense, I suppose; but personally I think I'd prefer a bag of multi-purpose from the garden centre.

The thunderbox on ANP Hill was as basic as they all were. One thing I will say for it, though: it had an amazing view. I think Pete must have thought I was a bit barmy when I commented on it. 'Some of the toilets in the world haven't got as much danger out there either,' he politely reminded me.

Fair point, Pete. Fair point.

*　　　*　　　*

That night I slept in the open on ANP Hill. It was stunning. There was a warm, gentle breeze and it was mild enough to wear just shorts, a T-shirt and a pair of flip-flops as I prepared to go to bed. I slept against a protective wall of sandbags on which some green ammo boxes were perched—a constant reminder of where I was, and that despite the pleasantness of the evening and the astonishingly beautiful ceiling of stars overhead, this was still one of the most perilous places in the world. There was a risk of being mortared on the top of the hill, but it was a small risk. The Taliban tended not to fight at night. In addition, throughout the hours of darkness the FSG would be sending up 'lumes'—flares that are shot up a considerable distance by 81mm mortars. They light up the surrounding ground, using either fluorescent light or UV light, which requires night-vision goggles. This enables the FSG to spot any approaching threat. Despite the small risk, and the occasional firework-like noise of the lumes going up, I slept well.

I woke with the sun. Members of the Fire

Support Group were already up, taking advantage of the relative cool of the dawn to catch up on their exercise. The place looked like an open-air gym. Some lads cycled on exercise bikes that looked somewhat out of place here; others performed stomach crunches and elaborate contortions hanging upside-down from a pole. There were a lot of tanned pecs and biceps on display, but this wasn't mere vanity. The guys understood that they would be expected to go out on patrol at some stage and as I well knew, carrying 35 kilos of kit in 50-degree heat could take it out of you. They needed to be fit.

While they attended to their physiques, I took the opportunity to admire the breathtaking surroundings. The mountains were lit up against the rising sun. It was an awe-inspiring sight. The town of Now Zad and the desert that surrounded it were unspeakably beautiful and there was a stillness all around. A real sense of peace. Never was such a sense more misplaced, of course.

Once the camera team and I were up and moving, we headed back down the hill and returned to Now Zad DC. A *shura* was scheduled to take place between Mick Aston and some of the village elders. I had seen David Robinson conduct the *shura* at the end of Operation Lastay Kulang when the villagers of Jucaylay had asked if they could visit the caves the Anglians had just bombed in order to check there were no dead civilians, but this was different. Bigger. Its purpose was twofold: to start up friendships with the significant locals and to gather intelligence. As far as the villagers themselves were concerned, their motives were simpler: they just wanted to get on with their lives without being caught in the crossfire between us and the Taliban.

There were smiles all round as the villagers—four or five of them—were allowed through the gates of Now Zad DC. The Afghans had deeply lined, almost biblical faces. They were robed and bearded, but it was clear to everyone that the smiles and cordiality masked other emotions. And the smiles fell away somewhat as they were politely but firmly asked to remove their headdresses and the rest of their bodies were searched meticulously for explosives. It was a humiliation for them. There is a strict pecking order in Afghan society and for these elders to come into the DC and be felt up by young British soldiers no doubt constituted a big disrespect for them. But B Company knew there was a small risk of suicide bombers, so the body search wasn't up for negotiation.

It was also hard to determine exactly what the politics were between the two parties in this *shura*. As far as the Afghans were concerned, we were an invading force that was stopping them from returning to their homes; Mick and his men, on the other hand, could not be sure just where these people's loyalties lay. Were they edging towards us or to the Taliban, and could we accept what they told us during the course of the *shura* as the truth? More importantly, were they dickers for the enemy? There were rumours that anyone seen fraternizing with ISAF forces could have their legs broken. They could even be killed. Either these men had come here in secret (and certainly they appeared less than thrilled that we had a camera rolling on them), or the Taliban knew they were with us and would be posing their own questions when they returned to the green zone. It was impossible to say quite what the situation was and the chances were that we'd never know.

Mick and the Afghans sat around a long, low table. He greeted them with great politeness. 'I understand you're busy with your tribes and the work and harvest that's going on at the moment and I very much appreciate you taking the time out to come and speak to me today.'

A translator—one of the Afghans—converted his words into Pashtun. He was in a particularly precarious position: the rumours were that if anyone was caught translating for the British forces, the enemy would blind them, torture them and cut out their tongues before killing them.

One of the elders returned Mick's greeting. 'We are very pleased that you have come here.

May God protect your stay.' I wondered if his words concealed his true feelings.

Mick set about trying to gain some intel from the assembled elders. 'How many Taliban do you think are in the area?' he asked directly.

It was a question that caused a good deal of heated discussion among the Afghans. 'Around 1,000 to 1,500,' the translator finally said.

A thousand? That seemed like a lot of Taliban. Were they here all the time, or did they come and go? The Afghans started talking among themselves—it was obviously a matter of some debate. Mick just kept quiet as the room filled with the sound of chattering Pashtun. The consensus, if there was one, appeared to be that they came from all round the surrounding area, but that recently two strangers had been observed, Taliban from Pakistan. Their names were a mystery to the elders, one of whom admitted that they were forced to provide food for the Taliban in the green zone.

Mick smiled and turned to the translator. 'Tell this gentleman here that the next time the Taliban come and ask him for food, I'll give them all the food they want over here. The Taliban can come and eat here.'

The Afghans laughed. How funny they genuinely found Mick's wit, I'm not quite sure.

Once they had left, I asked Mick how useful the *shura* had been. He explained to me that the rule of thumb they worked by was to divide everything by ten, so when the elders said there were 1,000 Taliban in Now Zad, the likelihood was that there were only 100. It sounded to me like a much more realistic—and manageable—statistic. Aside from that, however, there was very little to go on.

Either the elders didn't know much about the Taliban's movements, or they didn't feel inclined to tell us. Whatever the truth, I couldn't help feeling that the locals were stuck in the middle and the information with which they were supplying us was distinctly unreliable.

*   *   *

The following morning at 02.00, members of 5 and 7 platoon of B Company set out for a patrol of Now Zad. I joined them.

The crescent moon hung brightly in the sky like a cradle and there was tension in the air. It was on just such a patrol—though admittedly one that went into the green zone—that Private Chris Gray, a nineteen-year-old from A Company, had lost his life just a couple of months previously. His patrol had come under attack by Taliban carrying small arms, heavy machine guns, RPGs and mortars. Private Gray's section had seen a group of Taliban just 15 metres away. They engaged the enemy and several Taliban were killed; but Chris Gray took a bullet through the side of the torso—the bit not covered by body armour. He was triaged as a category T1 and a Medical Emergency Response Team was immediately called in. They administered morphine, pumped his heart and drained the terrible chest wound before loading him into a Chinook so that they could perform a casualty evacuation, or casevac. The Chinook hurried down the Helmand river towards Camp Bastion with the MERT taking it in turns to pump Chris's chest and keep him alive. At Bastion he immediately underwent emergency surgery but it was no good. He died soon after his arrival in camp.

I was shown by one of Chris's colleagues some helmet-cam footage of the moment he was shot. It made uncomfortable viewing: violent and brutal, and to watch the panic of the soldiers knowing they were on the verge of losing one of their muckers was gut-wrenching. It was a reminder to all of us that even though everything sounded quiet out in Now Zad in the thick of that Afghanistan night, you could never afford to be complacent. You could never tell what was just around the corner.

Sergeant Canepa of 5 Platoon briefed his men before the off. He was a young soldier from Gibraltar, the Royal Gibraltar Regiment having strong links with the Anglians. Canepa had been promoted to Platoon Sergeant when Keith Nieves was sent home. He explained to me that the guys on ANP Hill had recently mortared Taliban positions in the town and there was no way of telling if the Taliban had laid booby traps in the town centre. It would be difficult enough to see these during the hours of daylight; at night it would be almost impossible.

We left the compound apprehensively and started walking deeper into the town of Now Zad than I had yet gone. It was like a ghost town. Silent. Eerie. I felt as if we were the last survivors of some terrible disaster and in a sense, I suppose, we were. It was hard to imagine that this place was once a vibrant, busy centre.

We spoke in whispers, not knowing if anyone was within earshot and not wanting to alert them to our presence if they were. The soldiers looked out into the night with the benefit of a heat-seeking camera. For a long while the camera picked up nothing other than the multicoloured shapes of 5 Platoon picking their way through Now Zad.

But then Sergeant Canepa received word. A heat source had been detected 400 metres away. There was something—or someone— out there.

I could almost taste the tension. No one knew what the heat source was. It could have been a dog; it could have been an innocent villager; or it could have been a Taliban soldier. The Platoon approached with care;

but the heat source disappeared. I didn't know what to make of that. The town was interlinked with underground tunnels that led up into the compounds. It was well known that the Taliban used these little rat runs to move around and to get up close to British forces. Maybe one of them had appeared nearby and then ducked down one of these tunnels when he realized we were there. Or maybe it really had just been a wild animal. There was no way of knowing.

The sun rose. It took away the threat of the darkness but it brought with it the inevitable heat. Before long we were patrolling in 40 degrees. We didn't need heat cameras or night vision to see movement now and it was just as we were heading for home that movement was indeed spotted. The platoon divided itself into two, each group flanking one side of the suspicious area. They approached with caution, fully prepared for a contact with the enemy.

But it wasn't the enemy. It was some locals packing up a vehicle. They must have been the only stragglers left in this part of Now Zad, taking the last of their belongings, firmly locking up their compound and getting the hell out of there.

As I looked around that war-torn, deserted place, I couldn't really blame them.

*   *   *

162

Now Zad was tense. Everywhere in Helmand Province is tense. But Mick Aston had been right: the tempo here was a lot slower than it had been in Jucaylay during Operation Lastay Kulang. There was a risk that the soldiers would become stale. Not bored, exactly, but perhaps lacking some of the excitement they had come to expect. Something needed to be done to keep morale high. A distraction. Fun. So it was that B Company decided to put on its own talent show: 'Mr Now Zad'. *X-Factor* Afghanistan-stylee.

Everyone was involved—5, 6 and 7 Platoons plus the Fire Support Group. Tim Newton was the MC; Mick Aston, 2ic Dave Middleton and I acted as judges, the British Army's answer to Sharon Osbourne, Danii Minogue and Simon Cowell, though I'm not saying which was which. The lads threw themselves into the proceedings with gusto. To start off with there was a shooting competition. Someone drew a load of heads—mine, the OC's, various others—which were pinned to a wall and then shot at with Browning pistols. There was the obligatory *EastEnders* skit with some hilarious Grant Mitchell impressions. Penis-pulling, bollock-twisting and other eye-watering genital puppetry seemed popular. Robert Foster showed how brave he was by licking the toe jam out of one of his mate's toes. He also raided the inadequate kitchen at Now Zad

163

where he found chilli sauce, tomato sauce and mayonnaise which he then licked off someone else's feet. There was stand-up, singing and a lot of in-jokes aimed at the company's resident luvvie—me—including plenty of piss-taking about my character in *Ultimate Force*. The platoons competed against each other in a massive, heated tug-of-war. As a prize I offered tickets for any Premier League football match when the tour was over: it gave the event a whole new dimension of competitiveness. In the end, Private Hirsch was crowned Mr Now Zad—a title to be desired if ever there was one—and he went to watch Liverpool vs West Ham when he finally got back to England.

'Mr Now Zad' was a lot of fun and you could tell the effect it had on B Company. Morale, which had been flagging slightly, was lifted; and though this display of bravado and silliness might have appeared daft to the man in the street (not that there were any men in the streets of Now Zad), in fact it was a crucial moment for the lads, boosting their flailing spirits and making the relentless nature of their tour of duty a bit easier to bear.

I had been in Now Zad for about two weeks and my time here was coming to an end. So was my time in Afghanistan. It had been an eye-opening few weeks, to say the least. The myth that modern wars are fought electronically and at a distance had been well

164

and truly debunked in my eyes and I had seen at first hand something of what these young British troops were up against in Helmand Province. I had seen how they lived and how they fought; and even though I was strictly a noncombatant, I had experienced to some extent the fear and excitement of battle. If I had learned nothing else, it was to respect the job that these remarkable young men, some of them still teenagers, were doing in the service of their country.

But what was it, I wondered, that drove them? Were they as surprised by the intensity of the fighting out here as I was? And just who were they fighting for? The answer to that final question was answered in no uncertain terms by the group of lads with whom I sat around in Now Zad DC just before the time came for me to leave. 'For each other,' I was told. 'At the end of the day, Queen and country aren't holding a rifle on each side of you. You're relying on every bloke that's around you that's got a weapon system keeping you alive as you're doing for them.'

So what about the people back home? Did the lads think that they appreciated what the soldiers were going through out here? 'I don't think they fully understand,' came the reply. I had to agree with that and I hoped that what I was doing would go some way to filling that gap in the public's understanding.

One of the soldiers told me how much

money he earned: his take-home pay was about £1,000 a month. It didn't seem like a whole lot to be paying someone for putting their life at risk on a daily basis and I certainly sensed that although morale was high in terms of B Company's self-belief, there was an underlying dissatisfaction with more general aspects of life in the army, and an agreement among them all that when this tour was over, they'd be getting out. It was only partly to do with money. As Lance Corporal Blewett succinctly put it, 'Once you've done a tour like this, you can't go back to Brecon and throw Chorley grenades and fire blanks at someone.'

I could see their point; but I was also aware that battle weariness and homesickness were surely kicking in. I felt it myself and I hadn't been out here for half as long or undergone nearly as many contacts as this lot. I wondered how many of them, back in England and in the cold light of day, would really be resigning their positions.

Not many, I suspected, and in the event I was right.

10. BLUE ON BLUE

At the time it was by no means certain that I would be returning to Afghanistan. I wasn't sure that I wanted to. Coming back home was, to say the least, peculiar.

Having spent so much time in the desert, your eyes become accustomed to the ever-present sandy colour. As I flew back over the fields of England, the patchwork of summer greens was almost hallucinogenic in its intensity. Home Sweet Home.

If only.

For the first week I went out every night and got drunk; I tried to exhaust my girlfriend; during the day I was in a lethal mood, a pig to be with. I'd only been out in Afghanistan for a month, but I'd come very close to taking a bullet. That alters your perspective on life, at least for a while. You feel angry with people around you for not understanding what you've been through. Having been with a bunch of guys who were managing to keep up morale in such difficult circumstances, who were always there for each other, I found it galling to walk down Earls Court Road and see everyone so wrapped up in their own affairs. I couldn't help wondering if they'd got their priorities wrong. They didn't have a clue about anything, surely? With hindsight, of course, I can see how skewed my attitude was. These people were just living their lives. Why should they stop doing that just because I'd been in Afghanistan? But when you come back from a war zone, it's sometimes difficult to think straight. I didn't know it at the time, but I was experiencing in microcosm the problems soldiers have when they return from a tour of duty. If I was like this after one month, what would B Company be like after six?

What was more, I felt guilty about the fact that I had come home while the rest of the lads were still out there. I wasn't a proper soldier; I wasn't one of them. But I had grown to know them well. To like them. I missed the camaraderie and the simplicity of life: eat, sleep, keep yourself alive.

I also felt in some way closer to the people they had left behind. So it was that when I went to visit Helen Gray, the mother of Private Chris Gray who had lost his life in the green zone just under a klick from Now Zad DC, it was an emotional moment for us both. As we sat in the comfort of her home, she spoke with a piercing, desperate eloquence of the trauma she was suffering at the loss of her son. 'I just want him to walk through my door,' she wept, 'and dump his bag and raid the fridge. And plonk himself down. I don't sleep very well: I can't get to sleep at night and I wake up constantly through the night. It's like this massive brick wall that's been built and I can't

168

get over that brick wall. And I feel like some days I'm never going to get through it. He said, "I'm going to bring you home a medal." I told him I don't want a medal. "I just want you, Chris. You make sure *you* come home." '

Chris Gray wasn't coming home. He would never again raid the fridge, or dump a bag of washing on the floor for his mum to do. He would never plonk himself down on the sofa. I had a tear in my eye as I listened to Helen's heartfelt words. And I couldn't help but reflect on the fact that what had happened in the green zone of Now Zad would affect so many people—family and friends of the departed—for the rest of their lives.

After a stint in Afghanistan my perception of what was dangerous changed. Needing to keep busy, I travelled to East Timor to film an episode of *Gangs*. By most criteria it was an edgy couple of weeks: we found ourselves caught in the middle of a massive riot, with burning buildings blazing all around us. The place next to our hotel was set on fire. I got tear gassed. Nobody could say it was a walk in the park, and yet it wasn't Jucaylay: I didn't have a Taliban fighter shooting AK rounds directly at me. I was shown the East Timorian gangs' weapon of choice, a hand-fashioned dart called a *ramba ambon*. It was a wicked-looking thing, and could do you a lot of damage. But it wasn't an RPG.

Gradually I acclimatized. Life started to get

back to normal; I went back to being a rat in the rat race. I suppose I became once more like those people on Earls Court Road. Afghanistan, though, was always there, at the back of my mind. It would be going too far to say that I longed to return, or that I was addicted to the place. All I knew was that being out there had been one of the most intense times in my life. Surrounded by all that danger you somehow feel more alive. Back home seemed like a bit of a let-down after that adrenaline rush. What was more, I felt that the story hadn't fully been told, that there was more for us to film and to learn about the soldiers' lives out there. As their tour of duty progressed I wondered how they were coping. How they had changed.

I decided that I wanted to go back.

*   *   *

I was standing in my kitchen the week before I was due to return to Camp Bastion when the news came through. My ears had long become attuned to picking up details about the war in Afghanistan on the TV or radio and today was no exception. It was with a creeping sense of horror that I listened to what had happened. Three British soldiers had been killed by friendly fire. An American F-16 had dropped ordnance on their positions.

The three soldiers were members of the

First Battalion The Royal Anglian Regiment.

All manner of thoughts flashed through my head. Who had been killed? Was it any of the soldiers with whom I had struck up a relationship? Where had it happened? *How* had it happened? How were the survivors coping? And just what were the families of the dead men going through? To have your son or friend killed by the Taliban is a tragedy; to have him killed in an avoidable accident like this was unimaginable.

Gradually more information started to filter through to the media. The friendly fire incident—or 'blue on blue', as the troops refer to it—had happened in the village of Mazdurak, near Kajaki. Kajaki is one of the most isolated British bases in Helmand Province, at the top of the Sangin valley near the border with Kandahar Province. It's Taliban heartland. Kajaki is home to a huge hydro-electric dam. At the time it was working at only half its capacity. Plans were afoot to install another turbine: when that happened it would supply electricity to nearly 2 million people in southern Afghanistan. The dam is a main target for the Taliban. Whether they want to destroy it or control it is not entirely clear. Nevertheless, defending the dam is a major operational imperative for the ISAF forces in Helmand Province and its continued operation is crucial in the battle for hearts and minds.

It transpired that B Company had been engaged in a fierce firefight with the Taliban. They had called in fast air support to bomb the enemy's positions but something had gone horribly wrong. The dead, members of 7 Platoon, were Private Robert Foster, Private John Thrumble and Private Aaron McClure. I remembered them well, especially Robert Foster, who had been such an enthusiastic participant in the Mr Now Zad competition. It seemed impossible that they were dead. As I made my final preparations to leave, I could only imagine what sort of effect this incident would have had on the rest of the company. My mood was both sombre and apprehensive as for the second time I boarded a military transport from RAF Brize Norton to Kandahar Airport and then on to Camp Bastion.

The surviving members of 7 Platoon had been moved to Sangin District Centre for a short while to do sentry duty and get them away from the scene of the blue on blue and give them time to start coming to terms with their loss. A Company were stationed at the DC at the time and would be going out on patrol on a regular basis; but the B Company boys were excused that for the time being, and rightly so. I had been to Sangin once before, during our attack on Jucaylay. The lads then had been in reasonably high spirits as we swam in the river and prepared for the rigours of

172

Operation Lastay Kulang. As we left Camp Bastion in a Chinook and flew low over the desert, I knew I couldn't expect them to be in the same frame of mind this time round.

The moment we arrived in Sangin, an army liaison officer came up to us. The lads from B Company were in a bad way, he told us. We weren't to approach them or talk to them. It was a bit of a blow. I knew they probably wouldn't want to talk about the blue on blue, but I thought we might at least be able to spend a bit of time with them. At that very moment we saw Sergeant Michael 'Woody' Woodrow and Lieutenant George Seal-Coon from B Company. They immediately contradicted what the liaison officer had said and specifically invited us to come and join them. They wanted us with them and that felt good.

7 Platoon had their own little compound at the back of the base, where they had been left to their own devices for a few days. We joined them there. One of the platoon, a Brummie territorial by the name of OD, was quite a bit older than the others. He offered them a lot in the way of emotional support; he was also a bit of a negotiator and had managed to blag some flour to bake bread and pizza bases. It's amazing how something as simple as that could rekindle flagging morale. Nevertheless, it was clear that they weren't in the mood for talking about the incident. Not yet. So I

approached Ian Robinson, the Regimental Sergeant Major and the man in charge of discipline and morale. I asked them how the boys were coping. He explained that a single section from 7 Platoon had received all the casualties. 'They were remarkable, to be honest,' he told me. 'I was expecting quite a lot of anger. I was expecting a fair amount of shock. But as I've said previously, the guys have really grown up a lot on the tour, not just as soldiers, but as men as well. They were very, very sad, very low, but in the last week or so they've pulled themselves back up again, and that's really to the credit of them as individuals.'

The deaths of these three young soldiers had taken the number of Royal Anglians killed in action up to nine. I wondered if the RSM had a number in his head before he came out here, an estimated casualty figure. Ian admitted that he had. About ten, but he hoped he was being pessimistic and it would be a lot less than that. It looked as if pessimism was the order of the day, however. What was more, the Anglians still had one sixth of their tour to complete and as Ian quite rightly put it: 'For the enemy, each day's the same as the next and they don't mind whether they kill us on day one of the tour, day thirty of the tour or the last day of the tour.'

A sobering thought.

*　　*　　*

If I'd thought that my reintroduction to Helmand Province was going to be gentle, I was wrong. We hadn't been there long before we went out on patrol to a nearby village with A Company commanded by Major Dom Biddick. About eighty of us set out at midnight from Sangin DC. Walking anywhere in Afghanistan is difficult enough because of the rubble, ditches and craters underfoot; walking in the dark is twice as difficult. You stumble all over the place; across the wadis in the green zone you feel your face being whipped by the low-hanging branches of willow and mulberry trees. Add a heavy HD camera into the mix and it's very hard going indeed. For this trip we had a new cameraman, Fred Scott. Fred and I only gradually became adept at swinging the camera over the wadis and irrigation trenches as we tried to keep up with the patrol.

The last time A Company had gone out at this time of night they had come into contact with the enemy in about four minutes. To say we were apprehensive would be an understatement. All around us, dogs howled in the darkness. They didn't just sound spooky: they were constantly giving away our position no matter how quiet we tried to be. We patrolled with caution, going firm for a while to get our breath and check the lie of the land, then moving on; going firm, moving on.

175

Progress was painfully slow. More than once, as we crossed the irrigation ditches, we found ourselves up to our waists in water.

At around a quarter to four we reached a cornfield on the outskirts of the village where we were headed. We laid up here, trying to ignore the smell of the human shit that had been used to fertilize it. The temperature had started to drop severely as it does at that time in the morning. We experienced a severe drop in body temperature. In addition, my skin was clammy from sweat and from wading through the irrigation ditches. I started to shiver from the cold; the shivers became trembles and before I knew it I was rattling inside my body armour like a tortoise rattling in its shell. I'd never been so cold. It felt as if the sweat was turning to ice on the back of my neck; half of me thought I was going to fall asleep and never wake up again. I couldn't move my arms and as I lay there in the cold, soggy, shitty field, I wondered once more what the hell I was doing here.

Dawn arrived, and with it the call to prayer from the village. The company started to rouse itself. It hurt just to stand up but we needed to get moving. We must have been an odd sight, rising like the dead from that dung-covered cornfield in the half light of morning. Something from a zombie movie. That's certainly how I felt. We continued unwillingly into the village, where Dom had a *shura* with the elders. They informed us that the Taliban had left some time ago: either our intelligence had been wrong, or they'd cleared out, or the people we were talking to *were* the enemy. Whatever, it looked as if there wasn't going to be any contact that day. We continued our patrol nevertheless.

At 11.00 we stopped for ten minutes. I was so exhausted that I fell asleep standing up and leaning against a wall. Come the afternoon, we started heading for home. I was, in military jargon, snapped. My feet were hanging off, I was cut to pieces and I felt as if I could sleep for week. An hour or so later there was the sound of gunfire in the distance. The Coldstream Guards who were mentoring the Afghan National Army had got into a contact, so Dom ordered that we turn back on ourselves to help them out. At that moment I started feeling mutinous.

In the end our presence wasn't required— the Coldstream Guards managed to get themselves out of their hole—so this time we really were headed for home. We finally got back to base at 19.00, having been on the move for nineteen hours with no sleep.

Welcome back to the army, Ross.

*   *   *

As far as we were concerned, Sangin was just a stopover. The soldiers from B Company who had been involved in the blue on blue couldn't stay there indefinitely. When the time came for them to return to Kajaki, we were to go with them. On the day of our departure we rose early. As I pulled on my clothes I noticed that already the material had started to stiffen where my sweat had evaporated. They call it human starch. A soldier's clothes are often in tatters, full of rips and holes: when they reach this starched, stiffened state they become brittle and tear easily.

A Chinook arrived at the landing zone to take us on the dangerous journey up the Sangin valley. Not long previously, seven men had died when a Chinook was shot down by Taliban fire as it approached the British base at Kajaki. In order to avoid a repeat performance, the immensely skilled helicopter pilots vary their landing patterns at the base, approaching from different heights and different directions. Our new cameraman, Fred Scott—very experienced and as brave as you get—strapped himself to the aircraft and hung out the back to get the shots he wanted. At one stage there was more than half of him hanging out, but he managed to capture the sublime nature of that journey. And though the constant threat of ground-to-air fire somewhat took the edge off the spectacular trip, it was indeed spectacular. The wide, still waters of the enormous lake at the top of the Sangin valley—one of the biggest stretches of inland water I've ever seen—were an intense, crystalline, Mediterranean blue; the mountains were craggy and sublime in the distance; the dam itself was like a massive rocky plug in the valley. We flew over the lake above the dam to approach the landing zone—the Taliban don't have any boats, so it's a safer way to approach. It's a beautiful way, too. In less troubled times, this part of the Helmand river was a prime destination on the hippy trail. The Afghan royal family used to come on holiday here. The tourist industry in Helmand Province has tailed off a bit since then. Anywhere else, you'd actively want to take a trip like this; but then you probably wouldn't have an Apache attack helicopter as a chaperone, hovering overhead as you came into land, ready to take out anyone who opened fire on you.

The buildings that form the base at Kajaki, set in the craggy hills above the dam, look like some kind of austere, Soviet-era ski lodge—very different from the residential compounds I'd seen elsewhere. The inside of the base is divided into a number of rooms, giving the soldiers somewhere to bunk down; but it's very basic. I was billeted with the 2ic, Dave Robinson. That meant I had the benefit of the only bit of air conditioning at the base—a luxury that can't be overstated. Our quarters were, however, hardly five star, not least because we had a terrible mouse infestation. Each night I was there we spent more time

179

trying to splatter mice than sleeping. It started to resemble the Monty Python mouse organ sketch where Terry Jones thwacks his musical rodents with big hammers. Either that or a scene from *The Shining*. The little critters got everywhere, searching for any crumbs of food that might happen to be lying around. I would wake up with them on my chest and in my ears. Alternatively I'd be woken by Dave—a very mild-mannered bloke—screaming 'Fuck!' at the top of his voice, which was normally a prelude to us crawling round the room with our head torches on trying to exterminate our room mates.

To one side of the base there is a contingent of ANA (Afghan National Army); on the other side there's an ANP (Afghan National Police) position. Rumour around the camp was that the ANP would pass information over the radio to the Taliban about the British forces' movements. I never had this confirmed, but I'm inclined to believe it was true. These ANP recruits were local Afghans: they knew perfectly well what would happen if the Taliban came knocking on their door and they refused to play ball.

In addition there are three observation posts at Kajaki: Athens, Sparrowhawk East and Sparrowhawk West. Look out from one of these OPs—a crucial exercise if you're going to keep the Taliban from advancing—and the surrounding territory looks as if it's been shat upon by a thousand seagulls. These white markings indicate mine positions: Kajaki is littered with them, a hangover from the days of the Soviet occupation. It was the most heavily mined part of Helmand I had yet been to. It's as tactically important as it is dangerous, as I found out from the new OC of B Company. Mick Aston was no longer with them. He'd joined a recce platoon that would go out into the desert for a month at a time, gathering information about enemy positions. So hardly shifting down a gear, then. In his place was Tony Borgnis—a man who had quickly won the respect of B Company and with whom I got on extremely well. He explained to me that the Kajaki dam was crucial to the battle for hearts and minds in the province: ensuring the supply of electricity meant better facilities and a greater chance of regeneration of the local area.

Kajaki is regularly attacked using long-range rockets and the British forces are constantly engaged at the FLET—the Forward Line of Enemy Troops. The FLET runs north to south of the base and for the last ten days B Company had been unable to engage the Taliban at the FLET because, with 7 Platoon at Sangin in the wake of the blue on blue, they were undermanned. This meant that the enemy were growing stronger in the area. They were getting closer to the dam. This couldn't be allowed to continue, so B

181

Company were preparing to go on the offensive—and I was preparing to go with them.

Before I accompanied them out into the field, I wanted to speak to the men involved and find out just what had happened on the dreadful day of the friendly fire incident. Sergeant Woodrow and Lieutenant Seal-Coon agreed to speak to me.

B Company, they told me, had entered the village of Mazdurak when they came under heavy fire from the enemy based in the neighbouring village of Kavalabad. The two opposing forces were separated by only a couple of hundred metres of dried-up wadi. Fast air was called in to drop a bomb on the enemy positions. Woody, who was in the reserve section behind the compound, heard the jet overhead; when the bomb hit it was clear that something had gone wrong, but at first he thought it had simply landed in the wadi.

It hadn't, as George Seal-Coon was very well aware. He was on the roof of the compound with Corporal Parker, Private Leigh, Private Thrumble and Private McClure. There was a bright flash and a sudden, deafening shockwave. George described to me how it pushed him into the rooftop. He hunkered down, and when he got back on his feet in the wake of the explosion, he saw four casualties lying around him. It was a miracle that he had remained largely unhurt.

When Woody realized what had happened, he advanced on to the roof. The first casualty he came across was Private Thrumble. His helmet had been blown off and his clothes had been blown away. He appeared to be dead. Private Leigh's clothes were in a similar state; he had a bad eye injury and was in a lot of distress, but he was at least alive. Woody got him off the roof and then heard the bad news from a medic who had arrived on the scene. Thrumble was T4.

The medic went to work on Private Leigh as Woody started to get Corporal Parker off the roof. Stu Parker's body armour had been blown open, his clothes were also blown away and his ribs were crushed and broken. The Taliban continued to rain down heavy fire on them as the dead and wounded were evacuated from the compound. Private McClure was pronounced dead at the scene and the company retreated.

Away from Mazdurak, Woody went through the list of guys who'd been on the roof. McClure, T4. Thrumble, T4. Leigh, wounded. Stu Parker, wounded.

It was only then that they realized someone was missing.

Private Robert Foster had been inside the compound, firing from a loophole in the wall. Now the building from which he had been engaging the enemy was little more than a pile of rubble. Somebody had said, 'I think he's gone back with 6 Platoon.' But now, with a cold, sickening sense of horror, they realized that Private Foster was still under that rubble.

Night had fallen by the time they returned to Mazdurak, a moonless night that gave the soldiers very little light by which to search for their fallen colleague. They were determined to find him, however, and not only because recovering his body was the right thing to do. If the enemy had retrieved the corpse of a British soldier, especially one killed in a blue on blue incident, it would have been a propaganda coup for them. So it was that these shocked, numb soldiers dug through the rubble piece by piece with their bare hands. Tim Newton was on his way home for leave at the time of the incident, but he immediately returned to the scene, bringing with him the Brigade Reconnaissance Force.

They found his rifle first. Foster himself was buried beneath a thick layer of rubble. His army mates took some small consolation from the fact that he was more than likely killed immediately in the explosion. He was almost precisely underneath the location where the bomb had hit.

George Seal-Coon and Michael Woodrow appeared numb as they described these events, grown men on the edge of tears. It was clear to me that what happened that day would stay with them, and with everyone involved, for the rest of their lives. Woody, who was a father figure to the platoon, put it simply but movingly. 'You can't help but get attached to them,' he told me quietly. 'That's the hardest thing. And then to pull their bodies out of the rubble. As a father myself, I couldn't think of anything worse than to bury children.'

The men were experiencing such a complicated mix of emotions. Sorrow, of course. Anger. But also guilt. Guilt not only that they had left Private Foster in that pile of rubble, but also that they had survived while others—randomly, indiscriminately and through no fault of their own—had died. The guilt of soldiers who survive is a powerful thing. It is one of the reasons why, with almost no exception, they shun the label 'hero' that is so often forced upon them. They don't feel like heroes; they just feel like the lucky ones.

I wondered if there was any anger directed towards the Americans who had dropped the bomb on B Company's position. To my surprise, there was none whatsoever. Up on Athens, one of the OPs overlooking Kajaki, I had the chance to speak to 5 Platoon for the first time since we had been on patrol together in Now Zad. They had found the blue on blue as traumatic as everyone, but their attitude towards the Americans was uncompromising. These things happen in war, I was told, and there's no point trying to find a scapegoat.

I told them that back home, there had been

185

a lot of anti-American reporting in the newspapers—'The Yanks bomb our boys again.' Was this how they felt? Absolutely not. The lads understood only too well that this was sensationalist, inaccurate reporting designed only to sell papers. The reality was that if it weren't for the Americans, the troops on the ground would have virtually no fast air support. I had seen for myself how crucial that support was and how often it was called in. What happened in Mazdurak that day had been a tragedy that affected them profoundly, but without the Americans, they would be fighting a very different kind of war. A war in which a lot more of them would be killed.

It's still not clear what happened on that day, and the investigation is ongoing, but it seems that in the heat of the battle, information transmitted from ground to air and air to ground became confused. The truth be told, the mistake didn't sound to me like a very difficult one to make; in fact, it's a surprise it doesn't happen more often. Since that time I've heard the question asked more than once as to why troops on the ground, with all the technology that is available to us, don't have some sort of electronic beacon that alerts fast air to their position. It would, at the very least, be some kind of safeguard against this kind of incident happening again.

B Company might have been feeling sadness and guilt after the loss of life, but they were also feeling the need to avenge that loss. And so it was that preparations were made to take the fight to the Taliban once again. The enemy's radio chatter had been intercepted by army intelligence. The Taliban knew that B Company were nearing the end of their tour. They believed them to be tired, demoralized and unwilling to fight. The guys were going out into the field to prove to the enemy just how wrong they were. The Taliban had caused some of their mates to be killed. B Company were ready to return the favour, with interest.

11. FIGHTING IN SOMEBODY'S HOUSE

The missions and tasks were easily explained.

We were briefed by Dave Robinson, my mouse-crushing partner in crime. The faces in that briefing room were serious, angry and ready for war. In the ten days since the blue on blue, the depleted B Company had been unable to keep the pressure up on the Forward Line of Enemy Troops. All that was about to change. They were to deploy to the southern FLET. Once there, they were to locate the enemy's position and engage them. Once they were engaged, fast air would be called in to destroy their positions. The same fast air, it was lost on nobody, that had been called into Mazdurak with such cataclysmic results.

Our route would take us along the 611 highway. This is little more than a dirt track and most of it can be surveyed from Sparrowhawk East and Sparrowhawk West, the two OPs at Kajaki. Not all of it, however: there are certain blind spots, which meant that the Taliban could easily have planted mines or IEDs—improvised explosive devices—along the way. IEDs were usually constructed from explosives taken from anti-tank mines that have been attached to artillery shells. They have predictably devastating effects. The Taliban have a rich source of material for constructing IEDs, namely the mines littered around the country that were left by the Soviets. It is a horrible irony that during the 1980s it is said the SAS taught the Afghan Mujahideen how to construct IEDs. Now that knowledge is being used against British forces and IEDs can be made by anyone with the bottle to dig up a mine. Talk about being hoist by your own petard.

I was to travel with the Fire Support Group. When we approached the FLET, B Company would split: 6 and 7 Platoon would enter the green zone to flush out the Taliban, and the FSG would move to high ground to provide covering fire. This was going to be a serious contact. B Company were being thrown right back into the deep end and I heard no complaints about that whatsoever. For them, it was payback time.

We made the journey early in the morning while it was still dark. Our convoy travelled slowly, all of us well aware of the danger of this journey: IEDs are difficult enough to see during the daytime; during the hours of darkness practically impossible. The crew and I travelled in a WMIK, an open-top Land Rover. A mine would make very short work of a vehicle like this one. I could sense everybody hoping that the people in the observation posts had been vigilant enough over those areas of the road that they could see to ensure that nobody had dug anything in. When we reached

189

the hidden stretches of road, the convoy would stop and the track ahead was swept with minesweeping machines. These are essentially advanced metal detectors, although metal-detecting an Afghan road isn't quite like looking for Roman coins in a ditch. The minesweepers have a nervy, dangerous but ultimately crucial job—especially when it's done, as it was on this occasion, under cover of darkness.

Once the road was declared safe, the convoy moved on. 6 and 7 Platoons moved past us towards the enemy positions in the green zone. I waited with the FSG for dawn to arrive so that we could leave the road and head up on to the higher ground overlooking the southern FLET. If the journey up until now had been dangerous, this would be doubly so. The Taliban knew that this was the only location from which we could offer fire support, the only place where our weapons systems could get the necessary arcs down on to their positions. So the likelihood was that they would have left us a little welcome gift. It was a vigilant FSG that edged up that hill when first light arrived.

Their vigilance paid off. As we approached our firing position, some picks and shovels were noticed nearby. Nobody was under the illusion that the Taliban had been digging potatoes. Once more the convoy halted and the mine detectors were brought out. It was light by now, but in the rough, stony earth it would still be nigh-on impossible to locate the tiny pressure pad that would explode a mine, so yet again our safety was down to the skill of the men handling those metal detectors.

They didn't let us down.

Only a few metres ahead of us, bang in the middle of the path we were taking, they found the mine. All that was visible of it was the pressure pad—an innocuous-enough-looking bit of metal, but if the guys had failed to locate it and one of our vehicles had driven over the mine, it would have been blown to bits, along with all the soldiers in it. We drove around the mine and reached our final positions.

Ivan Snow, who was in charge of the Fire Support Group, explained that they would be splitting into two groups. The dismounted FSG, led by Corporal Si Thorne, would act as a sniper team with fifty-cals and Javelin anti-tank missiles from a separate position; the remainder would stay on the top of the ridge with their vehicle-mounted weapons. In the distance we could see an area called Big Top, which was where we knew the Taliban commanders were. Snowy had a pretty good idea which compounds in the green zone each of the two positions would draw fire from, and also how the battle would go. We knew where the Taliban were; the Taliban knew where we were. This was a fight that had been played out in the past.

191

'Basically,' I said to Snowy, 'it's a bit like "I'll meet you at the bike sheds at quarter to four," then everyone goes back home and tomorrow they do the same thing.'

It's exactly like that, Snowy told me. Exactly.

There seemed something a bit farcical about this Groundhog Day-like situation, but in fact it was crucial that B Company kept the Taliban regularly engaged along the FLET. The previous year the enemy had got so close to the Kajaki base that they could fire down on it from the surrounding hills. It was essential that this didn't happen again. Even if B Company weren't gaining any ground in these encounters, they were stopping the Taliban from advancing and getting any closer to taking the base.

The FSG set up their positions. And then they did what soldiers have to be prepared to do. They waited.

All around us there was silence. It was the silence of anticipation. We knew that at that precise moment 7 Platoon would be moving deep into the green zone, advancing on the enemy positions.

Half an hour passed.

The FSG surveyed the green zone with quiet, determined care.

An hour.

I suspected that when the sound of contact came, it would be sudden and intense. I wasn't wrong.

After two hours of sitting on the hill, there was a loud bang. The ground troops were gaining entry into a compound with a bar mine—long planks of explosives intended as anti-tank mines. A telltale cloud of smoke rose from the compounds in the green zone. It was like a starting pistol: suddenly the air was filled with the fire-crack of rounds. The FSG slipped effortlessly into action: Snowy yelled an order that the WMIKs, mounted with fifty-cals, be driven up to the ridge. Immediately they started raining down heavy fire on the enemy positions to support the two platoons, which at that very moment were eye to eye with the Taliban. The dismounted FSG fired Javelin missiles; through the image intensifier of that weapon they could see a Taliban commander giving orders to his troops.

It was an awesome display of firepower. Clearly it was causing the Taliban some difficulty, because almost immediately we ourselves started taking incoming fire from one of their positions. The rounds flew over our heads, landing just a few metres behind our position. We had gone from silence and anticipation to a deafening, brutal frenzy in a matter of a minutes; and there wouldn't be any let-up for a long time yet.

The contact lasted for three hours—three long, aggressive hours, during which our ears were constantly filled by the grating, metallic boom of the weaponry and by the shouts of the soldiers around us. I already knew that war consisted of long stretches of boredom punctuated by moments of extreme action, violence and terror. This was one of those moments. 7 Platoon were pinned down a mere 18 metres from the Taliban positions; 6 Platoon fired upon the rear of the enemy from a roof 250 metres behind them. The FSG continued to pour down fire from the ridge and between them, despite the fact that they were taking a good deal of incoming, they managed to suppress the enemy. The two platoons and the FSG had a single aim: to get the Taliban into a position where they couldn't escape when the fast air support was called in. When the Americans dropped their bomb, they wanted to make sure they killed as many of the enemy as possible.

The order came through to stop firing. The air was still for a moment, but then I heard the now familiar whizz of rounds shooting past my head. The enemy were still firing back, but they were hemmed in, pinned down, and they wouldn't be there for long.

Because at that moment I heard the order we'd all been waiting for. 'OK! Call in air!'

The American F-16 took about four minutes to approach. I strained my numb ears to listen for the sound of the aircraft; when the droning noise arrived and started to get louder, I plugged my ears with my fingers. I knew what was coming. The F-16 roared over the enemy positions and started to disappear. But not before it had delivered its package. There was a short pause as its bomb fell to earth.

And then the explosion.

It rocked the surrounding area like a small earthquake; a flash of orange on the ground and then an enormous dust cloud billowed from the enemy compounds. A direct hit. No one in the range of that bomb could possibly have survived it; and if there was any lingering doubt about the accuracy of the American fast air after the blue on blue, this was enough well and truly to put it to rest. The F-16 performed a strafing run. This is when fast air comes in and delivers a burst of fire from a low altitude, in this instance using thirty-cal HE (high explosive) rounds; followed by a slower flyover as a show of force.

In the wake of the Americans' ordnance, the gunfire stopped. It was time to extract. The F-16, however, remained in the area, circling high up ahead and making sure that 6 and 7 Platoon achieved a safe extraction from the green zone. The same was true of the FSG. They remained on the ridge, weapons systems at the ready, covering the ground troops until they had managed to pull out to a position of relative safety. They are always the last to leave and as we prepared to get back down the hill, I was very aware of the fact that there was nobody supplying fire support for the Fire

Support Group as we travelled carefully to the main road to meet up with the others.

Back at base, we received encouraging news. The Taliban radios were silent. It meant that several of the enemy had been killed. The operation had been a success.

More importantly, though, it was good to see everyone safe—especially Woody, George Seal-Coon and the other members of 7 Platoon who had been so affected by the blue on blue. This had been their first contact since being returned to Kajaki; it would have gone some way to exorcizing the demons that were still with them. And I hoped that this would help them as they prepared for their next task: returning to Mazdurak, where the incident had happened, where they had lost their friends and come very, very close to losing their own lives.

*   *   *

The assault on Mazdurak would serve two purposes. Firstly it would enable B Company to reassert their authority on the northern FLET, just as they had done to the south. But there was another, perhaps more important objective: to destroy any equipment from the compound involved in the blue on blue and so deny it to the enemy. It was crucial that no British Army equipment fell into the hands of the Taliban: it could give them intelligence as

196

to the army's methods or even a propaganda tool to persuade the locals that they were winning the war.

The return to Mazdurak would not only be an emotional operation for the guys: it would be a particularly dangerous one. The enemy's morale would be high in the wake of the blue on blue; they would know that it had made international news. Moreover, B Company knew that there was an accurate sniper covering the village, probably using some kind of fifty-cal weapon system, as well as some highly effective machine gunners. It was clear that B Company were not going to regain the initiative in Mazdurak without a fight. Dave Robinson articulated well how he and the men felt about returning to the scene. 'On a personal level,' he told me, 'there's nothing I'd rather do less. On a professional level, we've got to get back up there and we've got to reassert our authority.' It was one of those moments when I was reminded of the accomplished, businesslike attitude these soldiers had to the job in hand. It was to be an emotional operation, but there was no time for emotion. Just professionalism.

The mission to Mazdurak was not aided by the fact that we had a false start. At 03.30 on the day we were supposed to hit the village, the operation was spiked. Elsewhere in Helmand Province a British soldier had been killed and five more injured. The MERT was therefore not available to us. We would have to wait another twenty-four hours before being given the orders to advance.

So it was that the following day we reassembled before first light. The plan was to cross over the Helmand river and then advance north along a dried-up wadi. The assault would be spearheaded by 6 Platoon—accompanied by me and the crew—while 7 Platoon and the FSG moved to the high points of Essex Ridge and Barakju to provide fire support. Our first objective would be the compound where the blue on blue happened. We were to wait until the RAF had dropped two 1,000lb bombs on it, then clear the compound and continue our assault on the village of Mazdurak.

For this operation, we had two extra members of the company—not human but canine. There are a lot of dogs in Afghanistan, both domesticated and feral. Often they get adopted by the ISAF forces and they stick around as long as there is food for them to eat. These two animals had had a particularly rough time of it. The Taliban, it was said, knew that they had been fed by ISAF troops. Consequently, when they returned to their village, the animals had had their bollocks cut off with a wire. Perhaps it wasn't any wonder that they preferred our company.

03.22. We left the base in silence. The cover of darkness would, we hoped, protect us from the unwelcome attention of the Taliban sniper that we knew was in the area; but we didn't want to alert ourselves to him by making too much noise. Moreover, earlier in the morning thirty Taliban had been seen moving to the west. Our advance into Mazdurak would not be a secret from them for ever, but we wanted to retain the element of surprise for as long as possible. Negotiating the treacherous ground in the dark was difficult; but it was a hell of a sight better than the alternative.

It took an hour to come to a halt in the wadi near Mazdurak. By this time we were a good couple of klicks away from the safety of the base, but only 400 metres from enemy territory. Above us, I heard the distant hum of the fast air as it circled, waiting for the order to unload its bombs on the compound. Apart from that, and the urgent whispers of the command team around me, there was a deep, threatening silence. The sort of silence that can only be a prelude to something worse.

As we waited, however, on the outskirts of Mazdurak, we received some good news. Taliban chatter had been intercepted: our enemy was bragging, and along with the fact that twelve men had just been identified in the area, it was possible to predict an ambush and pinpoint its location. They say that careless talk costs lives. With a bit of luck, in the Taliban's case, this was going to be true.

I wondered how the enemy knew we were

coming. Specifically, I had a suspicion that the Taliban had been tipped off by the members of the ANP stationed above Kajaki. Major Tony Borgnis didn't seem to think so. The enemy knew we hadn't patrolled into Mazdurak since the blue on blue, so they knew it would only be a matter of time. Now, though, they had given away their hand.

The morale boost this gave the troops was immense. As Tony put it, unable to stop the smile showing on his face, 'We should kill more Taliban this morning than we might have done.' What was more, we had the equipment to do it. The fast air was still nearby and in the light of this new information, the plan changed. They would still drop ordnance on the compound where the blue on blue had happened; but first they would bomb the hell out of another compound—the one where the Taliban were waiting in ambush.

6 Platoon advanced. By 05.46, in the grey light of dawn, we were just 300 metres from Mazdurak. The only thing that separated us from the village was a patch of open ground and the knowledge that the Taliban were lying in wait. But not, if everything went according to plan, for much longer. Tony Borgnis made a final check that the pilots circling overhead were aware of 7 Platoon's position in the neighbouring village of Barakju; once that was done, the order was given and the jets cleared to attack.

The drone of the planes grew louder as they approached.

The bombs were dropped and the aircraft receded.

The length of time it takes for a bomb to hit its target is always a surprise. You hold your breath; you feel the tension all around you. I suppose at the back of your mind there is the constant, nagging worry that things can—and do—go wrong.

I heard someone announce fifty seconds to impact.

'Thirty-five seconds.'

Splash.

When it hits, the relief is immense. And on this occasion, it was unerring. The ground shook and in the distance the familiar huge cloud of dust mushroomed into the sky. It was followed immediately by the booming sound of mortars back at Kajaki as the FSG fired on the enemy position while the fast air approached once more, this time to drop a bomb on the blue on blue compound and deny it to the Taliban.

The explosion seemed to light up the morning sky. It was our signal to advance.

To get into Mazdurak we had to cover about 250 metres of open ground. The only way to do this was on foot. The Taliban ambushers might have been hit, but we didn't know how many of them had been killed. Moreover, there was probably still a sniper in the region. The only thing we could do was put our heads down and run like hell.

We made it to the halfway point, where we took shelter behind the wall of a compound. We caught our breath, and then received news over the net that eight Taliban had just left the ambush position. Whether the others had been killed or not we didn't know. It made the remaining 150-metre sprint into Mazdurak edgy to say the least, but we couldn't stay there in the open ground. In our hurry to get to the village, we started bunching—something I knew we should never do because it meant we presented an easy target to the enemy. But once it happens, it's difficult to sort out. We were lucky to reach the entry point of Mazdurak unscathed.

Even from the outside wall of Mazdurak, it was clear that the village had been bombed to hell. The wall was littered with shell holes and we entered through a massive gap in the wall that had simply been reduced to rubble. The thought passed through my mind as I ran into the village that no matter how hard you try, you're never going to make yourself popular with the local population if you destroy their towns and villages like this, no matter what your justification. The bombsite around me used to be people's houses; indeed, it had been people's houses for the last 200 years. Now it was a scene of devastation.

Our orders were to clear Mazdurak and

then push on to the town of Kavalabad, the Taliban front line. In order to do this, we needed to clear every single compound. I thought back to the few days I had spent on Salisbury Plain with B Company as they underwent their training exercises in preparation for their tour. No one could have said that their FIBUA training was an unqualified success—truth to tell, it had been a bit shambolic. What a difference six months makes. The troops around me went about their business as though they'd been doing it all their lives. They knew the Taliban could be hiding in any of the compounds we were entering—every corner or doorway we approached could be a Taliban firing point; and we knew their sniper was somewhere in the area. It didn't stop 6 Platoon clearing each compound with a rigorous efficiency. They used bar mines to blast their way into the compounds. Once an entry point had been made, fragmentation grenades and smoke grenades were used to ensure that the compounds were empty.

What followed was an hour of high-intensity house clearance. They call it 'going red'— using maximum force to clear every compound. Bar mines and grenades exploded constantly; the air was full of smoke, dust and the urgent shouts of the soldiers performing this dangerous but necessary work. I was jumping out of my skin. The further we penetrated into Mazdurak, the clearer the extent of the devastation in that village became. I found, embedded amongst the rubble, a sharp, twisted piece of shrapnel. This was the casing from one of the bombs that had been dropped on the place. The idea of this wicked-looking hunk of metal spinning through the air and crashing into a compound was a pretty sobering one—it gave a good idea of the kind of damage these bombs can inflict. It could easily have ricocheted off a wall and split someone in two. Maybe it had.

After an hour of this high-octane manoeuvring through the village, it became clear that Mazdurak was deserted. And it was hardly a surprise—we had burned through a lot of ammo in that hour. Any Taliban who had been here had retreated and we were now only a couple of hundred metres from Kavalabad, where the enemy were holed up. From this new position close to the enemy's front line, 6 Platoon were able to identify enemy positions. The situation changed immediately. No longer were the soldiers focused on house clearance: now they were focused on assaulting the enemy front line, and they were going to use everything in their arsenal to achieve that.

The crew and I were told to keep our heads down. We didn't need telling twice. Just over the wadi we could see Kavalabad. The Fire Support Group, from their position up on the hill, started raining down fifty-cal fire on to the enemy positions while Tony Borgnis called in another fast air strike. Two bombs were dropped. The boom of the second ordnance was 6 Platoon's signal to join the attack. They did so with gusto. Climbing up on to the roofs and walls of the compound we were in, they unleashed an awesome number of rounds into the Taliban positions in Kavalabad.

The enemy were behind a tree line about 300 metres away. When 6 Platoon added their fire to the party, the Taliban were forced to take action. They started a flanking manoeuvre, moving to either side of the line of trees in an effort to divide 6 Platoon's fire. Ben Browning, the Platoon Sergeant, ordered the fire to be redirected. It continued with the same blistering intensity and the flanking manoeuvre was suppressed.

Now, though, we had a different problem. Every soldier's worst nightmare. The rate of fire over the last couple of hours had been so intense that 6 Platoon were running out of ammo.

The order came to slow down the rate of fire. But the weapons were starting to overheat—smoke was pouring from a few of them—and the platoon's arsenal was almost depleted. There was no more ammo coming up the line, so there was only one option left. Ben Browning ordered a 'fast extraction'. Or, to put it another way, we were told to get out of there. And quickly.

We sprinted back through the decimated remains of the village. We needed to get back to the riverbed from where we had watched the fast air bombing Mazdurak. But in order to do that, it was necessary to cross back over the open ground. This left us dangerously open to a counterattack and so, despite the 45-degree heat, I ran as fast as my little legs would carry me. It was knackering, and I wasn't even carrying a weapon system or a camera. Eventually we reached the security of the riverbed, where we were able to catch up with Tony Borgnis and find out from him how he felt the operation had gone.

Despite the sudden need for a fast extraction, he could barely contain his delight. 'Extremely successful,' he told me. Not only had they scuppered the enemy's ambush: 'We also engaged a number of firing points, heavy machine gun and mortar positions, as well as snipers. It doesn't get better than that in terms of operational success.'

As we stood in that dried-up riverbed, Tony flashed us a charming smile. 'I've got to go, lads,' he told us, and off he ran.

Which left three of us—me, Fred the cameraman and John the director. We looked around for the rest of the soldiers and suddenly realized that everyone else had disappeared. We stared at each other as the penny dropped that we were the last ones left.

You've never seen a bunch of guys move so quickly. We absolutely legged it until the rest of 6 Platoon came into view.

'Thank fuck for that,' I muttered under my breath as we joined them and walked back in the midday heat towards the safety of the British base at Kajaki.

12. THE KNOCK ON THE DOOR

The Royal Anglians' six-month tour of duty was nearing its end and the time had come for me to say goodbye to Helmand Province once more.

I approached my departure with mixed feelings. There were plenty of things I wouldn't miss: being shot at, living in hot, sticky, dirty conditions, eating army rations. The soldiers, of course, had more reason than me to look forward to their return. After all, they'd been shot at a whole lot more; they'd lived in bad conditions for longer; and they'd eaten a hell of a sight more army scoff than me. Josh Hill and Ben Browning spoke almost dreamily of tucking into fish and chips when they got home and I knew what they meant.

But there were things I knew I would miss. The camaraderie for a start—I had forged strong friendships with some of the guys, friendships that I hoped would last for a long time. And I had come, in a strange kind of way, to forge a bond with Afghanistan itself. It is, of course, a highly dangerous, deeply troubled place and I wouldn't want to express any misplaced bravado or naivety about going there. But it is also a truly beautiful country. A place that can take your breath away, despite the ugly nature of what's going on there. As if

208

to highlight this, one of the last things I did before I left Kajaki was take a swim with a few of the guys in the cooling waters of the lake above the dam. It's a treat only those stationed in this northern outpost of Helmand Province can look forward to and there's no doubt that, in the midst of the intense heat of the Afghan summer, it was the best swim of my life. Immersed in the clear, chalky blue waters of the lake, you could almost forget that the craggy slopes all around you are littered with mines, and that you are swimming under armed guard. It almost seemed like a metaphor for something, a reminder that when you're surrounded by danger and death, the small things become of great importance.

Sergeant Ben Browning echoed that feeling. In the time since he had been away, his little boy had learned to talk. A momentous time in any father's life, but doubly so for a father who has been absent in a foreign land, knowing that there is a very real possibility that each day could be his last. 'I'm definitely going to appreciate things a little more,' he said. I hoped that the same would be true of me.

It was also clear to me in that summer of 2007 that the ISAF forces' involvement in this war-torn country would last for a long time to come. Men like those I had come to know in the Royal Anglians would be facing similar dangers to the ones they had faced while I was with them tomorrow, and tomorrow, and

209

tomorrow. The remit of the soldiers was to win the hearts and minds of the Afghan people, but while they were involved in a fight against an intelligent, determined enemy willing to die for what they believed in, this was an almost impossible task. They were there to improve the infrastructure of Afghanistan, and they wanted to do this; but all I witnessed was destruction. The end of the road, if indeed the road was ever to end, was a long way off. The journey would continue to be hard.

My own journey was almost over. The day before I was to leave Kajaki a few of us were sitting around outside, drinking tea, smoking cigarettes and chewing the fat. On the ground around us there was an expanse of tough, straw-like grass. One of the guys decided to clear this grass away by burning it, just to neaten the place up a bit and make it a nicer environment to hang out in. He sprinkled some petrol over the ground and set it alight. This was an area where unused rounds were emptied out of the weapons systems, especially the FSG's fifty-cals. Out of the blue, the air was filled with the sound of rounds banging off all around us, some whizzing over our heads. We hit the deck as this discarded ammunition burned and exploded randomly. It was a miracle nobody was hurt and highlighted that for a soldier, surrounded by the lethal tools of your trade, you sometimes don't even need an enemy to come to mischief.

Like, I imagine, many of the soldiers at the end of their tour, I was feeling demob happy. But as I took my final journey back along the Helmand river towards Camp Bastion in a Chinook, I was reminded that in Afghanistan you can't let your guard drop even when you're going home. From the back of the chopper, flares erupted into the air, their trails twirling and spiralling impressively. This wasn't a bonfire night display, however: it's standard procedure for aircraft traversing Helmand Province. The flares act as heat sources. If a heat-seeking missile is aimed at the chopper and locks on to the hot engines, the flares are there to confuse it.

As the Chinook carried me away from Kajaki, I remembered what Ian Robinson had said to me only a couple of weeks before. 'For the enemy, each day's the same as the next and they don't mind whether they kill us on day one of the tour, day thirty of the tour or the last day of the tour.'

The Royal Anglians had already lost nine men. I hoped and prayed that they would have lost no more when I saw them next.

*   *   *

The banner, carried by two excited-looking children, was large, colourful and festooned with balloons. It lit up the drab surroundings of Pirbright Barracks, Surrey. England. Back where my association with them had all started.

The message emblazoned upon it was simple: 'Welcome Home Daddy'.

There were a lot of kids congregated to welcome their daddies home the day I travelled to the Anglians' base, and a lot of wives and girlfriends too. It seemed a lifetime ago that the lads had left and I imagined that their families and friends must have scarcely dared think about this moment for fear of tempting fate. Bunting surrounded the parade ground. As we waited for the guys to arrive it struck me how different this was to the environment in which they had been living for the past six months. Bunting and balloons are in pretty short supply in Helmand Province. The guys would have had a couple of days' decompression in Cyprus to help them acclimatize, but it was going to take a lot more than that for them really to become used to no longer having to live in a war zone.

You could feel the thrill as the coaches trundled into view. Conquering football teams are given open-top buses and streets lined with cheering crowds. None of that for these young men who had risked their lives on our behalf; nor, I imagine, would they have wanted it. Just plain white coaches bringing the boys home from war. The cheers from the families, however, as the guys spilled out on to the tarmac in their desert gear, were enthusiastic

212

and, for me, highly emotional. The sheepish grins on the faces of the soldiers told their own story. I stood and watched as children ran up to their dads and allowed themselves to be embraced. Six months is a long time for a soldier in the field, but it's even longer for a young child. It must have seemed to them half a lifetime ago that their dads went off to war. I felt something of an intruder as tearful wives embraced their husbands. Few words were spoken. Sometimes that sort of relief and joy can't easily be expressed. I had seen many of these men turn into experienced and efficient fighters; but today I was witnessing a side of them that barely had the chance to reveal itself in Helmand Province: they were family men, people like you and me, just glad to be home.

And then, among the crowd, I saw a familiar face. Familiar, but different. Corporal Stuart Parker had been on the roof in Mazdurak when the blue on blue incident had occurred. His body armour had been destroyed, his clothes blown away, his ribs broken. But he had been one of the lucky ones. Unlike Foster, Thrumble and McClure, he had survived. As he put it, he had fallen asleep in Helmand and woken up in Birmingham and he joked, with a spark of his old humour, that the two places didn't look a lot different. I could tell, however, that his repartee masked his feelings about the severity of what had happened to him. Stu was thin and drawn. He looked pale

213

and walked on crutches. I told him I was expecting to see him in a wheelchair, but he brushed off anything that sounded like sympathy. That wasn't what he was there for. The sight of him standing there with Sergeant Woodrow, the man who had helped him off the roof in Mazdurak, dragged him from the rubble and probably saved his life, was a poignant one. Woody, of course, would never ask for or expect a word of thanks, but it seemed to me that there was a bond between these two men that would never go away.

'We went through a lot, didn't we, mate?' Woody said. His voice was full.

Stu agreed. 'A few short months took a long time to get through.' I didn't doubt that there were plenty of men surrounding me who would agree with that sentiment.

*   *   *

As overjoyed as everyone was to have returned home, nobody forgot that there were nine families for whom this day was not one of celebration. Nine families for whom the worst had happened. Nine families whose young men had not come home alive. For them, the aftershock of the war in Afghanistan would be felt every day, most probably for the rest of their lives. They say that the Royal Anglians are a family regiment so they too would be feeling something akin to the loss of a family member. It was important to everyone involved that the deaths of the fallen were commemorated in an appropriate way. A month after their return from Helmand, a service was held. It seems a small thing, but it was a ceremony of immense importance to everyone.

I was unable to attend because I was filming abroad. The first I saw of it was on the screen when we came to edit the last episode. I saw the wide eyes of the men I knew so well. They looked confused, as though they were trying to make sense of it all. They looked as if they were trying not to cry. I saw children and the elderly there to honour their loved ones. I heard the heart-rending swell of 'Nimrod' from Elgar's Enigma Variations. I heard Ian Robinson read lines from Laurence Binyon's 'For the Fallen': 'At the going down of the sun and in the morning, we will remember them.' I watched families light candles in memory of their loved ones.

I wept. And I defy anybody who watches it not to do so.

I was invited into the home of Private Robert Foster. In many ways, meeting a bereaved family is more difficult than being with the men on the front line. As always, I was amazed by the quiet dignity with which Robert's parents, Lisa and John, and his sister Lauren conducted themselves. Lisa's account of hearing the news was heartbreaking. 'As I was walking down the stairs, putting my dressing gown on, I was thinking, Please, let it be the police. Something's happened in the road. Let it be the police. But as soon as I opened the door, I knew. The officer standing there introduced himself and he didn't have to say any more. And my first words were, "Just tell me it's not the worst." And he said, "I'm afraid it is." I said, "Now tell me you've made a mistake." He said, "I'm afraid I haven't."'

Somehow she managed to hold back the tears as she spoke. Or maybe she had just cried them all.

The feelings that must have surged through the family at that moment are unimaginable. Now, every time I hear of a death in Afghanistan, I remember Robert Foster's family and their description of that knock on the door. It seems to me that it's being repeated too often.

Back on the parade ground at Elizabeth Barracks on the day B Company returned, Stu Parker had attempted to draw a line under their tour of duty. 'Everyone's back now,' he had said gruffly. 'That's it. Over and done with.'

Well, up to a point. The tour might have been over and done with, but the after-effects weren't. Nor was the battle for Helmand Province. The Royal Anglians had returned, but other young British men had taken their place in the field. They would continue to fight the Taliban, come what may, and they would continue to die for their country.

The war wasn't over by any means.

PART TWO
Herrick 8

13. THE JOCKS

I had seen only one small part of Afghanistan. To be more precise, I'd seen only one small part of one province in the southern part of the country. But I felt drawn to it. Drawn to its beauty and other-worldliness. And drawn too, I suppose, to its danger. When your life is at risk, you appreciate it all the more. No doubt I would feel differently as a real soldier, stuck in the middle of a real tour of duty and having to undergo major firefights on a daily, and sometimes twice-daily, basis. But I'm not a real soldier. I'm just an observer, and in the year that followed my first major excursions to Afghanistan, I knew that I wanted, at some stage, to go back. Maybe I was addicted to the thrill of it. Maybe, when you've been to a war zone, the rest of your life seems a little bit bland.

There were other, less selfish reasons for going back. I wanted to see what had changed in a year. I wanted to see whether the Taliban had been pushed back from those areas where they had been dominant and who was really winning the war. I wanted to find out for myself whether conditions for the soldiers had improved at all. And perhaps most importantly, I wanted to see if the sacrifices that had been made by all the young British men and women—both those who had given their lives and those who had been traumatized by the experience—had, in the final analysis, been worth whatever territorial and political gains had been achieved. I'd been gone only a year and I wasn't expecting miracles; but I hoped to get some sense that the British Army's operations had made progress.

The MoD would allow us to revisit some familiar places; but there were now locations we could visit to which it would not have been possible to go the previous year. In 2007 the town of Musa Qala, an important strategic position for reasons that I would understand once I got there, had been entirely under Taliban control. This was no longer the case, although the Taliban presence was still strong and it was now the scene of some of the fiercest fighting in Helmand. It was decided that Musa Qala would be top of our list of places to visit.

We would also need to attach ourselves to an entirely new group of soldiers. A number of possibilities were suggested. At one stage it was mooted that we would be billeted with 2 Para, based in Sangin. Their CO, however, wasn't keen on the idea. Fair enough. Another suggestion was the Royal Irish Regiment, who were in Helmand as part of an Operational Mentor and Liaison Team (OMLT, pronounced 'omelette'). This meant that the Royal Irish were accompanying and mentoring members of the Afghan National Army (ANA). It would have been very interesting to work alongside an OMLT, and I wasn't averse to spending some time with them, but I felt that it wouldn't have much resonance for our British viewers, so we decided against it.

In the end we were posted with the Argyll and Sutherland Highlanders, 5th Battalion the Royal Regiment of Scotland, or 5 Scots for short. The Argyll and Sutherland Highlanders was formed in 1881 and has a long and distinguished battle history, from the First and Second World Wars through Korea, Suez and the Falklands. The Royal Regiment of Scotland's motto is 'Nemo Me Impune Lacessit'—which I'm told means 'No one assails me with impunity'. Or to put it another way, no one tries it on with me and gets away with it. By the time we were assigned to 5 Scots, they were already well into their tour of duty. I wondered if the Taliban were feeling the truth of that motto.

The men of 5 Scots were posted at Musa Qala District Centre. The camera team and I would meet them for the first time when we arrived in that war-torn town—no training exercises or bonding sessions with the lads to ease us in this time. Instead we were thrown straight in at the deep end, with the now familiar journey to RAF Brize Norton in order

223

to board a flight to Kandahar. We were to be transported in one of the RAF Tristars that are used exclusively for transporting troops. These are very elderly aircraft and they are delayed on an almost routine basis; our flight to Kandahar was no exception. We arrived for an 08.00 flight; the delay was announced and true to type almost every British soldier who was due to be on that plane cheered enthusiastically. It turned out that the plane had sprung an oil leak and the oil had got on to the brakes. Obviously not an ideal situation. The aircraft teams, of course, professional to the last, picked up the problem straight away; not for the first time, however, it struck me that our armed forces should be better equipped for the jobs they have to do. Those Tristars are substantially older than most of the passengers they carry and although delays like this might not seem such a serious problem in the grand scheme of things, they can have a cost in terms of the troops' morale. I got talking to a few lads who were on their way to Afghanistan for the first time, having been posted in Germany. They'd been waiting four days for a connecting flight. I don't suppose they were too sad to have their journey delayed; but if the boot were on the other foot and they were delayed on their way home for R and R, it would have been a different story. I'm sure the Tristars are safe but surely they're due for an update.

We were delayed for twelve hours while another aircraft was brought in and all the gear swapped over. We finally took off at 20.00. Having made this journey a couple of times before, I knew what to expect. However, you never quite get used to the sight of those stretcher beds at the front of the plane with their straps and oxygen masks; you can never quite take your eyes off them. And despite the fact that I had been to the region before, it would be a lie to say that I wasn't nervous. I was. Very. But my nervousness was tinged with the excitement that always accompanies going to a war zone. Of course, there were no air hostesses with gin and tonics to calm me and my fellow passengers down. Orange squash, as always in the British Army, was the order of the day, and it doesn't do much to settle the butterflies in your stomach.

Because of the delay at Brize Norton we had to land at Kandahar during daylight hours—not something the pilots like doing because of the risk of mortar attack as they're coming in to land. No matter how edgy a nighttime landing in full darkness is for the passengers, at least it stops you from being a highly visible target. As the aircraft touched down I was greeted with a familiar sight. It looked like mist rolling in along the runway; in fact it was sand filling the air, billowing up as though to welcome us back to Afghanistan.

We spent one night at Kandahar. I was

225

surprised, and I suppose gratified, to meet so many people who had seen and enjoyed our first Afghanistan film, which had been broadcast since I had last been here. Not everyone, of course, was a fan, but in general it seemed we had the support of the troops. The next day we kicked around the base, buying a few supplies from the American PX—sweets, a knife, a new pair of sunglasses. There was time for a quick walk round the boardwalk and by nightfall it was time for us to board our C-130 Hercules bound for Camp Bastion.

Last time I had taken the short hop west from Kandahar to Bastion, we had done so during the day. Now, however, things had changed and the pilots prefer to make such journeys during the hours of darkness. They wore special night vision goggles. They told me that they could see further with these than with the naked eye during the day; but the bigger advantage, of course, was that the Taliban couldn't see our aircraft and take pot shots at us. I wasn't going to argue with that.

Since I had left the previous summer, the British base in Helmand had doubled in size with the construction of what had become known as Camp Bastion 2. It seemed to me that this expansion of the base had occurred somewhat under the radar; certainly I didn't recall it being widely reported in the UK. It was a clear indication, I thought, that the British intend to be in Helmand Province for a

226

long time to come. Outside the new general headquarters, a monument had been erected to the fallen, with a list of all the British soldiers who had died since the occupation began. It was a long list, with names of people I had known. It had not been updated since February of that year. At that moment, if it were to be updated, another twenty-one names would have to be added. Clearly the tempo of the fighting had not decreased. Clearly the war was very far from being over.

Bastion was a different place to the camp I had spent time in a year ago. An immense amount of construction work had occurred in the intervening months. Many of the canvas pods had been replaced with hard-covered accommodation units. Much of the Hesco had been replaced by concrete walls. There were new facilities, including a hospital. I couldn't help but think back to the tented accommodation a year before. It was hardly recognisable. I was able to take a quick tour and meet some of the doctors and nurses, having been told that they had some of the best trauma surgeons in the world.

In the operating room lay an Afghan national. His leg was being lifted up by a steel handle and had been perforated with holes the size of a golf ball. His ankle was hanging off by the ligaments and looked like a drawing from a medical textbook. The guy was out cold while the surgeons, wearing magnifying glasses, sutured his arteries with what were essential soldering irons. The room reeked with the smell of burning flesh—it was hi-tech and medieval at the same time. There were also two other adults and a child in there. I was informed by the head surgeon that they had been caught in an IED strike in Musa Qala, which did little to ease my growing anxiety about returning to the front.

As I walked around the wards and had my photo taken with the nurses—much to the befuddlement of the Afghan nationals—I noticed a young Afghan in a coma with an oxygen mask over his face. He'd been shot by ISAF forces while trying to fire an RPG. The Northern Irish doctor tending him had given him six pints of his own blood. (He joked that there may have been some Guinness in there too.) He was interested to know what the boy's feelings would be when he woke up and realised his life had been saved by infidel blood.

In all, I couldn't have been more impressed by the dedication of the staff at the hospital, and in particular by the love and care they gave to the young Afghan amputees around the wards.

Elsewhere, I saw that a well had been bored so that the camp could have its own water. The cookhouses had improved immensely. And of course, with the construction of Camp Bastion 2, adjoined to the original base by just a wide strip of heavily protected dead ground, the sense of scale was much greater.

There wasn't time, however, for much sightseeing round the new facilities. Because almost as soon as we had arrived, we were loaded up into a Chinook and ferried to the town of Musa Qala.

*   *   *

Control of Musa Qala has changed hands a number of times in the past few years. In the summer of 2006, UK troops occupied the DC at the request of the then governor of Helmand Province. Subsequently, a mix of Danish and UK troops held the position. The garrison was repeatedly attacked, difficult to resupply and became somewhat beleaguered. Following a ceasefire, the Helmand governor and the elders of Musa Qala reached an agreement in October 2006 and ISAF forces left the DC. A 5 kilometre exclusion zone was agreed, and no ISAF forces or Taliban were permitted to enter. There is some disagreement about the extent to which the Taliban infringed upon the agreement, but after a senior Taliban commander was killed by a US airstrike just outside the exclusion zone, the Taliban took full control of the town in February 2007. For many months it remained a no-go area for foreign troops.

Then, in December 2007, a couple of

months after my first visit to Helmand, ISAF forces working alongside the Afghan National Army moved to regain the town. They dropped leaflets warning civilians of the impending invasion; the Taliban prepared to welcome the invaders by mining the town heavily. Operation Mar Karadad—or the battle for Musa Qala—was a success. British troops took up residence in an old hotel in the District Centre, or DC, and the Taliban were forced to withdraw. However, they remained in significant numbers on the outskirts of Musa Qala and it was certainly true when I arrived that the British forces' 'occupation' of the town was limited to a relatively localized area around the DC. For this reason, they had to make regular patrols towards the outer edges of Musa Qala in order to keep a ring around the town and stop the Taliban advancing on the DC (though they could, of course, still walk around the town with impunity if they weren't carrying a gun).

There are strategic reasons why Musa Qala was so hotly contested. The town itself is built around the meeting points of two rivers, one of which stretches to the very north of Helmand Province and the Taliban stronghold town of Baghran. The riverbeds, dried out in the summer, are important commerce and travel routes. It's impossible to stop every vehicle that travels up and down them. Further south, at Sangin, the Musa Qala river connects with the Helmand river, making Musa Qala a staging post for anyone wanting to travel from the north of the province to the south. As such, it is an essential location in the poppy trade. Control Musa Qala and you control the flow of opium from vast swathes of northern Helmand Province. Arms, too, pass through here on their way from Iran and Pakistan. No wonder the Taliban are so keen to get what they perceive to be their town back.

In addition to all this, there is a fragile and complicated political situation in the area. Musa Qala is the home of a powerful Afghan warlord called Mullah Abdul Salam, a veteran of the anti-Soviet resistance of the 1980s. Mullah Salam has strained links with the Taliban, but is also rumoured to be receiving money from the American government. He is rumoured to be a producer and transporter of heroin and it is said he collects so much protection money from some of the villagers that they often run their little businesses at a loss. Mullah Salam might be on our side, but he's no angel. It may sound galling that the Americans should be protecting such a man, but such is the intricacy of Afghan society that it is impossible to judge such a situation by our Western standards. If keeping Mullah Salam on side means bringing peace to Musa Qala, it seems inevitable that we should have to accept his less acceptable activities. There were plans for me to meet him in return for a packet of

231

his own drug of choice—Viagra (and with six wives, who can blame him?)—but they never materialized.

It is said that the success of ISAF's mission in Helmand Province rests or falls by what happens in Musa Qala. That alone made it sound to me like a dangerous place. Perhaps I shouldn't have been surprised, then, that within minutes of stepping out of the Chinook that had ferried us from Bastion and into the dusty surroundings of the Musa Qala landing zone, I was told that the very next evening I would be going out on patrol. For four days. Into one of the most battle-torn parts of Helmand. Forty-eight hours previously I'd been in London. Well, I told myself philosophically, that was what I'd come here to do . . .

We had flown in low and fast to avoid enemy fire. (Weeks earlier a Chinook carrying the governor of Helmand Province to a meeting with Mullah Salam had an RPG smash between its rotor blades and they had to be replaced.) The good news about the forthcoming patrol was broken to me in the shadow of the Chinook by Alan 'Goody' Goodall, Company Sergeant Major of Delta Company 5 Scots. 'You're guaranteed to see what you came to see, mate,' he told me in his broad Scottish accent.

I gave him a nervous smile.

Our liaison man was Captain Stevie Rae.

We would become good friends during my time in Musa Qala and he was one of the most impressive soldiers I have ever met. Sorry to make you blush, mate. He had previously been an RSM and to have done all this at such a relatively young age was testament to his abilities. He was modest too, and didn't want to be mentioned or appear on camera; but without Stevie our time in Musa Qala would have been very different, if not terminal.

I was taken to the DC—an old hotel that the Taliban had used for the same purpose when they were in charge of the town. It looked like a cross between a bombed-out NCP car park and a half-constructed concrete monstrosity on the Costa del Sol. There was evidence that it had been used for purposes other than housing troops. Brown stains on the inside of the walls indicated that some previous residents had been refining poppies into brown heroin sludge that could then be transported far and wide. On the roof, satellite transmitters stretched up to the sky and machine-gun posts gave a 360-degree arc of fire.

To one side of the hotel was a line of cubicles. These housed the satellite phones. The soldiers are given a set time to phone home. Their calls are good for morale but largely uninformative for the families, not so much for reasons of security but because the guys simply don't want to worry them with talk

233

of the dangers they've been facing. (More than once, after our first documentary was aired, I had soldiers coming up to me complaining that their family had become ten times more nervous about their tours of duty now that they had seen what life on the front line was really like . . .) The only time phone privileges are withdrawn is when a soldier is killed. Regimental gossip being what it is, the authorities have to do what they can to stop rumours spreading before the next of kin can be informed.

Beyond the hotel was a wadi, about 500 metres at its widest point, and a wall surrounded the whole area. Delta Company were billeted in tents up against the wall, so it was here that we were to make our home for the next few weeks. Our sleeping quarters were surrounded by high walls of protective Hesco and, like the soldiers, we tried to make our surroundings as restful as possible. It was difficult. We didn't have much in the way of creature comforts and the area stank of piss— clearly someone had taken a leak here pretty recently. A small gap between the top of the Hesco wall and the roof let the light in. Unfortunately it also pointed in the direction of where the oil drums of shit got burned on a daily basis. Air freshener Afghanistan-style— every morning I would wake and cough up a horrible brown sludge thanks to breathing in the stench of burned faeces every night. Still, beggars can't be choosers and at least we were protected by Hesco not canvas. We barely had time to unpack before we had to start preparing for our patrol the following day and head off to the briefing.

The briefing was given by the OC of Delta Company, Major Nick Calder, a military man from a military family. One brother was the 2ic of 5 Scots, the other had been 2ic of the Royal Anglians when I was out there on Herrick 6 and was now in command of the Fusiliers. Nick was astute, friendly and intelligent with a cut-glass English accent—but if ever there was a man under pressure, it was him. You could see it in his face. Nick told me that wherever he travelled, he took with him a box. It contained a picture of his wife and kids. Every morning he'd get it out, look at the picture, then return it to the box and put it away. That ritual over, he'd turn his attention to his other family: Delta Company, the seventy or eighty men whose lives and wellbeing were his direct responsibility.

Nick stood in front of the men and indicated a large military satellite map of Musa Qala. You could clearly see the convergence of the two wadis, and the DC where we were stationed. Every compound in the town, and there were several hundred of them, was individually numbered so that they could be easily identified, especially by fast air when the necessity arose for a bomb to be dropped accurately.

Nick explained that the four-day op was the longest they had yet embarked upon. The going would be difficult: the green zone would be filled with fields of maize a couple of metres high and in certain areas the soldiers' vision would be restricted to 5–10 metres. It would give the Taliban ample opportunity to hide and ambush. The enemy would definitely be in the vicinity, so we could expect what Nick called 'a considerable amount of activity'. I'd been in the green zone enough to know what that meant. 'Hopefully,' Nick concluded, 'we can give them a good bloody nose by the end of the four-day op.'

Hopefully indeed.

I took the opportunity to grab some one-on-one time with Nick Calder. I wanted to know how soon after leaving the DC we could expect to come under fire from the Taliban. Within about 2.5 klicks, he estimated. Not a huge distance, although I knew it would take a long time to walk. Not only would the patrol have to zigzag through the town, but in the rough terrain of the green zone you can hardly walk a few paces without twisting your ankle. The going can be both painful and painfully slow. Nick predicted that we were going to get dicked from the moment we left the DC, and that the Taliban would have a good idea of just where we were at any given moment. As we headed north, the contacts would be sporadic but frequent.

He was right about that.

Delta Company were four months into their tour of duty. Before I went out with the men, I wanted to get to know a few of them. They were incredibly welcoming to us—this was largely down to the fact, I think, that most of them had watched the first series. Some of the lads had put up a Queen Vic sign, and they'd got hold of a promotional picture of me which they'd stuck on to a Page three girl. So now, instead of reading *Ross Kemp on Gangs* it read *Ross Kemp on Porn*. Pretty basic humour, but well meant and we hit it off immediately. As we sat round together, I was shocked by how thin they all looked. Too thin, some might say, to be fighting. Nearby there were seventy or eighty Americans, separately billeted. They were buff—well fed and fit as you like. Every week or so, a couple of Sea Kings would fly in and deliver fresh food for the US troops. It was maddening to see how much better treated the Americans were. *That* was something that hadn't changed in a year. I would soon learn, though, that even if the Jocks—as 5 Scots refer to themselves—weren't the biggest men in the world, they were some of the toughest in a fight.

The youngest of their number, Private Nigel Campbell who looked like a young Gordon Brown, was eighteen. He had the bearing of a much older man. He spoke with pride about the fact that when he'd gone home on R and R, he was the only one of his friends who was actually doing something with his life. I wondered how the lads felt about the Taliban. They spoke in terms of respect. They were a good enemy, hard fighting and brave to take on the ISAF troops, especially with the assets they had at their disposal. Sergeant George McCafferty told me a story of Taliban being attacked by Apache helicopters overhead and taking them on with RPGs. Either brave or stupid, but certainly formidable. The Taliban were well organized, I was told, and trained. One particularly worrying example of this was that they had started putting anti-personnel mines and IEDs in the ditches that criss-cross the green zone. They had learned that when a soldier is under fire, he will dive for the nearest cover and the ditches served that purpose. In order to warn the local population about the presence of the IEDs, the Taliban would leave markers nearby. But these were difficult to see in the heat of battle; moreover, the enemy normally placed them on the opposite side of the IED to the direction from which they expected our troops to approach. It added a new sheen to the whole business and I was beginning to think that the enemy's skills had come on a bit since I was last out here.

But, as ever, what struck me most was the soldiers' camaraderie. Sergeant McCafferty stated that his platoon were the best soldiers he'd met in his fifteen years in the army; he knew that when they were 'in the shit', which they had been a lot lately, each could rely on his mates. I came away thinking that 5 Scots had had a particularly brutal time of it; and I was starting to become even more concerned about the wisdom of going out on patrol with them the following day.

In the event I got a stay of execution. Temperatures the next day were nudging 50 degrees and it was decided that we should stay at base for a while longer to acclimatize. So it was that I watched Delta Company step purposefully out of the DC, tooled up with their weapons systems—the GPMGs, Minimis and SA80s. Even though they looked like they were carrying too much lead for their thin bodies, they were a formidable-looking force and I knew from having spoken to a few of them that they were ready to meet whatever was thrown their way.

I would follow the next day when they were resupplied, and would spend the next three days with them while they were doing their job: fighting the Taliban.

*　　*　　*

Delta Company's foray into the green zone was dubbed Operation Cap Fox. I was to join them on day two, but word came in before we left that they'd already had contact with the

Taliban. It was an apprehensive Mr Kemp who donned his body armour and helmet in preparation for the trip.

The men of 2 Scots were to drive us north in their Mastiffs. The Mastiffs would resupply Delta Company and drop us off, and the joys of war would begin. 2 Scots—the Royal Highland Fusiliers—are an infantry battalion, but for their deployment in Helmand they had been turned into an armoured vehicle unit. As I'd noticed before, in the army you get what you're given and you do what you're told. They had adapted to their new role amazingly well, given that their pre-deployment training involved driving Land Rovers around Salisbury Plain. It was a relief to know, however, that they would be transporting us to our positions in Mastiffs, rather than the Vikings so common during my last visit. There had been Mastiffs last year, but not enough. This had changed and rightly so: these vehicles had made a huge difference to the troops, as their V-shaped undercarriages were designed to deflect the blast of mines and IEDs. The Taliban were adding more explosives to their devices; but in any case, having seen the damage a mine could do to a lesser vehicle— not to mention the men inside it—I was very pleased to have the benefit of this extra protection.

Just after 14.00, and in the relentless, burning heat, our convoy trundled north along the dried-up wadi under the protection of fifty-cals and grenade machine guns, kicking up dust as it went. Inside the Mastiffs, little monitors displayed camera footage of the surrounding area. There were very few people, at least in eyeshot. In the distance beyond the town rose the craggy peaks of what the British had dubbed Mount Doom. Occasionally we stopped and the guys brought out the metal detectors to sweep the wadi for mines. Soon enough, though, the time came to disembark. It's always a dangerous moment: no doubt the enemy had watched the convoy approach. While we were moving, we were encased in steel; but as soon as we stepped outside, we were vulnerable. Admittedly we had a guy on top with a fifty-cal machine gun but that, as I well knew, wasn't always enough to stop the Taliban having a pop.

On RV'ing with Delta Company, the plan was to zigzag further north until we reached an area known as the Garden. Here the vegetation was so thick that spotter planes simply couldn't see into it, which meant that it was an ideal place for the Taliban to congregate. They couldn't just artillery the Garden because there were also Afghan nationals living there, whom the Taliban used as cover. The only way to identify the enemy was to go in on foot and draw them out.

First, though, we had to make contact with Delta. They had taken cover in a compound on the edge of the wadi, and it was here that we caught up with them. Nick Calder described to me the circumstances of their contact with the enemy that morning: there were two confirmed enemy deaths and another had been seen limping away. He grinned at me almost cheekily. 'A reasonably good day,' he observed.

But the day wasn't over yet, as the Icom chatter confirmed. Icom chatter can be a blessing and a curse. No one would want to be without it, but the Taliban, who know we listen in, are cute enough to plant red herrings and try to obscure what they're saying. *The melons are ready.* A phrase like that can play on your mind. What does it mean? Has an IED been planted? Has an ambush been set up? Or are, in fact, the melons just ready, and the Taliban are taking the piss? Interpreting the Icom is a skill in itself.

On this occasion, the chatter suggested that the Taliban knew where we were and at that moment were preparing to attack us with RPGs. Delta Company's compound wasn't safe any more. We were a marked target and it was time to get out.

We stepped gingerly into the fields of maize, acutely aware that an ambush could happen at any time. These fields are particularly treacherous. Anyone or anything can hide in those high crops; the Taliban would be able to hear us coming and they would be able to see

242

us too on account of the antennae from our lads' comms equipment. The enemy could just spray rounds indiscriminately across the field and have a pretty good chance of hitting a soldier. I expected to hear the burst of AK fire at any second.

We reached the Garden. More Icom chatter: the Taliban still knew exactly where we were and they were preparing to attack. Sweat poured from my body; my mouth went dry with that familiar feeling of terrified excitement.

I'd only been on the ground for a matter of half an hour and already I could sense that a contact was minutes away . . .

14. THE GARDEN

We crept through the Garden. Ahead of me was Sergeant Danny Carter; behind me was the cameraman and Stevie Rae. The TAC were to our right. Sweat dripped from my nose. You could tell it was about to go off because of the silence.

No one spoke unless it was necessary, and even then only in a tense, hushed whisper. Danny Carter relayed some intelligence. 'The Taliban are in the Garden.'

My pulse rate increased.

'They know we're walking into their line of fire.'

Silence. The calm before the storm?

We pushed forwards along an irrigation ditch on the side of a maize field. There wasn't much cover.

And then it came.

I hadn't missed that sound, the noise of a round whizzing over your head, dangerously close. 'Get down!' I shouted at the cameraman, but I needn't have. Everyone around me hit the dirt, though the soldiers did not hug the ground quite as enthusiastically as me. That first round was like a trigger: in an instant the air was filled with the firecracks of weaponry.

A boom.

'IDFs!' Danny shouted. Indirect fire. We all pressed ourselves further against the earth as the Taliban's mortars flew randomly into the Garden. And then . . .

'RPGs!' I heard the whoosh as they went over us. 'Fuck!' someone shouted. 'That was close!' And when a soldier says that, you know it was.

The Taliban were no more than 30 metres away and we were pinned down. I knew that the enemy had their sights on us in particular because I could hear the sound of their AK-47 rounds cutting the maize 7 inches above my head. My pack was so big it was being used as a target, so I rolled over onto my side so that the plates of my body armour were facing the incoming fire. Rounds zipped over my hip, which flinched from the air pressure. It was perhaps the closest I've ever come to being shot. The FOO was shouting, 'Enemy there! Enemy there!' We were caught between the flanks of an L-shaped ambush.

Staying put wasn't an option. The longer you sit still during an ambush, the greater your chance of being scoped out. Danny decided that we should advance through the enemy's fire. We started to crawl along a small trench that divided the maize field from a compound wall. For a moment it felt that the firing was no longer aimed at us. Then two rounds came very close. We couldn't move. 'Fuck, that was close!' We started to laugh—a way, I suppose,

245

of releasing the tension that had been building up over the past few minutes. The laughs didn't last long. Another AK round whizzed above our heads again. We were once more in somebody's sights and needed to keep moving. 'Keeping fucking low!' came the instruction. I did as I was told.

The air was full of lead and it was almost a fluke that we hadn't been hit. Danny made the decision that we should get into the ditch itself which meant making ourselves that little bit more exposed as we climbed out of the cornfield and into it. By now it was a two-way range but that didn't help us. The ground shook as the IDF grew closer. I felt my pack weighing down on me as we crawled through the marshy bog of the irrigation ditch. My clothes and boots were soaked with warm mud, and something else too: human shit, putrefying in the heat. Not something I'd have chosen to crawl though, but frankly that was the least of my problems. The pungent smell of fresh mint hit my senses—a delicious, fragrant smell but one that created a strange counterpoint to the turds and to the battle raging all around me. Roast lamb will never be the same again. The enemy were still on two sides of us, rounds were still flying, getting closer. I turned to camera. 'Here I am again,' I said, 'in Afghanistan, in a ditch.' A round whizzed close by my head again. 'Oh, fuck off!' I said in a slightly camp voice.

246

We had to keep pushing on, despite the fact that we were clearly in the sight of their snipers. More than once the call came to get down, either because of a burst of AK fire, or because of mortar or RPG attack.

On TV, it looks like we were in that ditch for five minutes. In fact it was more like 35 as we slowly crawled on our hands and knees. The ditch ended with a small bump which we had to go over, so making ourselves momentarily more exposed. We reached a place where two compounds joined and there was a covering wall where we thought we could take cover. Other members of Delta had made it there and it represented safety, for a while at least. But in order to reach it we had to cross several metres of open ground: a dangerous operation when Taliban snipers know where you are. But there was no point waiting. I pushed myself to my feet and ran like hell.

It's hard to describe the relief of getting to those walls, or the thrill of knowing we'd made it through an ambush alive. We were still surrounded, of course, but with the high walls of the compound we had better cover. A chance to get our breath and wipe the sweat from our faces.

It had been quite a welcome back to Afghanistan.

I asked Danny to give us a sit rep. The Taliban had four different firing points, but Delta had advanced towards their positions nonetheless. To the east, another platoon was under mortar fire. As I tried to light the cigarette—a real Afghan lung-gasper—of Private Govern, who was crouched against the wall next to me, the Taliban opened fire on our positions. An AK round ricocheted off the wall and passed inches from my outstretched hand. Jesus. Even the safe places weren't safe. We had to change our position and take refuge in the cover of a nearby wall.

It was while we were here that the word came through to expect an artillery strike. Forward Operating Base Edinburgh was about 7 klicks away on the other side of the wadi. Delta believed, thanks to the Icom chatter, that they had located the compound from which most of the incoming fire was originating. More importantly, observers believed that the Taliban commander who was directing the rest of the forces was stationed here. Take him out, and it would leave the men on the ground without any instructions. We braced ourselves for the sound of artillery shells being rained into the compound.

I looked around me. The men were exhausted. I saw one of Delta Company's snipers. He was used to being in a fire support position, away from the actual thick of the fighting. No less a soldier, of course, but practised at a different job. This was his first time on the ground. He had what is known among the men as the '1,000-yard stare', an unfocused gaze of shell-shocked disbelief common to anyone new to the stress of close combat. It wouldn't be helped, I thought, by the whistle and boom of the artillery shells. They slammed into the Taliban compound with a crash that shook the whole ground. We waited for the last of them to hit their target and then, inevitably, we continued moving forward.

For a while there was silence as a whole group of us crept along the wall of the compound. For a short while. It was punctured by the blistering noise of what sounded to us like mortar fire. We were under attack again. Urgently we took cover in the nearest building. Only when we were under shelter did the word come through: the boom had not been mortar fire at all but American F-16s, dropping bombs on another Taliban compound. 'Calm *doon*!' Danny's broad Scottish voice rose above the nervous chatter of the soldiers. 'Calm fucking *doon*!'

We took the opportunity to rest and listen to the F-16s and the continuing artillery strikes. Each time they hit the target, I felt my whole body shake, my bones rattling against my body armour. Not the guys around me, though. They hardly blinked. You could tell just by looking at them as they sat louchely on the ground, smoking cigarettes with their backs against the walls, that this was something they dealt with every day. That isn't to say, however, that there weren't a few more 1,000-yard stares. Maybe it was something to do with the adrenaline rush of the contact: it makes your eyes bulge, your eyesight better and your senses more acute—the human body's natural reaction to danger.

19.00. The Taliban guns had fallen quiet. Darkness was approaching. Nobody was complacent stuck out here in the green zone; there was a general expectation that the Taliban were less likely to attack after nightfall, although Nick Calder said—as calmly as though he were discussing a game of bowls—that there was the possibility of a small contact before sundown so that the Taliban could make it clear that they knew where we were. So that was something to look forward to, then. Nick did not seem remotely fazed by what had gone before. Tomorrow, he said, they would try to outflank the Taliban and continue pushing north. Such relentless, ruthless professionalism: when most people would be begging to go home for tea and buns, Nick was plotting how to continue the scrap and win.

My first day back in the saddle, and I'd seen as intense a day's fighting as any I had yet experienced in Afghanistan. It seemed astonishing to me that we hadn't taken any casualties and I was glad it was nearing its end. But more than anything, I was acutely aware that for the soldiers around me, what had happened that afternoon was just a regular part of their everyday life.

As night fell I joined a few of the guys and we chatted about what they were doing here. The sentiments I heard from the men of 5 Scots were very similar to those I'd heard with the Anglians: that they were here for their mates, not for the politics. That if anyone out here tells you that they are not, or have never been, scared, they're lying through their teeth. No bravado. Just the quiet reflection that being on the front line seems to bring. And as one of them succinctly put it, 'I didn't expect Afghanistan to be as bad as this. I don't want to come back here ever again. It's just too damn dangerous.'

Not unreasonable, I thought, under the circumstances.

*   *   *

It was not the first night I had spent in an Afghan compound, but tonight was different in that the owners were still there, a couple of tough old boys if ever I've seen any. They were putting themselves in danger with the Taliban, letting British troops into their home; and of course being close to us meant they were in the line of fire. There are also certain indignities involved in having your compound occupied by a company of soldiers. Not to put too fine a point on it, a man's got to do what a man's got to do. It wasn't as if there were five-star toilet facilities in the vicinity, so playing host to the army means allowing them to take a dump in the corner of your compound. Clearly these fellas thought this was worth it for the payment they received from us for the use of their living quarters. But often our troops are commandeering deserted compounds. Everyone knows that the key to the war is winning the hearts and minds of the locals; and I wonder how well disposed I would be to thirty guys who broke into my house and took a shit in my garden.

In the heat of summer, the Afghans tend to sleep outside, on rickety beds made from intertwined branches on which they lay thick roll-up mattresses. They raise these beds up from the ground on wooden stilts to keep cool air underneath them. I got on well with the forward operating officer, a real character named Axel. Between us we hit upon what we thought was a very good idea. One of the problems with sleeping outside is that the stars in the Afghan sky are so bright that they can keep you awake if you're not too tired. We decided to sleep in the space between the ground and the owners' beds.

At first our plan seemed an excellent one. Blissful shade, and perhaps a good night's sleep. However, we had made just one tiny miscalculation. Our Afghan hosts clearly had a liking for lentils—or at least they'd eaten

252

something for dinner that had a similar effect on the alimentary canal. I'd been under one of these beds for a matter of minutes when I heard a rumbling. It wasn't an artillery shell in the distance, but it was just as explosive in its way. What followed was a cacophony of trumping that had Axel and me surrounded by a fog of Afghan fart. There was no way we were going to get to sleep there, so we gathered our gear and started looking for a less fragrant place to rest our heads.

If you've got a platoon of men around you, chances are there's going to be some snoring (and I'll freely admit that I'm the worst culprit of all). Stevie Rae had advised me that the secret of a good night, therefore, is to get to sleep first, because once the snoring starts, it ain't going to stop. There was no way I was able to do that now, so my only option was to sleep as far away from the others as possible. I ended up with my head in a doorway and what followed was hardly the most refreshing night's sleep of my life, especially as the guys that were on 'stag'—lookout duty—kept walking in and out of it. Still, you live and learn. I wouldn't try to sleep under an Afghan again.

The temperature dropped dramatically overnight. It was terribly cold when we arose at 04.00 on day three of Operation Cap Fox. The men were already up and about, pulling water from the compound's well. The well is surrounded by an old oil drum; the 'rope' is a

253

tyre that has been split and meticulously unwound. It's an ingenious piece of engineering. The only problem is that when it goes wrong, the elders send little girls down the narrow well to fix it. Why little girls and not little boys? Because girls are less valued in Afghan society than boys and it's a potentially dangerous job.

Most of the water I drank when I was with 5 Scots was well water. It was important to sterilize it with chlorine tablets and although this made it taste like swimming-pool water, it was better than the alternatives: diarrhoea and vomiting or cooking from the inside through dehydration. Some of the guys would flavour their water with a powdered drink known as 'screech', or Lucozade powder. It made their drinks more palatable, but had the disadvantage of clogging the mouthpiece of their water pouches up with sugar—a magnet for bacteria in the heat.

We left the compound while it was still dark. It gave us an advantage over the Taliban as they didn't have night vision and we did. But NV only gives you the upper hand at night; dawn came soon enough.

We were pretty sure that the Taliban knew where we were, but the plan was to perform a flanking manoeuvre that allowed us to skirt around them. In addition, as the previous day's fighting was so tough, Nick Calder had decided to call in a bit of extra firepower. So it was that, a few klicks south, as we were leaving the compound and the call to prayer was heard above the rooftops of Musa Qala, a convoy of Mastiffs emerged from the DC and made their careful, threatening way along the wadi, along with their fifty-cals and GMGs.

Delta Company started pushing north, towards Mount Doom. Their objective: to use air and ground assets to draw out the Taliban, force the enemy from their positions and eliminate them. It promised to be another very lively day.

As we headed north, it became clear that the local compounds were deserted. Their inhabitants had moved out to the other side of the wadi. For us, that was a clear indication that the Taliban were there, ready and waiting for us. We walked with care, accompanied by the sound of the Mastiffs trundling up the wadi. It was as we were patrolling along the edge of a maize field that the firing started. Our boys had seen the enemy and engaged them first, but the Taliban's retaliation was swift. RPGs flew above us as we hid in the maize and the word came through that an Apache attack helicopter had just been despatched from Camp Bastion. This was cheering: brave as they are, the Taliban really don't like Apaches. We got to our feet and started heading along the edge of the maize field, but as soon as we moved, the cry went up: 'IDF!' We were being mortared, so we hit the ground again and waited for the firing to subside.

But we couldn't stay still. We left the cover of the maize field to make faster progress. As we did so, the interpreters told us the Taliban had lined up another ambush.

The vegetation in this part of the green zone was so thick that nobody could see through it. We knew the Taliban were close, but we didn't know just how close. Delta Company needed to be prepared for everything. The order came down to attach bayonets. That happens only when there is a risk of hand-to-hand contact.

The air filled with the thumping sound of PKM fire. The PKM is the Taliban's version of the General Purpose Machine Gun, Russian-made and brutally effective. I buried myself in the thick vegetation that covered the ground of the green zone. The enemy was getting closer. We could hear it.

Nick Calder decided to call in 2 Scots in their Mastiffs so that they could silence the Taliban with extra fire support and give Delta the opportunity to make it to safety. The vehicles moved up the wadi towards our position, mounted with fifty-cals, GPMGs and Javelins. As soon as they approached, the men of 2 Scots scoped out a Taliban position and decided to take it out with a Javelin. Just one problem: we were pinned down between the Taliban and the Mastiffs. I remembered the moment, so many months ago on Salisbury Plain, when the Royal Anglians had been practising with this weapon and one of the missiles fizzed, failed and landed 30 metres away from us. 2 Scots *had* to be on target. I steeled myself for the impact and waited.

The missile was launched. It sounded like an aircraft speeding overhead and exploded with a force that made my whole body jump off the ground it was hugging. And then I started to laugh. There was nothing funny, of course. But it's amazing how many times you find yourself giggling, and I wasn't the only one.

The javelin had scored a direct hit, but it had taken out only one of the enemy positions. The thundering of PKM fire continued to fill the air and we were still pinned down. Time, therefore, for the British troops to play their ace card. An Apache had arrived and started circling overhead. It was out of the range of the Taliban's RPGs, but the enemy knew that its Hellfire missiles would make short work of them; even its thirty-cals, which could engage from 3,000 feet, would turn them to slush. The firing stopped. The Taliban were apparently saying, 'Hold your fire till the fly goes away.' We had to seize the moment. Under cover of the Apache, we found the nearest compound in order to regroup.

11.13. The temperature was soaring. It was a relief to get into the compound, find some shade and drink some water. During the middle of the day, when the sun is at its hottest, we had learned to expect an unofficial ceasefire: the Taliban didn't want to fight in the heat any more than we did. It was a relief that we could expect a few hours of downtime after our thrill-a-minute morning. Nick Calder crouched in the shade of wall and smoked a well-earned cigarette. His alternative family had put a lot of trust in him over the past two days, and followed him into some dangerous contacts. The pressure he was under, with the safety of so many men his direct responsibility, was unimaginable.

'Shitty' compound, as the troops started calling it, had a well. We pulled up a bucketful of water: Evian it was not. There was a thick scum on the top, home to a colony of fly larvae. Clearly it hadn't been used for a long time—at least I *hope* it hadn't. In one corner of the compound was a sprawling pile of dried-out poppy stalks. One look at them told us that whoever had processed them had been thorough: they had leached the sap out of the head and removed the seeds, ready for next year's crop. What remained would be used as kindling in the winter.

The compound belonged to an old woman. She had fled, leaving her belongings and a rather mangy dog that lolled in the midday heat. Among her belongings was a letter, which our interpreters translated for us. The letter was from her son, who had decided that he wanted to devote his life to Islam and become a mullah. He had travelled to a religious school in northern Pakistan in order to train for his religious calling. He didn't know that this school was a training ground for suicide bombers, extremists and religious soldiers. His 'teachers' told him that if he wanted to become a religious leader, it was his duty to defend his country from the infidel. He tried to leave but he was soon found, beaten up and forced to stay. What followed, we might imagine, was a process of indoctrination and brainwashing; the letter itself stated that the son was, at the time of writing, training to become a religious soldier.

A young man who wanted to devote his life to doing good had been turned and it didn't sound like he'd had much choice. It was a sad story, and an enlightening one.

We would normally expect hostilities to start again at around 16.00; but just a couple of hours after our arrival at Shitty compound, our sentries spotted movement in an area where the Taliban were known to be. So much for the unofficial ceasefire. Intelligence confirmed what the sentries' eyes had suggested. The Taliban were advancing. Worse still, they had sent a special commander from the town of Qats to organize a battle against us. And even worse than that, they were surrounding us on three sides: to the north, the west and the east.

There were a lot of them. They meant business.

Nick Calder had a difficult call to make. We were compromised on three sides; and we didn't know for sure that we weren't compromised to the south. There was no air cover, since all our air assets were in use elsewhere. The base at Musa Qala DC was 4 klicks away. If we moved south, we risked running into an ambush; if we stayed still, we risked being overrun on all sides. Nick remained improbably calm—on the outside, at least—as he made his decision. We couldn't stay where we were. We had to head south.

There wasn't a man among us who didn't leave that compound on tenterhooks and in total silence. I practically tiptoed out of the compound; even my breath seemed too loud as we crept south, hoping desperately that we weren't walking into a trap. The next ten minutes passed very, very slowly.

So far, so good. Nick Calder had made the right call, though I still found myself holding my breath.

And then we found out that the Taliban had entered the compound. They'd just realized we'd escaped. From what Delta Company were hearing, it seemed they were extremely upset that their plan had been scuppered. As you can imagine, we all felt terribly sorry for them.

*   *   *

We spent one more night in the green zone. As the next day dawned—day four of Operation Cap Fox—we started to see more Afghan nationals returning to their compounds. This was a good sign: it meant the Taliban had retreated from the area. We chatted to an Afghan man. He was welcoming to the troops and told us that his family felt safe when the ISAF forces were in the vicinity. He came across as friendly and genuine enough, but I didn't know if he'd say the same thing if the Taliban were around. Somehow I doubted it. His two children—a boy and a girl—looked on as we spoke. I took the opportunity to give each of them a sweet, and then watched as the boy openly stole the girl's. She didn't complain.

We continued tacking back down to the DC as the temperature soared. Sweat poured from me: the villagers looked at us in bemusement. One local spoke to me in Pashtun. I could well believe that he was saying, 'Why are you moving about in this heat with all that equipment and with a tin can on your head?' It was a pertinent question. Both Nick Calder and I started to experience the symptoms of heat exhaustion that day. I felt sick, my mouth became unquenchably dry and my head started to throb. It was like being drunk, but without the good bits. I knew the dangers of heat

261

exhaustion. Before I had arrived in Musa Qala, another journalist had gone for a walk around the DC. Her core body temperature had soared to fatal levels—levels at which the internal organs start to cook—and a Chinook had had to be called in to medivac her back to Bastion. She died on the chopper and had to be brought back to life by the MERT.

I wasn't the only one to feel the effects of the heat. As the day progressed, one of Delta Company's men went down with heat exhaustion. The Mastiffs were called up the wadi to collect him; but the rest of us had to continue down to the DC on foot. By now it was getting dark and we still had 2.5 klicks to go. Nick had to make another major decision: should we stay out another night or should we make for home? He decided that we should push on down to the DC.

We needed to get back to base as quickly as possible, but we couldn't go through the green zone at night, as we'd be stumbling in the dark. Moreover, there was a chance of IEDs, which didn't bear thinking about in the dark. So we headed for the wadi. That way we could be sure of heading in the right direction despite the darkness. Nick didn't want his company to walk in the middle of the wadi because we would be too exposed, so we stayed to the side. This had its own problems, however. One minute the edge is on a level with the riverbed, the next it is 9 metres high. The ground was as treacherous as it was undulating, especially in the darkness. We couldn't see where our feet were going; we couldn't see the huge cracks on the edge of the wadi that went down into water pools. I could hear blokes stumbling and every time I heard a splash I knew there was water ahead.

In the darkness, my other senses became acute. An eerie sound drifted across the wadi: the baying of jackals in the desert. It made my blood run cold. From another direction came the lone voice of a holy man chanting the call to prayer. A creepy, echoing wail. All around me the soldiers were stumbling blindly, and so was I.

We couldn't stay on the edge of the wadi for long. It was too treacherous, and sooner or later someone was going to fall and break their ankle. Trying to medivac someone out from that position in the darkness was more than anyone could face. So we walked down into the wadi proper. The going was easier here, but my heart was in my throat. Bunched up, unprotected and illuminated by the rising moon, we were an easy target. My body temperature started to drop dramatically; at one point John the cameraman and I had to wade up to our chests in cold water as we carried the camera over our heads to keep it dry. The jackals and holy men continued to wail. I felt as if I was walking in a surreal dream and I couldn't wait for it to end.

It was a moment of bliss when we walked back into the gates of Musa Qala DC. Even now the soldiers couldn't just kick back and relax, however: they immediately had to clean their weapons, knowing that the base was vulnerable to attack at any time. Then everyone did what they had been waiting to do for the past four days, during which time they had eaten nothing but cold ration packs. The kitchen had stayed open and there was even a treat in store: steak, as opposed to the omnipresent tinned spam. It was the only time during my whole stay that we were given fresh meat. The men fell on the hot food like famished vultures. I did the same.

It was good to be back, but the howling of the jackals and the wailing of the call to prayer would stay with me for a long time to come. Goody turned to me and said, 'Did you enjoy that, mucker?' as he slurped his soup.

An unrecognisable me turned round and said, 'Yeah, let's do it again. Same time next year.'

But I knew we'd be going out again much sooner than that.

15. THE MUSA QALA SHUFFLE

Delta Company's next operation was scheduled for two days later. In the meantime the troops were given time to recuperate from Operation Cap Fox. We hung around the DC, playing ball and washing out of our gear the dirt that had accumulated during our recent foray into the green zone. A delivery of mail was made to the camp: the surge in morale was noticeable as the lads opened packages containing such delights as smoked sausage and tins of fruit. These packages are a chore for the people in charge of the army's mail, as they slow down the system; but the benefit they give the troops is immeasurable. I was given a coconut biscuit the morning the mail arrived. After the stresses of the green zone, it put a big smile on my big face. A taste of home.

The officers and sergeants performed a debrief at which they went through the details of the latest op and assimilated what knowledge they had gained from it about the enemy's positions and how they reacted to our strategies. Nick Calder considered the operation a success—not least because Delta Company had chalked up two confirmed kills, thanks to the sharp shooting of Lance Corporal Gordon Pollock, who was going to have a much more interesting tour than he thought. 'For the lads to come across two Taliban bodies is a good thing,' he told me. 'It makes them realize they're having an effect on the enemy and getting a bit of their own back on the Taliban.'

Nick seemed sure that the sight of a couple of dead Taliban would be a boost to the guys' morale, and I didn't doubt him. I wondered, though, if there were any other feelings these young men experienced having taken another person's life. Guilt, perhaps? Sorrow? I was soon put right. Private Nigel Campbell was the youngest guy in the company and he had also taken a man's life. 'I don't feel guilty,' he told me. 'He shot at us first. If it had been any of the other boys, they'd all have done the same thing.' The lads sitting around nodded their agreement. There was no misplaced bravado. They weren't gung-ho. Private Campbell admitted to me that he was sad it had fallen to him to pull the trigger; but there was a shared acknowledgement among the men that this was their job. If the situation called on them to kill, they would kill, and they all knew that the opportunity to do so would be presented to them once more in just a couple of days.

Or at least it would have, had circumstances not dictated otherwise.

It was the second morning after we had returned from Operation Cap Fox that the first cases of D and V were diagnosed. After that, the guys started dropping like flies, including Nick Calder and his second in command. The camp medics identified it as a viral outbreak, which meant that those who had succumbed to the illness had to be quarantined from the rest of the base. The sick men were placed on camp beds and covered with a dome-shaped netting. They were given water and rehydration sachets and left to sleep. As the day went on, the outbreak grew worse. People started projectile vomiting spontaneously and the medical team had to work flat out to control the virus. Medic Lance Corporal Andy Pettiford gave me a guided tour of the isolation area. It looked like a scene of the plague in days gone by. Even in the open air, you could smell the illness, a horrible mixture of vomit, shit and that nasty sweet odour that pervades hospitals all over the world. The men were absolutely wretched, lying in the shade of their beds, barely able to move and with a sickly pallor on their faces. I noticed again as I looked at them just how thin they all were. Andy agreed with me. 'Too thin,' he said. 'Well, underweight compared to what they should be. I've lost three and a half stone since I've been out here.'

If the D and V continued, there would be a lot of weight loss to come. 'On a scale of one to ten, ten not being very good, I'd say it's a close nine.' (Nick Calder himself lost three stone during the tour, weight he couldn't afford to lose, and a stone of which came off during the D and V outbreak.) What none of us knew was that the medics' resources were about to be pushed to the very limit. On a scale of one to ten, we were about to hit fifteen.

It was a day into the D and V outbreak that the word came in. Afghan nationals had been wounded in some unspecified incident. The injuries were bad enough for them to risk the wrath of the Taliban insurgents and seek help from our medics. The British base was, after all, the only place for miles around where they could get emergency treatment.

As soon as they knew that casualties—six of them—were on their way, Dr David Cooper and the team of medics he headed up started making space for them, setting up beds and preparing equipment. With twenty D and V patients under their care at the same time, the medical team must have felt more than a little harassed, but they appeared calm enough as they waited for the Afghans to arrive. Until, that is, the base started to receive indirect fire. A 106 rocket flew over the DC and, thank God, exploded in the wadi beyond. Had it been on target, it would have killed a lot of people.

All thoughts of IDF and D and V went out of the window, however, when we saw the state of the injured. A number of them were children, one of them small enough to be cradled in the arms of the soldiers who were all rallying together to help. An older man had a wound to his abdomen. A good handful of his guts were hanging out of his body like fresh offal and he moaned with untold agony as the medics cut the clothes from his thin body. A six-year-old girl wailed pitifully. She had a shrapnel wound to her back and was clearly in terrible pain. An older Afghan man—her father perhaps, or even her grandfather—held his gnarled hands to her head; but he seemed unable to find any words of comfort. How *do* you explain something like that to a child so young?

It was as the medics were trying to tend to the injured that the cultural difference between the Afghans and ourselves was thrown into sharp relief. Dr Cooper and his team had to access the wounds of the injured, a number of whom were female. For an Afghan female to show her body in public is, of course, contrary to the custom of that part of the world. So it was that some of the older men held a flowery sheet in front of the women as a makeshift screen so that the doctors could get to work on them. The look on the faces of these men made it quite clear that, even though the British troops were trying to save lives, they found the whole situation quite frustrating. That moment taught me a lot about the Afghan peple and how difficult it is to judge them by the way we live.

In a matter of minutes this basic outpost in the middle of the Afghan desert had become a bustling emergency room. Everyone momentarily forgot the D and V outbreak as the medics treated these people, whose injuries were genuinely life-threatening. A baby girl, injured by shrapnel and her little face distorted with distress, wriggled around on a military stretcher as two medics did what they could to save her; her condition remained serious. I had assumed that the man whose guts had been exposed and who was now lying motionless with an oxygen mask over his face was the most critical, but Dr Cooper corrected me. The casualty who worried him the most was the six-year-old girl. He'd had to put his fingers into her side to pull out shrapnel, but she also had a serious chest injury, which had caused internal bleeding. A chest drain had been inserted to help her breathing, and they had decompressed the chest itself by inserting a needle into the cavity. Dr Cooper explained that if there is air on the outside of the lungs, the lungs can't open up and you suffocate. Had the little girl not been brought into the DC, that's what would have happened.

It was heartbreaking to see these children in such a state of distress, and it was clear that the situation could deteriorate at any moment. 'The one thing that I've learned since being here,' Dr Cooper told me, 'is that kids will hang on and hang on until suddenly . . .' He clicked his fingers. 'They go very, very quickly.' I looked at one of the children, a pretty little girl, who was sucking on a lollipop, a gift from the troops. She occasionally cried out as tiny bits of shrapnel were pulled from her back and neck. Dr Cooper also explained to me that these Afghan children were so undernourished that when treating them he prescribed only a fraction of what he would give a healthier Western child; a normal dose of morphine would kill one of these kids because they are so much smaller for their age.

The medical team did everything they could. Their facilities, however, were limited and it was vital, once the patients had been stabilized, to evacuate them to Camp Bastion, where they could receive better treatment. As we waited for the MERT to fly in, I watched one of the soldiers cuddling an injured baby as if it was his own child—an image that will stay with me. The baby was momentarily soothed by the attentions of its surrogate father, even if the soldier had blood spattered over his latex gloves.

The MERT arrived in a Chinook, its blades kicking up a dust storm all over the landing zone. The wellbeing of the injured was out of Delta's hands now. In fifteen minutes they would be at the new hospital in Camp Bastion. As the Afghan nationals were ferried away, I was left to reflect on the realities of this war.

Since British troops had gone into Afghanistan, nearly 150 had been killed. A substantial number. But we have absolutely no idea how many civilians have died. Nobody keeps a statistic, almost as though it's not worth knowing. But I can assure you of this: it's a lot more than the ISAF forces and it's a lot more than the Taliban.

What I had just witnessed was simply a small snapshot of the horrors the Afghan people have had to undergo. It was a great relief to all of us that they had been sent to Camp Bastion and word later came through that they all made a full recovery. Many more don't.

*   *   *

In retrospect, I suppose that having a guided tour of the D and V isolation area wasn't my best idea ever. It was only a matter of time before I came down with the dreaded lurgy myself. The night after the casualties were evacuated to Bastion, I started to feel the first rumblings of what would become a very nasty bout of that vicious little virus.

The whole camp now had the high, sweet smell of illness and I started to feel rough as evening approached. My body ached, so I took myself off to bed and fell asleep. It was the middle of the night when I awoke. I was shivering, my head was thumping and I went from very cold to very hot. It was, I knew from experience, a bit like having malaria. I also knew that the world was about to fall out of my bottom. Climbing out of bed, I fitted my head torch—a dusky red light, as white light can be more easily seen by any enemy spotters—and started the urgent, uncomfortable walk to the thunderboxes.

As I approached, the smell of shit and sick hit my nostrils. Certain of the thunderboxes had the letters 'D&V' scrawled on them to stop the spread of the disease. I'd half hoped that I wouldn't get to see the inside of those cubicles; now it felt as though I was going to get pretty intimately acquainted with them. Inside my chosen thunderbox was a sheet of plywood with a seat and a metal drum underneath. The interior of the drum swarmed with flies even at night. As I glanced into it with the light from my head torch, I saw what I can only describe as a mauve-brown porridge. The porridge was moving, thanks to the flies that had settled on it and were now feasting among the little white islands of tissue paper.

I didn't have time to be revolted. I dropped my pants, sat my pretty little arse on the seat and evacuated my bowels. The process clearly disturbed the gourmet meal going on down below. The flies swarmed up between my legs, one of them scoping out the moisture on the corner of my firmly closed mouth with the pinpoint accuracy of an F-16 bomber. I knew perfectly well that the fly had just been dining on the porridge, so I flicked it away in a movement that must have made me look as if I was suffering some kind of muscular spasm.

My mouth wasn't the only area of moisture. I'm sure nobody reading this really wants to picture the crack of my arse, but in the interests of accuracy I have to report that the flies found their way there too. Yum.

I cleaned myself up as best I could and then started to stumble back to my bed. By the time I was halfway there, however, I had to turn back again. A matter of urgency—all of a sudden you forget about the flies in the need to rid your system of this stuff. You can't quite forget about the smell of poo and sick, however, so as I retook my seat, I held my breath and had my T-shirt pulled up over my nose, knowing that the smell of vomit would eventually make *me* vomit.

All I wanted to do was lie down on my bunk and die; but each time I tried to get to bed, I had to do an about turn and run back to the thunderbox. My tender backside grew increasingly sore the more it was wiped clean. The trouble was that every time I stood up and started to move, it set off the need for another bowel movement. So it was that I found myself sitting in the cubicle and shimmying like a teenager at a disco. Well, perhaps not *quite* like a teenager at a disco. I wasn't the only one to hit upon this technique to rid myself of the foul liquid my body was trying to expel. All the lads did it. In fact it even had a name: the Musa Qala shuffle. There was a definite skill to getting it right, though somehow I doubt it will ever find its way on to *Strictly Come Dancing* . . .

The sanitary situation in the middle of that viral outbreak was like something out of the Crimea. But what else could anyone do? It wasn't as if there was a fully appointed bathroom with marble tiles and a bidet out there in the desert. Far from it: the following morning a couple of the Jocks would have to remove those metal drums full of sloshing excrement from the thunderboxes and set fire to it. You can imagine the smell. Or maybe you can't.

The next day I was given a handful of rehydration sachets and told to go back to bed. Having been up all night, I was happy to oblige. Delta Company's next operation was only a day away and like the rest of the men I wanted to make sure that I was fighting fit. But before I hit the sack, I padded off to the thunderboxes yet again. Time for one more Musa Qala shuffle. Better safe than sorry, after all.

*   *   *

To the north-east of Musa Qala, in the shadow of Mount Doom, were two towns: Qats and

275

Small Qats. These were Taliban strongholds and the targets of Delta Company's next mission. The D and V outbreak had subsided—this was the day after I had been sent to bed with my rehydration sachets; whether everyone was fully well enough to go on what promised to be a very dangerous mission was a different matter. We couldn't become complacent, though. Delta had to take the fight to the Taliban if they were to stop the insurgents overrunning the town.

As Nick Calder briefed his men under Hesco that morning, he explained that intelligence reports suggested there could be high-ranking commanders in these towns. There was also some slightly less useful information, courtesy of the Afghan special police force, the NDS. According to their top-secret intelligence, we could expect there to be enemy in the areas through which we were travelling. We'd be able to recognize them because they'd be wearing sandals.

Thanks, NDS. I really don't know what we'd do without you.

Operation Small Qats was to last twenty-four hours, departing at 14.00 that day. There was a definite sense of apprehension. As we were sitting in the Mastiffs driven by 2 Scots, Alan 'Goody' Goodall admitted to me that he had been to church the previous Sunday— 'church' being a service held in a tent by the company chaplain. It's not uncommon for the men to turn to religion more as their tour of duty progresses, some of them to give thanks for the fact that they are still alive, some of them to deal with the doubts and insecurities that inevitably arise when your life is being threatened—to get rid of the voice in their head asking what the hell they're doing out here, or at least to get its volume turned down. Goody had been given a shiny souvenir coin for going to church. He never struck me as being a superstitious man, but he carried that coin with him for good luck. 'Not that we'll need it,' he said. 'Because we'll be fine.'

Hope you're right, Goody. I really hope you're right.

Each Mastiff was armed with a fifty-cal or grenade machine gun and a Javelin weapons system. You'd have to be suicidal to launch an attack on a convoy like that. Trouble is, the Taliban sometimes are. As always it was an uncomfortable ride with the threat of incoming from above and IEDs from below, but not as uncomfortable as it was for the guys in the lead vehicle, who were unable to drive in anybody's tracks, so avoiding the threat of a mine strike.

An emaciated man, Nick Calder had a plan. Normally Delta Company headed north from the DC in order to launch their attacks on the Taliban positions. On this occasion, however, we travelled east along the wadi and into the desert. Once we had moved out of the range of any Taliban dickers, we would head north. The Mastiffs would drop us off in the shadow of Mount Doom, where we would rest up overnight. The following morning we would be able to attack Qats and Small Qats from the east and, with a bit of luck, catch the enemy by surprise.

We made slow progress—four hours to cover 7 klicks. The ground ahead of us had to be constantly swept for 'legacy' mines—so called because they're a legacy of the Soviet occupation—so it was with some relief that we reached the base of Mount Doom in one piece. We overnighted there—cold scoff and no fires. I had a crafty smoke with one of the boys—even that was against the rules, as in theory the glow from the end of a cigarette is enough to give away your position—and then settled down to get some sort of kip. I lay on the ground, having kicked a load of stones away to make a reasonable place to sleep. It doesn't matter how hard you try, though. There's always one stone digging into you, making you feel like the princess and the pea. Nobody went for a piss more than two metres from the vehicles: a legacy mine had been found nearby and no one was sure if we were in a minefield.

Four hours later the sun rose on day two of Operation Small Qats. As we readied for the off, the lads organized a sweepstake on the time of the first contact. I opted for 07.45. We loaded ourselves on to the Mastiffs, which then dropped us on the outskirts of the green zone before heading back up to the higher ground in the desert to provide fire support and, should we need it, medical evacuation.

I marched with Delta Company into the heart of the green zone. It was eerily quiet: most of the inhabitants had bugged out, so we took that as an indication that the enemy had ID'd us and knew of our arrival. It was only a matter of time before the contact began—we'd poked our stick into the hornets' nest and the hornets were on their way. In order to spread out our forces, Delta split up into its platoons—one-zero, two-zero, three-zero and the TAC, which was OC Nick Calder and his team, including the forward observing officer Axel and Bruce, the JTAC. On this occasion I stayed with the TAC.

I was only metres away from Nick Calder when the firing started. I dived into a ditch, and then followed Nick to the cover of a compound wall. Nick looked back at me. 'Seven forty-five,' he said with a grin. 'Bang on!' Looked as if I'd won the lottery, but the popping sound all around wasn't the opening of champagne bottles. It was the crack of AK rounds, and then the whoosh of an RPG sailing over our heads. We pushed forward, one-zero platoon giving us covering fire from about 150 metres away. As we dodged the Taliban's fire, however, Nick received bad news over the radio. One of Delta Company had been shot.

His heart must have skipped a beat. I know mine did. The relief was indescribable when we heard that the wound wasn't serious. In fact, watching headcam footage of the incident afterwards, you'd be forgiven for thinking quite the opposite. 'Wee Johno', as he was known, had been shot in the foot—much to the hilarity of his mates. 'He's not going to be dancing for a while, is he?' someone joked.

Nick told me that Johno had been given morphine and that he should be fine. He was loaded into a Mastiff and taken back to Musa Qala for medical treatment. In the meantime the Taliban had been spotted in a nearby compound—Compound 109. Nick ordered his men forward to secure the compound. Delta Company followed his orders swiftly and professionally, but by the time the compound was theirs, the Taliban had done a runner. They were compound hopping, so Nick sent out a forward party to hunt them down while the rest of the company provided fire support in the form of light 51mm mortars and underslung grenade launchers. Accompanying the soldiers were members of the ANP. The camera team and I stayed behind with Nick Calder and the TAC, waiting for news that the surrounding compounds had been cleared. Nick called in fast air support, just in case.

Not long after the forward team had

left, word came through that they had apprehended someone. He was a fighting-age male and was claiming to be an ordinary citizen. The ANP weren't buying it: they were sure he was Taliban and had used their powers of arrest to detain him. They brought him back to us in Compound 109 while I prepared to come face to face with a man who, if the ANP were right, would have no hesitation in killing any of us.

If this was a member of the Taliban, it was clear he wasn't a commander. He had mascara around his eyes which was moist with tears of fear. His pink-painted nails were short, broken and bitten. His *dishdash* was stained with food and human issue and his sandals were the only other clothes he was wearing. The fact, however, that he kept pleading in Pashtun, 'Don't shoot me!' suggested he had more to fear than an ordinary villager would.

The prisoner was told to get on to his knees while a member of the ANP stood guard. I asked how sure they were that he was Taliban. The ANP member pointed to an area around the prisoner's left shoulder. It was red, bruised and raised—the kind of bruising that only comes from the kickback of a weapon. The ANP policeman said, 'PKM.' The prisoner denied this. 'My brother fought with me,' he announced. 'He hit me with his prayer beads.'

Prayer beads, hey? They must have been some pretty hefty ones. Prayer cannonballs, more like. The ANP weren't buying it any more than I was. They took the prisoner away for interrogation. There is a spray they can apply to a man's body which, if there is any gunpowder residue on his skin or clothes, will turn pink. Our man turned pinker than a fairy. Sounded like quite a scrap he was having with his brother.

We left the compound, turned south and zigzagged for another four hours. Our surprise attack had been successful—perhaps a little too successful. The Taliban had clearly retreated in order to regroup. Operation Small Qats was only ever supposed to last twenty-four hours, so just after 13.00 we met up with our Mastiffs, ready to return south to the DC. As we arrived at the RV point, however, the intelligence suggested that enemy forces were preparing to attack. It was a highly alert group of soldiers that climbed into the vehicles ready for the trip back home.

No matter how many times you experience enemy contact, you never quite get used to it. It felt good to be encased in steel once more— even if it was like an oven—and as I downed a bottle of water, Sergeant McCafferty gave me a succinct précis of the operation. 'Short and sharp. It was almost like a raid. Straight in, straight out. Job done.'

Job done indeed, wee Johno's toe notwithstanding. No confirmed enemy kills, but the Taliban on the back foot and a hostage taken. It was galling to find out later that the authorities thought there was insufficient evidence to detain him; either that, or he had friends in high places. Helmand Province—like much of Afghanistan—suffers from corruption at the highest level. Musa Qala itself, as I had already learned, was under the influence of the local warlord, Mullah Salam, and there was little doubt that certain contingents of the ANP fell under that sphere of influence. Despite the rumours that he was deeply entrenched with the Americans, it didn't seem unlikely that he would try to keep his hand in with the Taliban. He didn't know, after all, what the future held for Afghanistan. In truth, I think that Mullah Salam was too far gone: if the Taliban regained power I imagine he would seek some kind of diplomatic immunity.

Did our hostage have a hotline to the top man? Were the wheels of injustice greased? I don't know. All I can say is that he was released—ready, if indeed he was a member of the Taliban, to fire another RPG. Might he kill a British soldier? Might some Afghan children be wounded or killed in the crossfire? Impossible to say, but it was an insight into the difficulties of bringing peace to a place such as this.

We made it back to camp, thankfully without incident. Like many of the men, I was still suffering from the aftermath of the D and

V virus; but it would have been a gruelling twenty-four hours even if we'd been at the peak of physical fitness. It felt very good to be back home. I was looking forward to a rest. As I walked back to my bunk, helmet in hand, I passed the RQMS.

'All right, Ross?' he greeted me cheerfully. 'How are you?'

'Fucked,' I said. I think it summed things up pretty well.

16. GOING NATIVE

The base at Musa Qala was home not only to 5 Scots and 2 Scots. As well as the contingent of Americans, it was shared with members of the Royal Irish Regiment and the ANA. The Irish were there as an OMLT. Their duty was to accompany the ANA, instruct them in the techniques of modern warfare and in so doing get the Afghans a step closer to being able to defend their people and their borders against insurgents.

All things considered, the ISAF forces and the Afghans rubbed along pretty well. That's not to say there weren't big cultural differences between them. There were, and none so great as the rumours of what would happen on a Thursday night. For the Afghans, this was party night, a time for men to get together; on some occasions, the rumour was, they would get closer than others. As was the case in Ancient Greece, 'man love' is not stigmatized in Afghanistan. I saw plenty of young Afghans wearing make-up and nail varnish and holding hands. It was just part of the culture. Far from being something to be ashamed of—and even though it would appear to be at odds with their Muslim beliefs—it's an accepted phenomenon. It certainly doesn't make you effeminate and I wouldn't recommend that anyone reading this book goes out and calls an Afghan male a poof—unless, that is, you're getting bored of the company of your teeth and fancy a period of trial separation.

I never saw any actual evidence that Thursday night was man-love night, but I did witness enough fisticuffs resembling lovers' tiffs between members of the ANA to make it absolutely clear that there was some truth to the rumours. And, of course, it became a bit of a joke for the ISAF troops. 'What you doing Thursday night, Ross? Going up to spend it with the 'terps? Feeling frisky?'

Afghans, of course—at least, some of them—have a different view of Western sexuality. Apart from the occasional medic or intelligence officer, they see hardly any Western women and their view of them derives from the centrefolds and porn shots that are plastered over the soldiers' barracks. The streets of Musa Qala are not filled with rampant homosexuals any more than the streets of London are filled with girls getting their tits out, but these preconceptions are good examples of how cultures can be misunderstood and demonstrate the need, if you are occupying a foreign country, to spend time with its people and learn about the way they live their lives—and to control your sniggers on a Thursday night just because all the boys are dancing with each other. It was partly because of this, and partly in order to see just how the OMLT scheme worked, that we decided to go out on the ground with the Royal Irish and the ANA.

The ANA and the ANP are two very different beasts. The ANP are generally recruited from the locality of Helmand Province. As a result they have friends and relations in the towns and villages they are supposed to be patrolling. Afghan society being what it is, this leads to corruption. In Kajaki the previous year, there had been a rumour—unconfirmed, I should say—that the head of the ANP contingent there was related to the head of the Taliban at the northern FLET and was passing him information about our plans and movements. Other rumours suggested that certain members of the ANP swapped bullets and weapons for drugs: while they were seeing butterflies, the Taliban were getting tooled up. While it would be wrong of me to paint every member of the ANP with this brush of corruption, it seems unlikely that these rumours were entirely without foundation.

The ANA were a different matter. There were rotten apples, of course, but then that's true of any group of people. The Afghan army was recruited from all over Afghanistan and was much freer of the complicated cords of loyalty that bound the ANP in Helmand. And there was no doubt about it: the ANA was being slowly turned into a formidable fighting force. They were equipped more and more with American weapons and, as Officer in Command Major Dave Middleton explained to me, they were crucial to the ISAF forces' activities in the region. 'There are not large numbers of ISAF ground-holding troops here. It's the ANA that carries out a lot of the operations to push the enemy back. And the enemy *has* been pushed back.'

I wondered whether being part of an OMLT was a bit of a chore in British Army terms. One of Dave's lads answered me in a broad Irish accent. 'Babysitting. That's what I thought straight off. We're coming out here to babysit these people.' And when you've been on the front line as these guys have—Bosnia, Iraq and a previous tour of the Stan—I can see that this might not be a tempting prospect. But the Irish had come to a different point of view. 'When you start working with them and have some craic with them, ninety-eight per cent of the time you'll just fall down laughing. They're just crazy. But they're a good bunch of lads.'

I wanted to find out for myself if this was true and so it was that I prepared to go out on patrol with them into the bustling streets of the Saturday morning Musa Qala bazaar. The streets were, in general terms, off limits to all troops apart from the Royal Irish and the ANA, and for good reason: two suicide bombers had already hit the bazaar that year;

288

during the previous year in Afghanistan as a whole there had been 140 suicide bombs, and many civilian casualties as a result. The OMLT patrolled twice daily, but they had two advantages. Firstly they varied the times of their patrols so that suicide bombers wouldn't know when to expect them in town; and secondly they had the ANA with them. The presence of Afghan troops was a distinct plus. It meant that the villagers were a little less hostile to the presence of the occupying force; perhaps more importantly, the ANA were well attuned to the atmospherics among the population. In short, they could tell far better than the ISAF forces when things were likely to kick off—a useful asset somewhere as volatile as Musa Qala.

I was looking forward to the trip. Sure it was dangerous, though probably not as dangerous as a full-on attack on a Taliban position. But it would be the first time I had put myself in the middle of a real, working Afghanistan town, to see the sights and meet the people. It promised to be quite an experience.

As we approached the main street of Musa Qala, the ANA went first, sensing the atmospherics before the Irish arrived. I guess the locals knew what to expect, however, because as soon as we followed up the rear, all their attention was fixed on us. The Afghans are world-champion starers and as we walked up and down their street, they put their skills to good use. Some of the locals—young kids mostly—looked at us with smiles on their faces. But overwhelmingly we received stares that made me feel as if I'd just stepped out of a spaceship. Hardly surprising, I suppose, given the uneasy peace that existed there. John the cameraman and I attracted even more attention than the troops, probably because he was carrying a camera and we were dressed a little differently.

Old cars, motorbikes, tractors, donkeys with carts and men with wheelbarrows made their way along the street, which was lined by rickety buildings with makeshift canvas canopies. One of these buildings housed an opium den— everyone hanging around outside that place looked extremely relaxed. Another housed the bank: little more than a man with a wooden box full of notes. It looked kind of medieval, but in the final analysis I suppose that's all banks are. All manner of goods spilled out on to the pavements: hats, clothes, kitchen appliances, crates of fizzy drinks and, most temptingly, fruit and vegetables harvested from the fertile green zone. It was a thriving provincial market, noisy and bustling—in many ways no different to any market town in any country in the world. Given that all this fresh food was piled high so close to the DC, it struck me as faintly ridiculous that the British soldiers should be fed on tinned spam and rice. The ANP and ANA had a good business opportunity of which they took full advantage. They would buy crates of fizzy drink in the bazaar for a handful of Afghanis, and then sell them on at the DC. I'd be the last to begrudge someone the opportunity to turn a profit, but it seemed strange to me that the villagers themselves weren't given the chance to sell their wares directly to the troops. The Afghans are born businessmen and if anything is likely to build bridges between the locals and the occupying force, it's the prospect of a bit of trade. There are security issues, of course: fresh food can be poisoned, traders can be disguised suicide bombers. But it seems to me that these issues are not insurmountable in the battle for hearts and minds.

Back on the street, it was about to become uncomfortably clear to me why it was important that this battle was won. At the top of the street was Musa Qala's best-known landmark, a tall white monument that had taken a bit of a battering and was now surrounded by wooden scaffolding. The rumour was that the Taliban used to hang people from this structure. I couldn't find anyone who would confirm this; but I couldn't find anyone to deny it either. In order not to be targeted, we were told to keep moving; but it was difficult not to attract attention and I found myself chatting to a small group of children. Behind us was what was left of the old DC. It had been bombed to fuck when the

Royal Irish and the Paras had had to defend it from the Taliban just a couple of years before. To one side of the bombed-out building was a hospital, newly built by the ISAF forces. Lovely building—shame it was totally empty. The Taliban had made it clear that any doctor who dared work there would lose his head. On the other side the foundations were in for a new mosque.

The kids were an appealing bunch, inquisitive and with broad grins on their faces. I asked them what they wanted to be when they grew up. 'A doctor,' one replied. Well, that, at least, was hopeful.

Feeling like an alien, I wondered if they thought I looked much different from them. The kids shook their heads, although they confessed to being bemused at my lack of beard. All in all it was an amicable chat with some bright kids. Unfortunately, it was brought to a rather abrupt halt. Dave Middleton approached. His voice was tense. 'We know a suicide bomber has moved in to the western edge of the bazaar,' he told me. 'It's believed he's going to come across and target the bazaar.'

I turned to camera. My voice dropped a few octaves. 'Let's go,' I said.

In an instant the whole atmosphere changed. I started noticing things I hadn't seen before, like the group of men on a nearby balcony staring at us. They didn't look as if they were queuing up to be our best mates. In the past the bombers had predominantly been adults, but of late the Taliban had taken to using children as young as six. Even more disturbingly, these child bombers are often followed by another kid armed with a radio-controlled detonation device, just in case the suicide bomber has second thoughts.

The Irish and the ANA started to perform a hasty withdrawal from the bazaar, and who could blame them? As Dave Middleton explained to me, their continued presence in the centre of town was not only dangerous for us but dangerous for the locals too. The Taliban would like nothing better than to take out a couple of British troops; if it meant that they killed thirty or forty Afghans to do it, that was an acceptable loss.

It was with genuine relief that I walked back into the safety of the DC. Fighting an enemy that had guns, mortars and RPGs was one thing. What I had just tasted in the bazaar of Musa Qala, however, was a very different sort of fear, caused by the prospect of a very different kind of attack: that of the suicide bomber, driven on by religious fervour or blind terror, an invisible weapon whose presence was often known only when he or she exploded their hidden package.

In many ways, that kind of attack was more terrifying than what happened in the thick of the green zone. And the people of Helmand

Province have to live with the threat of it every day of their lives.

*   *   *

Having been out on patrol with the ANA, I wanted to meet some of their number. So later that day Dave Middleton arranged for me to have a chat with their senior officers. We met on the roof of the DC and I was immediately impressed by the resolute attitude towards the Taliban of Colonel Shadil, who was in charge of the ANA forces in Musa Qala. 'All of Musa Qala is under our control,' he said with the air, frankly, of a guy not prepared to take any shit. 'Our security posts are active. We won't let the enemy take Musa Qala.' No ifs. No buts.

It was clear that they liked working with the Irish and Dave Middleton returned the compliment. He singled out one of the officers in particular. 'We've been on some big operations together and he's a very brave man, I have to say.'

The officer rolled up his sleeve to show me one of his battle scars. It was a wicked-looking thing, stretching the length of his arm. He grinned at me. 'Sangin!' he explained. 'Nuff said.

Company Sergeant Major John Crown agreed with Dave Middleton's analysis of the ANA. 'You'll see them do things and you'll stand in awe of their bravery. I've stood sometimes watching them and thought, you're completely crazy or you've got no fear. It's like a hunt. They've seen the enemy in a compound and they'll go across open fields to destroy that enemy.'

In my view, John was touching on a crucial aspect of the Afghan psyche, one of the biggest things that makes them such a formidable fighting force. Many of them—both Taliban and non-Taliban—believe that the day of their death is pre-ordained. As a result, they don't fear fighting or bullets or suicide bombers. If they're supposed to die, they will die; if they're not supposed to die, they'll survive. Simple as that. I understood that it could make being alongside them a pretty lively experience and I asked Dave if he found it difficult reining them in. He nodded a bit ruefully. 'We call it riding the dragon,' he said. 'You never know quite where you're going to end up.'

The next day I was due to go out on an operation with the Irish and the ANA. I'd be able to ride the dragon for myself and find out how two different cultures, with two very different styles of fighting, operate under fire.

In order to stop the Taliban from taking back the town of Musa Qala, ISAF forces had built a ring of five fortified patrol bases around the town. To the south was a fortification known as US Patrol Base South. This had been in the hands of the Taliban, but just a week ago the Royal Irish and the ANA had retaken it. Things had been quiet there for the last three or four days, but before that it had been the scene of heavy fighting. At 06.50 on the morning after I had met the senior ANA officers, we prepared to head to the USPB, where we would unload our kit and then go out on patrol. We didn't really know what we'd find when we got there.

USPB South is one of the most exposed patrol bases in the Musa Qala area. The road leading to it at the time was frequently IED'd. I wasn't thrilled to be making the journey in a Pinzgauer; you really don't want to be in one of these poorly armoured vehicles if it goes up. The base itself comes under regular attack; as a result the roof of the base is armed with two heavy machine guns—a fifty-cal and a Russian DShK, or Dushka—and these would be supporting us as we went out on our operation. A contingent of the ANA were on the roof as I arrived, vigilantly looking out over the green zone.

I took the opportunity to speak to Bombardier Michael Hogan, who told me a bit more about what I could expect from the ANA when we went out in the field. 'They don't *look* very good patrolling,' he told me. 'They'll sometimes have their rifles on their shoulders and all that kind of stuff. You'd think that they're slack. But they can tell when something's wrong and straightaway you'll see them become so alert. The minute something happens they're there right beside you, firing.'

Only time would tell whether they would need to do that on this operation.

When the British soldiers go out on patrol, they carry a huge amount of equipment: weapon systems, body armour, water and ammunition. The ANA, on the other hand, travel light. Many of them decline to wear body armour or even helmets, choosing instead to put their faith in their religion; but it couldn't be said that they were totally free of vanity. As they lined up, a number of them had ammunition belts hung round their necks and bandanas round their heads. Rambo chic was the order of the day.

The ANA were tasked to lead this mission, checking the ground for mines and potential threats as we headed 2 klicks south. Everybody appeared pretty confident that we'd bump into the enemy at some point. The ground surrounding the USPB was bare, stony earth. No trees or fields of maize for cover. I felt vulnerable as we walked across it; I felt even more vulnerable when, as we left the base, the Royal Irish performed a test fire of their weapons. The guns were fully competent, but it also meant the enemy knew we were on our way.

We were able to rely on the full resources available to us. Fast air—and their accompanying 500-pound laser-guided bombs—could be called in from Kandahar Air Base. Heavy artillery was situated to the north-west of Musa Qala at Forward Operating Base Edinburgh. This was 8 kilometres away, but the 105mm shells that the Royal Artillery were able to fire from their light field guns were accurate over a range of 15 klicks or more. At the ops room in Musa Qala DC, Major Andy Thompson coordinated the operation. His team kept in contact with the troops on the ground by radio and he was able to benefit from one of the battle group's more temperamental assets. Radio-controlled spy planes—or drones—could be flown over enemy positions. They send back footage that is often difficult to interpret, but equally often provides invaluable tactical information.

All in all, then, some pretty formidable backup. But despite all the modern technology, battles are still won by troops on the ground. And it's easy to forget about spy planes when the only thing that separates you from the enemy is a bullet.

We started approaching cultivated land—maize fields and lines of trees. There was a deep, unnatural silence—the sort of silence of which I'd learned to be suspicious. As I crouched in a shallow ditch between two open fields with Dave Middleton, he agreed. Up ahead we watched as a couple of ANA scouts approached a local whom they believed to be a dicker. Dave explained that the ANA, even though they're not from Helmand Province, were more in tune with what was going on and in a better position to judge who was informing on us and who was not. But having the ANA along served another, perhaps more crucial purpose. There were farmers in the fields around us and it was no secret that these people would be very reluctant to speak to ISAF forces when they knew the Taliban were in the area. Afghan forces, however, were more approachable.

We started walking towards some nearby compounds. One of the ANA interpreters approached a local. He was poorly dressed—I was constantly reminded of how poor this country was—and crouched by an outlet of fresh running water. The local was happy to talk to the ANA man and he gave us good intelligence: that the enemy were concentrated in compounds to the south of where we were. Dave said it was a good sign that they were choosing to help us; and having been out on the ground without the ANA, I could already see what an advantage this was. But we hadn't come out to sit and chat with the locals. We headed south.

Passing through several more farmed compounds, we found evidence of Helmand Province's main cash crop. The poppy stalks had already been leached of their precious resin and were now stacked up high against a compound wall, ready to be used as kindling in the winter—nothing goes to waste in

Afghanistan. The sun grew hotter and more uncomfortable; so did the stares we received from the locals we passed. As we edged nearer to the compound where we believed the Taliban to be, there was clearly going to be no chance of collaboration, even with the ANA forces. In fact, for all we knew, the fighting-age men we were passing could actually *be* Taliban. On the high ground to the west we saw the telltale sign of a motorcyclist. Nobody seemed to be in any doubt that this was a dicker. The enemy knew where we were and were watching us. It was just a matter of time before they engaged.

More open ground. We crossed it at full pelt. As soon as we hit the cover of some compounds, the firing started. A round whizzed over my head and I dived backwards on to John the cameraman, cracking the camera's microphone in the process.

'You've broken the camera!' he shouted at me.

'Well,' I yelled back, 'that makes it 3–1.' (John had quite understandably dropped the camera three times under fire. Still, why let a little thing like a shower of AK rounds and a couple of RPGs get in the way of us having a bit of a bitch?)

The ANA broke into the compound and we managed to gaffer-tape the camera back together; meanwhile, some of the Irish went out in order to get an assessment of where the

300

enemy were. Word came back that we had enemy to the south engaging across open ground. It meant we had to make another dash out in the open while the soldiers provided covering fire. Rounds cracked in the air as we ran; it was an out-of-breath camera team that took refuge in a watery ditch running along a compound wall. From this position the soldiers could fire on the enemy, keep them pinned down and wait for fast air to be called in.

The Irish and the ANA traded fire with the Taliban. They knew where we were and were giving as good as they got. The Irish stayed low, protected by the ditch as they fired on the enemy position. Not so the ANA: I watched in astonishment as one of them stood up on the edge of the ditch and fired towards the enemy as casually as if he was watering his garden. Despite this show of bravery—some people might call it something else—we were now taking fire from the south and the south-west. The fast air had not yet arrived and so Dave Middleton made the decision to call in an artillery strike on the compound to the south-west.

The request was called into the operations room at Musa Qala DC, along with the exact location of where the Taliban were located. At FOB Edinburgh 7 klicks away they started adjusting their sights and loading the 105mm shells into their field guns. I watched from the ditch, waiting for the artillery to splash. When it did, you could see the devastation it caused just by looking at the cloud of smoke that was kicked up on impact. Five shells hit in quick succession while the lads back in the ops room coordinated the air strike. We sent up a plume of green smoke to identify our position to the incoming aircraft and waited for a very big bang.

The jet came from nowhere, filling the sky with its roar. The bomb hit the firing point to the south; the ground shook; another great cloud of smoke billowed up into the air. 'Splash,' Dave Middleton shouted. 'Bang on with a five-hundred-pounder.' If the remaining Taliban thought that was it, they were wrong: the artillery at FOB Edinburgh continued to rain 105mm shells into their compounds. They were taking a battering.

But the job wasn't done yet: we were still getting incoming. Back at the operations room, a spy plane had revealed enemy holed up in another compound 150 metres to the south of where we were. The ANA secured the compound next to which we were dug in and the troops entered while Dave Middleton took stock of the situation. The enemy were retreating towards an area known to the ISAF forces as Taliban Crossroads. Dave Middleton called in another 500-pound bomb to cut them off. It splashed right on target. The 105s continued to rain as we pushed south along the ditch towards the enemy. Shrapnel from the artillery was flying over our heads and hitting the compound.

The firing had stopped. In the compound the soldiers started to reload their weapons. Many of them had shaking hands—nothing to do with fear, but rather a mixture of extreme adrenaline, the shockwaves caused by the artillery and fast-air strikes and the strain of constantly firing their rifles. Looking back on the tapes of that day, I saw that I myself had the 1,000-yard stare. It had been a gruelling few hours. Now, though, the patrol was running low on ammo and Dave Middleton needed to decide whether to keep pushing south and see what state the enemy were in, or to return to the USPB. He made his decision snappily: we would return to base, and he called for covering fire to support us as we prepared to make the return journey over open ground.

But as soon as Dave made his decision, he had to change his mind. *'Cancel withdraw! Cancel withdraw!'* We had started taking yet more enemy fire. So far the Taliban had been hit with two 500-pound bombs, fifteen 105mm artillery shells and hundreds of rounds. But those of them left were still prepared to fight. No wonder the soldiers respected their enemy. Yet again the air was full of the crashing of weaponry. The enemy had returned to the compound that had been hit by the artillery. In order to engage them fully, the Irish and the

ANA were going to have to leave their own compound and return to the ditch from which they had been firing previously.

It was an Afghan soldier who managed to lob an RPG over the enemy compound wall. A direct hit; our Afghan Rambo looked distinctly pleased with himself.

Back in the ops room, another artillery strike was being prepared. In the meantime, the Irish and the ANA had to keep the Taliban pinned down. With ammo running low, they couldn't just unleash a barrage of firepower. They slowed down their rate of fire, but it was still enough to stop the enemy moving.

The artillery strike arrived, a massive explosion that we hoped would silence the enemy once and for all. We couldn't stay any longer—it was just a matter of time before we ran out of ammunition, and for the time being there was no air support, so we had to start the dangerous journey back to the USPB. The ANA continued to give covering fire as the order came down for us to leave the compound and start walking.

The company performed a leapfrogging manoeuvre, one group covering the other as they performed our tactical withdrawal. To be honest I was pretty lost at this point and didn't really know what was going on. It was a quick, exhausting extraction—sweat poured from me as I ran in the midday heat. Eventually we came safely within eyeshot of the base and then we stopped. We could see our destination; we could see the manned weapons systems perched on the roof. But between us and safety was 500 metres of open ground.

The sound of artillery shells in the distance was our signal to cross the open ground between us and the USPB. We had been told there was a risk that this ground had been IED'd, but I tried to put that thought from my mind. What else could I do? As we approached the base, a French fighter jet roared overhead. The noise of its engines was deafening as it looped upwards and then disappeared into the distance. This was a show of force, intended to intimidate any remaining Taliban. I couldn't say how well it worked, but it would certainly have had *me* running for cover . . .

It felt good to be back within the safety of the USPB walls. It had been an eventful morning. Ten unconfirmed Taliban kills and a number injured. We'd been out for six hours and it was now swelteringly hot. My shirt was so wet with sweat it was dripping. I thanked the ANA and had a quick chat with the Bombardier. His debrief was short and to the point: 'We took the fight to the enemy and we're all back in one piece.'

I washed my shirt out, then went off to find myself a much needed cup of tea with the lads.

17. 'THOUGH I WALK THROUGH THE VALLEY OF THE SHADOW OF DEATH'

Human beings adjust quickly to their environment. The soldiers at Musa Qala DC were in the zone, and so too were we. Weight might have dropped off me, my clothes and body armour might have been brown and stained from sweat and dirt, but I felt I had slotted into the routine of accompanying the soldiers out on patrol, doing what we did not in a blasé way but with a weird sense of normality. More importantly, I felt we had been accepted by the men of Delta.

My final patrol was approaching. We were to head north to the FLET. This was in the green zone and there was no ISAF patrol base in this area. Other patrol bases had open ground around them, but the trouble with setting one up in the green zone is that you're totally vulnerable to attack. Delta Company's task was to install themselves in the region of Compound 69 and engage the Taliban from this position, with a view to judging the response we got from the enemy and determining whether this was a suitable location to establish a new patrol base. A base in this part of the green zone would allow the ISAF troops to push the FLET further north and we were on a test run, to see just how badly the Taliban would react.

Compound 69 was about 200 metres to the south-west of Compound 71, which was the compound that had been demolished by bombs from the F-16 during Operation Cap Fox, my first with 5 Scots. We headed north up the Musa Qala wadi by Mastiff and I sat for the 3-klick journey with OC Nick Calder. Around us, locals travelled up and down the wadi, riding motorcycles or pushing wheelbarrows. Many of these wheelbarrows were ancient and held together by pins, reminding me that the Afghans live in a world very different from our disposable one. Anything that can be reused or recycled is; they can't afford to live in a throwaway society. But were these people ordinary civilians or Taliban dickers? Nick told me he would be 'very surprised if they hadn't seen us leaving the front of the camp. There's probably someone on a motorbike somewhere, or somebody out on the ground with a communications system, telling commanders where we are and what we're doing.'

We dismounted at the drop-off point on the edge of the green zone. It's never an easy moment, getting out of that protective metal shell and on to open ground. There's also a strange vibe between the soldiers going out on the ground and those driving the vehicles. 2 Scots were infantrymen too, and you could sense mixed emotions coming from them as they hoped we would be safe but also wished they were coming with us.

As we crossed open ground to leave the wadi, we were dangerously exposed. To add to the tension, Taliban Icom chatter started to come through, confirming that we were in their sights. Was that true, or were the Taliban just messing with us? Impossible to tell, and somehow that just made it worse.

We made it into the green zone without incident, but when we got there we encountered a problem with the radios. Some of Delta Company's radios had the wrong 'fill', which meant they could not communicate properly with the base. The controllers back at the DC wanted us to remain static in the green zone while they sent up new fills for the radios.

Nick Calder, always cool under fire, became uncharacteristically edgy as he delivered his orders. 'I'm pretty unhappy with that,' he said. 'It means we're static at this location. Tell them we'll push down south and give them an RV.' He stared at his map, paused, and then looked up again. 'In fact,' he announced, 'tell them to fuck off.'

'Yes, sir,' Bruce the JTAC murmured.

'Tell them to *fuck off* and sort it out. Do they know how long it takes to refill fucking thirty radios?'

Bruce gave a sheepish smile. 'Shall I use those exact words, sir?' he asked.

Nick didn't have time to reply. At that

moment the sound of an RPG explosion rang through the air. The OC was right: there was no way we could sit around here waiting for the radios to be fixed. We were vulnerable and needed cover. Once we were laid up within the safety of a compound, the guys could deal with the communications problem; but first we needed to make ourselves safe.

We edged through the maize fields towards the compounds. There had been fighting here recently, so the area was deserted, the civilians having left; but there was still a risk that the Taliban were present, or that they had booby-trapped the compounds in this vicinity, so we moved gingerly. Along with two-zero platoon, we reached Compound 69 safely. One-zero and three-zero took up positions in Compounds 66 and 67 about 100 metres to the south.

Compound 69 was seemingly deserted, but locked; the guys just kicked the door in and then entered to secure the location. When a compound is damaged in this way, the occupants can claim compensation. Some locals are too scared to do this, as it makes it look as if they're cooperating with the occupying force; others show the typical Afghan flair for negotiation and demand outrageous amounts of money before working their way lower.

Once inside the compound, the soldiers systematically checked each room for occupants or booby traps. They then satisfied themselves that there was a good arc of fire from the top of the compound walls. If the enemy fire came—or rather, when it came—it was essential that the Scots were able to counter-attack the surrounding positions. The guys had brought about twenty empty sandbags with them, which they filled from the dusty compound floor and placed on top of the roofs to give them some cover, as apart from some decorative nipple-shaped domes there was none.

And then we waited.

The company's intention was to draw fire from the Taliban so that the enemy would give away their positions and reveal how many of them there were. Members of one-zero platoon were sent out on the ground so that if the Taliban were to approach our compounds, the men on the ground could ambush them. After laying up in Compound 69 for two hours, however, there was nothing. Delta Company were joined by a group of intelligence officers whose role was to try a tactic that I had not encountered before. Lieutenant Bolin set up a loudspeaker on the top of the compound wall while Corporal Edwards explained what was to happen. They intended to send messages over the loudspeaker in an attempt to goad the Taliban into action. I was in two minds about the wisdom of this. There seemed to be no doubt that the enemy knew where we were; it

310

was, to my mind, likely that they would attack sooner or later. Why make things worse? In addition, it was the time of Ramadan, when Muslims fast during the day. It struck me as culturally insensitive at the very least to start disturbing the locals in this way; but I guess you sometimes have to look at the bigger picture, and Lieutenant Bolin explained that the locals were unlikely to become inflamed provided we didn't disturb the call to prayer. The Taliban, though, were a different matter.

The goading started. A member of the ANA spoke over the loudspeaker: *'In this month of Ramadan stay in with your families. Do not fight! Stay where you are, stay with your families.'* The words sounded peaceful, but the subtext was quite different. Though at the time, I was pretty dubious about this technique, about the wisdom of drawing more attention to ourselves, with hindsight I can see how effective it is. There was an immediate response. Within thirty seconds small-arms fire and RPGs flew over Compound 69. The 'Do you think you're hard enough?' approach had earned Delta Company a reaction—and given them a clue as to where the Taliban were firing from.

Intelligence gave us an insight into what was going on among the enemy. The airwaves were buzzing with instructions: 'Don't be tricked into giving away your positions. Don't fire any more RPGs because we don't have enough.'

311

Clearly the Taliban commanders knew what we were up to, but the grunts on the ground couldn't resist responding to the wind-up. Delta Company used their maps to work out the RPG firing point; in the meantime Nick Calder ordered the sound commander to continue his job of goading the enemy. Just one problem: the equipment broke. While they tried to replace a broken cable, they told me that the backup plan was to use an iPod to broadcast bagpipe music. I'm not sure if the 'Highland Fling' ranks highly in the Taliban top ten, but we didn't find out: a replacement lead was found and the machinery was up and running again. It had been a chaotic little incident and not, as I said to camera at the time, the British Army's finest hour.

While the sound commander was getting his DJ equipment up to scratch, Nick and his men believed they had identified Taliban firing points in compounds to the north. To the west of us, on the other side of the wadi, British troops were occupying the high ground at a location called Roshan Tower, home to a mobile phone mast. From here, Nick decided to call in an attack of 81mm mortars into Compounds 94 and 95, where he believed the enemy were holed up. However, one-zero platoon were lying in ambush, so he had to establish that they were not in the way before the mortars could be launched. The last thing anyone wanted was a blue on blue.

While the patrol's position was being determined, the loudspeaker goading started up again. *'Stop annoying the Afghan people. Do not fight. Try to stay at home with your families during the month of Ramadan.'*

More small-arms fire. Then I heard the sound of gunfire much closer: our own men engaging with the enemy. I scrambled up on to the northern roof of the compound to see what was happening. At the north-east corner were two soldiers, Hammy and Gordon Pollock. Pollock—too cool for school, with a laconic turn of phrase—was installed behind the somewhat ineffectual protection of some sandbags with a Minimi light machine gun. The FOO, Axel, was up on the wall about 12 metres away from him so that he could direct the artillery. To the north-east of us were the demolished remains of Compound 71. On the outskirts of the demolished compound, about 100 metres away, was a collapsed wall with an overhanging tree. This, as we were soon to find out, was a Taliban firing point.

We started taking incoming from the west. A burst of rounds went over my head. *'Fuck!'* I shouted as I got my head down. That had been very, very close. At this point Pollock, directed by Axel, opened up on enemy that he had seen in Compound 71. Everyone knew what a good shot he was. A to-and-fro battle went on for five minutes, then stopped.

A brief lull. Then, out of nowhere, a burst of fire hit Pollock's position and struck the edge of the roof in front of us. Pollock dropped. He got up again. Then dropped once more. Hammy took his place, and at that very moment I heard Axel's voice shouting the words you never want to hear.

'Man down!' he barked. *'Man down!'*

The air turned into a riot of rounds and shouting. Chaos. Axel's was a voice of calm among it all as he spoke into his comms. 'We need a medic up on the roof and we need more firepower. We need another gunner!'

For some reason Axel's request over comms for a medic up on the roof hadn't been heard, so I crawled across the roof leaving him and the cameraman as Hammy banged away at the enemy who were breaking through the tree line. I bellowed down to the others in the compound. 'Man down! Boys, we need a medic up here!'

Everyone sprang into action. It was no surprise to me that Stevie Rae was the first up on the roof: 'Where is he? Where is he?' I had my head firmly buried into the roof. All I could do was raise my hand and point as the soldiers took over. They bravely shuffled towards the firing position despite the incoming fire. Hammy fired the Minimi to give them cover as they clambered towards Pollock and escorted him down to relative safety inside the compound, but just then I heard Axel's

314

voice. 'Enemy!' he screamed. 'Enemy! Enemy! Two hundred metres in that direction!'

They were coming through the trees, approaching from the north. Delta Company engaged them with their SA80s while the Minimi was reloaded so that their advance could be suppressed. I took advantage of the covering fire to get the hell off that roof and back down into the compound. Down on the ground, I saw Pollock. His face was smeared in blood; so was his hand. True to type, however, he was still wearing his shades and when I asked him how he was, he told me simply that his arm was a bit sore.

As I say, too cool for school.

In fact he'd had a very lucky escape. It transpired that the rounds—three of them—had hit the bipod of Pollock's Minimi. The metal jackets of the rounds had splintered and sheared his left forearm in several places. He'd been unbelievably lucky. When you're lying prone in a firing position, your body armour is no good to you. Had the rounds not hit his bipod they could well have gone down his throat and he would have been beyond anyone's help. Along the top of his wounded arm he had a tattoo. 'Though I walk in the valley of the shadow of death,' it read, 'I will fear no evil.' Gordon Pollock had been inches away from taking that very walk.

The medic administered morphine to his right arm, and inserted an IV access so that he could get fluids into him should anything go wrong. But he was triaged as walking wounded. Everything was going to be fine. In the time that I had known him, Gordon Pollock had racked up two confirmed enemy kills and now he'd narrowly missed death with severe wounds to his arm.

A few of the guys from three-zero platoon escorted him down to the wadi so that he could be evacuated back to base by Mastiff. Meanwhile, it was only 17.30. If we were the jam in the jar, we were still attracting a lot of wasps. It wouldn't get dark for another two hours, so we knew that the contact was likely to continue.

Delta Company had established that the bulk of the Taliban forces were situated in and around the remains of Compound 71, about 200 metres directly to our north-east. While Pollock was being evacuated to the wadi, two-zero platoon increased their rate of fire towards the enemy in order to give them cover. I climbed back up on to the roof as the rounds of the Minimi zipped across the green zone. Then Axel called on Hammy to hold his fire: the time had come for the 81mm mortar rounds to be called in from Roshan Tower. Axel had a position on one-zero platoon and he passed the information down to Nick Calder that the mortars were being directed 500 metres from their position and 300 metres from ours. It didn't leave much margin for

316

error.

The mortars hit their target. Just as they did, the loudspeaker started up again. *'Taliban, Taliban, Taliban! You are the enemy of Afghanistan.'* 'Fuck,' I muttered to myself. Up on the wall of Compound 69, I didn't much fancy the thought of the enemy being goaded even more. *'Taliban, Taliban, Taliban . . .'*

Despite the mortar attack, there was still a lot of movement around Compound 71. In order to suppress the enemy further, the OC called in a strafing run. Compound 71 was very close by, which meant the strafing run had to be carried out with pinpoint accuracy. A phosphorus grenade was launched from an underslung grenade launcher into the enemy compound to give the aircraft an extra marker of where he should be aiming. But as we waited, I couldn't help remembering the scenes of devastation at Mazdurak when Foster, Thrumble and Maclure lost their lives in the friendly fire incident. I knew perfectly well as I lay on that wall that if the strafing run missed by a whisker, we wouldn't be going home.

In the distance, the sound of an F-16.

We waited.

A voice behind me. Tense. Bruce the JTAC, whose job was to liaise over the radio and coordinate the strike. 'He's taking his time about it for some reason.'

I wasn't filled with confidence. These

aircraft carry the latest imaging technology; the pilot should have been able to see exactly what he was aiming for. Truth to tell, he should have been able to see the sweat on my brow. But for some reason he was holding back.

We continued to wait.

'I think he might be looking in the wrong place.'

Great. Fantastically reassuring. Up above, we got a visual on the F-16. He was circling, but didn't seem to know where he was headed. You could almost taste the tension among the soldiers.

'I'm thinking of calling it off, to be honest.'

I turned to him. 'Call it off, mate,' I said. Quite where I thought my authority came from to make such an order, I don't know. I guess I was as nervous as everyone else.

Nick Calder gave his orders. The strafing run was cancelled. Instead, the F-16 was to complete the same trajectory, but simply give a show of force. Moments later, the pilot zoomed in, the engines roaring in our ears. He passed over Compound 71, dropping flares as he went that indicated where his line of fire would have been. Had he been strafing, he would have hit the enemy, not us. Reassuring, but in a situation like that you definitely want to be safe, not sorry.

The show of force supplied us with an extra piece of information. From the skies, the F-16

318

had spotted two dead bodies in the area of Compound 71. It looked as though the battle was over for the day.

Nobody could completely relax, of course. The soldiers went about the crucial business of cleaning their weapons systems ready for their next use; then they lit fires to boil water and heat through some hot ration packs. Everyone was tired, dirty and in need of food: it had been one hell of a day and tomorrow promised more of the same.

After sundown I took the opportunity to chat to Nick Calder and ask him how he felt the operation had gone so far. He seemed pretty pleased. We'd set out to gain entry into a compound and engage the enemy so that we could establish their positions and strength. We'd done all that, and we'd notched up two kills into the bargain. I suppose, though, that he was just as aware as I was that had one AK-47 round been diverted just a couple of millimetres, Gordon Pollock would have been dead and we'd all have been feeling very different.

Throughout the night, fluorescent lumes were pushed up from Roshan Tower to light up the green zone and any enemy movement there might be. I managed to grab some sleep, but was woken up in the small hours by the sound of something in the sky. I sat bolt upright and shouted: 'RPG!'

Stevie Rae was next to me. 'No,' he replied,

in a 'Calm down, Kempy' kind of voice. 'Lume. Go back to sleep.' I did as I was told; at least I tried to. It's difficult to sleep with explosions going on around you, no matter how innocent they are . . .

Morning came. We prepared to go out on patrol along with the Afghan National Police. The plan was to head east from Compound 69, loop up north into enemy territory and then head west to the rubble of Compound 71 to see if the two bodies that had been spotted by the F-16 had been taken away. Estimated journey time an hour and a half, but I knew from experience that it could well be longer, depending on what we came across.

The compounds around us were largely deserted, and we knew what that meant. It wasn't much after 06.00 and already the sweat was pouring from me. We saw a handful of locals farming in the fields—Taliban or farmers, who could say? The ANP stopped a man of fighting age and asked if the Taliban were in the vicinity. Apparently he didn't know, but what else was he going to say? As we passed along the side of one compound, I was given a taste of the Afghan's fighting spirit. A child stood by the path. Unbeknown to me, an interpreter up ahead playfully tapped the kid on the head with the antenna of his radio; in return the kid slapped me on the arm, clearly unperturbed by my body armour or the heavily armed men surrounding me. We did another circuit of the compound and passed him again. This time he whacked me across the chops with a big stick and a bigger smile. Kids today, huh?

We passed a compound that had people living in it and Delta Company decided to check it out. The old man who lived there was told to get any women out of the way because we were coming in; then he stood by, smiling, as the soldiers checked the rooms of his compound for hidden enemy. There was nothing. The interpreter thanked him and apologized for the disturbance. 'No problem,' he replied. 'God be with you.' I hoped he was.

We continued our patrol, through the green zone and along compound walls. After the bedlam of the previous day, it was eerily quiet. And it was eerie, too, to arrive at Compound 71. It was hard to believe that this was once a place where people lived. The compound was flattened. Sure enough, the bodies that the F-16 had spotted were no longer there. No doubt they had been taken to be buried before sunset the previous day, in accordance with Muslim tradition.

The dead Taliban were no longer there; nor were the living. We returned to Compound 69 to rest up in preparation for any further hostilities that day.

Back at the compound, everyone took the opportunity to get some food inside them and this included the members of the ANP. During

Ramadan, Muslims are supposed to fast during the day; but these guys had received special dispensation from the local mullah since they were out on the ground fighting. I watched as one of them—a serious-looking man with a long black beard—took some flour from his bag. He gave it to a younger man who, with the skill of a professional baker, kneaded it with water before flattening it so that it resembled a big pizza. Our policeman-turned-chef cooked the bread on both sides over a fire and then cut it into triangles and sprinkled sugar over it. Despite having been told not to, one of the ANP men rifled through the stores in the compound and found some chai. I was invited to sit down with them and eat.

The bread was as tasty as it smelled; the tea was delicious, but thick with sugar. We sat on a rug on the ground and, with the help of an interpreter, started to chat. No doubt some of what I'd heard about the ANP was true—that being selected from the local community some of them were pro-Taliban, or at the very least hedged their bets by passing information on to the enemy. But talking to my new bearded friend, I learned that there was another side to this story. He was from Musa Qala and he told me that his family lived in a Taliban-controlled region. Was he able to get in to see them?

He replied quite calmly. 'No, I can't. Only when that area is free. Then we'll be able to come and go. Not now.'

I wondered how long it had been since he had seen them.

'My friend, it has been around seven or eight months. God willing, when the Taliban are not there, I will go to see them.'

He had been with the ANP for four years. I asked him if he envisaged a time when it would be just the ANA and the ANP in charge of the security of Helmand Province.

'No,' he replied. 'ISAF won't go from here. They are our friends until the nation is built.'

Did he not want the Afghan people to control the Afghan state?

'First,' he told me, 'our neighbours should stop meddling in our affairs. Second, once our military is developed and has weapons and strength, then the enemy will disappear.'

Who did he mean by this?

'My friend, I suspect Iran and Pakistan. We have captured people here. They have left behind bodies, their injured ones and their prisoners.' He explained to me that the Taliban in his village had foreigners with them from Pakistan, Uzbekistan and Iran. 'There are even people from Chechnya! In the last thirty years, Afghanistan has been smashed into pieces because of these people.'

Did he think the Taliban would be defeated in this area?

'God willing, yes. Now that people know they are the enemy of the government, not friends. They burn schools, they burn the bazaar, they kill people. Eighty out of a hundred Afghans have turned away from them.'

I had heard British soldiers speaking in terms bordering on respect for the Taliban's fighting spirit. I wonder if my ANP friend felt the same.

'No, they are not good warriors. They are just creating disorder.' But then he proceeded to roll up his shirt and show me some wounds that these warriors had inflicted upon him. He had been shot thirteen times by the Taliban. His abdomen was a horrific mess of scars and healed wounds; he looked as if he had half his guts missing. I couldn't help the shock registering on my face. 'My arm has also been shot,' he told me with a faint smile. 'I cannot lift it up.' He showed me the injury—it looked as though the whole shoulder had been taken out. He laughed at my reaction; once more I was reminded what tough people these were.

'The Taliban are very brutal,' he told me.

I think you can say that again, my friend.

I had never come to Afghanistan to moralize about the rights and wrongs of the conflict; moreover, I was very aware that the Afghans accompanying British troops were likely to be those on the side of ISAF and that not everybody in this country thought the same way. But the conversation had been an honest and enlightening one.

It made me realize that, if the efforts of our troops could help this man be reunited with his family, then the hardships they were undergoing at least had a real, tangible aim. Was it worth the deaths of so many young British lives? That was a more complicated question; but at least I came away from that meal of sweet bread and tea thinking that what was happening here was not entirely in vain.

*   *   *

By now, the heat of the day was at its most intense. Along with some of the others I took myself away to get some sleep, but was suddenly woken by the sound of a bang in the air. In my half-awake state I suppose I thought it was night-time. 'Lume,' I muttered.

From near by, I heard Stevie Rae's voice. 'Lumes don't go up in the day,' he stated. 'RPG!'

It was an effective alarm call. Word went around the compound that the enemy were about to launch another grenade, so I put my helmet back on and waited to see how the game would be played out.

More news: the Taliban commanders were instructing that no more RPGs be fired until we left the compound. That suggested to Nick Calder that they didn't have many at their disposal. There was a suspicion that the RPG attack came from a Taliban dicker. My ANP friend told me that this had happened 'thousands of times'. It was decided that the ANP, who had powers of arrest, should wait by the entrance to the compound and if the dicker passed by again, they would run out and arrest him. 'OK, fine,' the ANP man told the translator. 'Tell him I won't let them go past.' He looked as though he meant it.

We waited for several hours. No more attacks. No movement. Then, from nowhere, a motorcycle, right outside the compound. The ANP were as good as their word. They stopped the motorcyclist, tied his hands behind his back and arrested him. The captive wore dark garb and had a swagger about him. The ANP removed his mobile phone and discovered on it some pretty incriminating evidence: phone numbers of people who were believed to be leading Taliban commanders, and video footage of dead bodies, killed in battle. Not the sort of stuff I'd want on my mobile, but maybe that's just me . . .

The ANP man wrapped a black scarf round the captive's eyes. He was led into the compound and put against a wall, all the while flatly denying the allegations that were levelled against him: that he was a dicker, about to report back to the Taliban commanders the ISAF force's position.

'Take me to anyone you want!' he babbled.

The ANP man was unmoved and unfooled. 'Yes, I will,' he replied, his voice calm. 'I will take you to Koka.'

Koka was the head of the ANP in Musa Qala. He was, by all accounts, one of the toughest men in this part of Helmand Province. It made sense. You don't get that kind of job with a degree from Harvard; you get it by being able to throw your weight around. I wondered if Koka would be any less impervious to the prisoner's claims than the ANP on the ground; I also wondered if the corruption that I knew to be so prevalent among people of authority in this part of the world would lead to our man being let off.

As it turned out, after further investigations by the ANP he was released without charge.

*   *   *

The remainder of the day passed quietly. We spent another night in Compound 69 and on day three of the operation Delta Company called for the Mastiffs to move up to an RV point on the northern wadi to pick us up and take us back to base.

I was happy to get back to the DC. Along with the rest of the guys, the first thing on my mind was to get some food down me: nothing special, but hunger is the best sauce and it was good to eat something that wasn't straight out of a ration pack. And it wouldn't be long before I was able to cook some food in my own kitchen, as this was my last night with Delta

Company before going home. I took the opportunity to sit with Nick Calder, Axel, Goody and Danny, to thank them for keeping me and the camera team safe over the past weeks and to see how they felt about their imminent return home. Nick seemed wary of becoming too blasé about it. Delta Company had been very lucky during this tour: he'd expected to have perhaps ten wounded and at least a couple of deaths; in fact, so far, there had been only five injuries and no fatalities. Nick knew that luck had been on his side; he also knew that he couldn't relax until all his men were on a Tristar out of Afghanistan, and that was a good fifty days away. I hoped that in the future I would be able to congratulate him on bringing all of Delta Company safely back home again.

As I prepared to leave, I contemplated what I had learned in my time with 5 Scots. The soldiers seemed more settled on the ground than they had done the previous year, and I had seen at first hand that they had a better working relationship with the ANA and ANP. That said, the fighting in Musa Qala had been intense—more intense, probably, than when I had been with the Anglians. The Taliban were fighting smarter, perhaps because their ranks were being swelled by professionals from Pakistan, Iran and, yes, even Chechnya. The strain on the British troops whose role it was to keep them at bay was immeasurable. I wondered how they would deal with being back at home; what would happen when they were in the supermarket and someone bumped into them without saying sorry. Can you really go from two contacts a day with advanced weapons systems to being just an ordinary Joe? Colour Sergeant Joseph Connelly maintained that you could. 'Because you've been here, getting shot at,' he told me, 'wee things like that don't bother you. It's insignificant.' I hoped that was true of every soldier who had fought in Helmand Province.

I caught up with Lance Corporal Gordon Pollock and he showed me the wound on his arm—three great gashes sewn together with black stitches. A fly rested on the moisture of the wound. Gordon himself, however, bore the relieved expression of a man who knew how lucky he was. I asked him what was the first thing he'd do when he got home. 'Hug my girlfriend, hug my mum,' he replied. I bet you will, mate, I remember thinking. And rightly so.

Before we left, Delta Company came out in force for a company photograph and I was afforded the honour of being part of that picture. And it was an honour. This was a group of very brave men. They were as tightly knit as any family and during the time I had been with them I felt that they'd allowed me to become part of that family.

The camera team and I left the DC for the

329

last time by Mastiff. We travelled up the wadi, and then west towards FOB Edinburgh, where we were to catch a Chinook back to Bastion. Unfortunately, Chinooks don't run to a regular timetable. We were stuck at FOB Edinburgh for four long, boring days. We didn't complain: we knew that the Chinooks weren't being delayed because of leaves on the line or the wrong kind of snow and that they were being utilized for more important missions than taking a guy off the telly back home. And we were reminded that in a war zone, boring is better than the alternative.

During the day, the pilot of an Apache needed to refuel before returning to FOB Edinburgh. We were all sitting in the mess tent having some scoff when he took off. Suddenly there was a dreadful noise from outside and everyone ran to see what was happening.

Taking off in a dusty desert is a difficult business because you can suffer from a 'brown out', where the dust cloud completely surrounds the aircraft and the pilot can't see what he's doing. This can be particularly dangerous when your Apache is laden with two Hellfire missiles. I don't know exactly what had happened when the pilot of this Apache had tried to take off in the brown out; all I know was that the tail of the chopper had broken off and was lying about 50 metres away from the main body. The crew were astonishingly lucky to walk away from it alive.

Moreover, had the Hellfires exploded, they would probably have taken half the FOB with them.

Now *that* would have made an interesting end to our stay . . .

*   *   *

As always, coming back home was bittersweet. I'd been out in Musa Qala for only a small fraction of Delta Company's tour, but you don't just slip back into civilian life that easily. I started having dreams. In one, I was playing football against the Taliban in the dark, and the ball was an explosive. They were wearing *dishdash*; I was wearing body armour. No one knew when the explosive was going to go off, so we had to keep passing it back and forth across the halfway line. I always awoke before the explosion, safely in my comfortable bed at home, a very long way from where the boys of Delta Company were still enduring the hardships of Musa Qala. It would be flippant of me to say I counted the days until their return as enthusiastically as them or their families; but I did look forward to them coming back, and so it was that I was pleased to be present at Howe Barracks in Canterbury when they were delivered back into the arms of their loved ones.

There was palpable excitement as the white coach carrying Nick Calder and his men turned into the parade ground. The bagpipes started playing; everyone waved Union Jacks. A full complement of men: exhausted, battle weary, but alive. Having been at Pirbright Barracks when the Anglians returned minus their fallen colleagues, I knew how different it could have been.

And so, it has to be said, did the families of the soldiers. They must have enacted the worst-case scenario in their minds countless times. Whether they fully comprehended what it was that the men of Delta Company had been through during their six months in Helmand Province, I didn't know.

But I knew this: the looks on the faces of the relieved wives and excited children said it all.

PART THREE
Herrick 9

18. ADAPT AND OVERCOME

Deep in the Surrey Hills, about an hour out of London in the genteel village of Headley, there is a place called Headley Court. It looks like a large country house, nestled in the tranquil surroundings of the North Downs. In fact it couldn't be more different, because this is a military rehab centre. In 2007, local residents objected fiercely—and ultimately unsuccessfully—to proposals to allow a nearby house to be used as a residence for visiting families. The feelings that this attitude raises in me are, to be honest, not suitable for print. I'd like to take any remaining protestors on a quick tour of the place, because if anybody has any doubts about the amazing work that goes on at the Defence Military Rehabilitation Centre Headley Court, one look inside would soon put them right.

In Helmand Province I had learned about the constant threat of mines and improvised explosive devices. Eighty per cent of casualties are caused by these explosions. Many are deadly; but there is an additional human cost that rarely makes the headlines. Headley Court houses, among others, those soldiers who have lost limbs in the Afghan conflict and are being repaired and rehabilitated. Physical therapy, occupational therapy, psychological therapy: all these are dealt with at Headley Court. I wanted to visit this place, to speak to the soldiers who were being treated there. I expected it to be a traumatic experience. In the end, it was an inspiring one.

One of the first men I met at Headley Court, whose name I won't reveal, had suffered a head injury. His mental faculties were fully intact, but he was almost completely paralysed. He was locked in a body that no longer worked and his only method of communicating was with a spelling pad and a pencil. He wanted to speak to me, and I sat by his bedside as he painstakingly spelled out a question for me.

'What . . . was . . . it . . . like . . .'

I felt pretty sure I knew how the question would end. 'To be in Afghanistan', right? Wrong.

'What . . . was . . . it . . . like . . . to . . . hit . . . Ian . . . Beale?'

We both had a good laugh, but then he started to get cramp in the arm he was using to 'write'. Can you imagine what it's like, having cramp and not being able to move the limb sufficiently to get rid of it? The nurse who was attending him began to cry; I felt myself welling up. The only sound he could make was one of frustration and pain.

Despite all this, he'd managed to have a joke with me and I couldn't help marvelling at this man's ability to keep his sense of humour up in such circumstances. And that remarkable uplifted morale was a feature of almost everybody I met.

Derek, a member of the Mercians, was a double leg amputee above the knee. As far as amputations go, that's about as bad as it gets. It means you don't have the benefit of the knee joint, so when your false leg is attached all the movements have to come from the hip. This makes it very difficult to learn to walk again, not least because it takes three times more energy to walk in this way; but Derek—whose legs were little more than stumps—was determined to do so. More than that, he lived for rugby and was determined to get back on to the pitch again, and even to compete at the Paralympics. We chatted as he was being fitted for a new set of legs and he explained what had happened. He was with an interpreter on the way to a meeting when the vehicle he was in—a WMIK—reversed over an IED. The device was constructed out of a 40-gallon oil drum, cut in half and filled with two anti-tank mines and 6-inch nails. The vehicle went up in the air and Derek was thrown 20 metres from the blast point. 'I can't say the amount of pain I suffered that day,' Derek told me. 'I couldn't compare it with anything. Before they came to rescue me, I looked up into the sky and I said a prayer. "Lord, I know that I won't make it today. But if you have a plan for me to be an inspiration to others, give me back life again."'

Now Derek thanks God every day that he's still alive.

Watching Derek jog down the corridor with his space-age metal running legs was indeed an inspiration, as was his attitude. I was also impressed to learn that some of the people who work on the legs making carbon-fibre casts—a delicate, hi-tech procedure involving laser measurements and computers—are RAF personnel also capable of working on aircraft in a war zone.

Royal Marine Peter Dunning, another double amputee, was also injured when his Viking hit an IED. He had no memory at all of the day of the explosion, but he showed me pictures of the vehicle. All four doors had been blown off and bits of the Viking were later found on the other side of the river, 200–300 metres away. The sharp, angular chunks of metal are not the only things that hit you when a vehicle like that goes up. Think about the oil, the gasoline, the acid in the battery, the hydraulics and the steel armour. The vehicles are pretty uncomfortable places to be at the best of times; blow them up and they turn into a poisonous hell.

Peter wasn't the only casualty that day. His driver, Dale Gosthic, took the full force of the blast and lost his life. 'Every day,' Peter told me, 'I count my blessings. With the driving, we'd just swap round each day. That day he was driving and I was commanding.' At the time of the incident, everyone around him was asking: how are you still alive? Peter told me he can't stop asking himself the same question.

Colonel David Richmond was the highest-ranking officer to have been injured in Afghanistan. He was also the Commanding Officer of 5 Scots. He had been shot near the town of Qats, north of Musa Qala. I sat down with him and we talked about how our paths had never crossed in Musa Qala and also about his overview of the conflict, which I totally sympathized with: that you have to have more troops on the ground if you're going to control the situation in Afghanistan and allow Afghans to lead a better life. He was also very much aware during his time in Musa Qala just how much political corruption there was. His overview of the future of Afghanistan enlightened me immensely; I didn't know it at the time but it was to be reinforced by other honest and perceptive people.

He described to me the moment he was shot. He was having a small debrief with a group of his men. Some Taliban had followed an American vehicle back to David's position. They'd opened up. Miraculously David was the only one hit. A round went into his leg. I asked him what was the first thing that went through his mind. He replied: 'That was close!' All the other rounds had gone past his head. If one of them had found its mark, he would never have seen his wife or daughters again.

Put into that kind of context, being shot in the leg isn't so bad. For the first ten minutes he was in shock and felt no pain, and he couldn't understand why. But once the adrenaline wears off, that's when it starts to hurt. *Really* hurt. I bet it did, David.

The process of repairing his leg had been long and complicated. The round had created dirty shards of bone, so the medics had had to cut open the leg and remove the shards. As a result of the loss of what had been cut away, one leg was 10 centimetres shorter than the other. David was given three options: reduce the length of the good leg, or undergo difficult, painful treatment to lengthen the bad one. Or wear a glam-rock-style high heel on one foot for the rest of his life. David, not being the Elton John type, opted for the leg-lengthening treatment. This involved wearing a metal brace around the top of his leg, which he had to lengthen on a daily basis. The broken bone inside his leg would eventually knit together, but it was important that this shouldn't happen until the leg itself had grown. Unfortunately it did—a testament to his fitness levels—so the injured bone had to be cracked again to allow the treatment to be successful. Ouch.

Derek, Peter and David had one thing in common: they refused to feel sorry for themselves. I know for a fact that many injured soldiers, on top of everything else, have to deal with complicated feelings of guilt, knowing that their colleagues are dead when they are alive, simply by fluke. 'I'm lucky' was a sentiment I heard any number of times, and that's not something you normally hear from the mouth of someone who's lost both their legs. These men all knew how differently their stories could have turned out.

I was astonished and humbled by the determination of everyone I met at Headley Court to stay positive and hold on to their sense of humour. In the TV show *South Park*, there's a character called Timmy. He's a disabled kid in a wheelchair and, with typical army wit, the amputees at Headley Court have adopted him as an unofficial mascot. The guys with amputated legs have developed a game called Timmy Tennis: two teams on either side of a low net, shuffling across the floor with rackets in their hands. The soldiers had lost none of their competitive edge or team spirit: I was allowed to join in one of their games and was comfortably the worst player on the court.

Our time at Headley Court was short, and though I came away feeling strangely optimistic about what I had witnessed there, I was also very aware that I had not quite seen the whole picture. No matter how brave a face these men put on their injuries, there was no avoiding the fact that for many of them life could never be the same again. Lucky or not, I felt sure that Derek, Peter and the others had their share of very, very dark moments. For them, conquering the psychological scars of their dreadful experiences would be at least as hard as overcoming the physical ones. And as I walked away from Headley Court, I couldn't help the words of one of the fantastic members of staff ringing in my ears. 'There are no happy endings here, Ross,' he said. 'There are no happy endings.'

Maybe. Maybe not. I'd seen a lot of positivity at Headley Court and I realised you could never really know what these men were going through unless you'd experienced it yourself.

*   *   *

My final trip to Afghanistan, in January 2009, promised to be different to the others. My ultimate destination was Kajaki—I wanted to return to the dam in winter to see how different the fighting was and also to judge for myself the increased threat of IEDs in the area. But first I headed to Kabul, the capital, to widen my limited knowledge of the country as a whole and see how the conflict was viewed outside Helmand Province.

We flew to Dubai, where we boarded a flight at what I jokingly named 'bad' terminal, because most of the places you fly to from there are pretty bad, by name and by nature: Islamabad, Jalalabad, Bad-dad (or should that be Baghdad?). The Mumbai bombings had

342

just happened, so security was at its highest and our body armour caused a lot of raised eyebrows and extra paperwork to fill in. On our civilian flight to Kabul, everybody around me was talking business—about how much money they were making in Kabul and what they were planning to do with it. I couldn't help raising an eyebrow myself and wondering just how these riches were being made in a place as poor as Afghanistan.

Kabul is situated nearly 6,000 feet above sea level, in a bowl surrounded by the magnificent mountain peaks of the Hindu Kush. It is a lawless place. The ANP and ANA patrol its borders in an attempt to keep suicide bombers out of the city. Crime is rife. But it was not always this way. In the 1960s and 1970s, Kabul was positively cosmopolitan, part of the hippie trail. It was a garden city with trolley buses and trams, with impressive boulevards lined with trees. People would come to Kabul on holiday from Pakistan. It even, for a short while, had its own Marks and Spencer. Make of that what you will.

But then the Soviets arrived. And after the Soviets, the civil war. And after the civil war, the Taliban. The Kabul of today looks nothing like its former self. Parts of it are more like a building site. It looks nothing like Helmand Province, either. The people speak a different language and among the *dishdash* wearers, you see people in clothes that would not look out of place in Europe. The population of Kabul is estimated to be somewhere between 3.5 and 5 million—there are no official figures; during the Taliban regime, however, there was a mass exodus and that number shrank to 500,000. Today, the Taliban exist in isolated pockets around the city, where they extort money and target victims, but they do not represent the same threat that they do in Helmand Province.

We stayed at Camp Souter on the outskirts of the city, but we didn't go anywhere in the capital unless we were accompanied by the army or a fantastic close protection team courtesy of Armour Group security. On patrol with both the Yorks and the Marines, I was struck by their techniques. Every time they turned a corner or crossed the road they would release a flare in the direction of any vehicle that refused to stop for them. It seemed heavy-handed, but I suppose that when everyone is a potential suicide bomber, you have to be careful. Still, I did wonder how it would go down if the sandal were on the other foot and we had guys in *dishdash* firing flares across the Shepherd's Bush roundabout.

I was used to sweltering in the Afghan heat, but winter in the north was a different story. On a journey up into the mountains surrounding Kabul the temperature plummeted to minus 12 degrees, reminding me that this truly was a country of environmental extremes. But the view was beautiful and I could see

344

how, in the past, people could fall in love with this place.

We had been invited to visit the British ambassador to Afghanistan, Sir Sherard Cowper-Coles. Cowper-Coles had previously been ambassador to Israel and Saudi Arabia—not someone to shy away from the hotspots, then—but by his own admission this was the most serious, difficult job he had ever done, or was ever likely to do, at probably the most highly protected British embassy in the world. 'There's no Ferrero Rocher here, Ross,' he told me. 'Maybe a can of Foster's after work.' I could well believe that the embassy staff might fancy a couple of cold ones at the end of the day. It transpired that the ambassador was aware of the programmes—or maybe I was just on the receiving end of some of that ambassadorial charm. One thing's for sure: by the end of the meeting, I could completely understand how Sir Sherard could hold positions of such high importance, even without the help of Ferrero Rocher.

The ambassador wanted to conduct our interview in a specific location, so we travelled from the embassy with his close protection team in two armour-plated four by fours through the streets of Kabul as he pointed out the sights. While admitting that Kabul looked rather like Berlin in 1945, he appeared genuinely optimistic about its future. 'One of the exciting things,' he told me, 'is how it has

345

grown since 2001. Buildings have been put up again, roads have been resurfaced, telephone cables are up again. And you can see that there's a lot of economic activity going on.' Of course, it wasn't all rosy. 'There's a big terrorism problem here, but there's also a law and order problem associated with the drugs trade—local petty warlords, kidnapping. What worries ordinary Afghans as much as terrorism and the Taliban is the threat to law and order—guns everywhere, people are poor and unemployed and they take matters into their own hands.'

During the Taliban regime, of course, the law and order problem was much less pronounced—not least because if you stole, you had your hand cut off. In Kabul today, there is still a small contingent that would like to see the Taliban return for precisely that reason: they see them as offering swift justice. These people are in a minority, however. Cowper-Coles was of the opinion that most Afghans knew they had had a 'test drive' of Taliban rule and had no desire to return to it. To emphasize his point, he was taking us to a location that served as a grim reminder of the realities of Taliban rule.

It was a swimming pool, empty and unused, on a hill that dominates Kabul. It had been built by the Soviets for altitude training and it enjoyed a spectacular location with its view of the Hindu Kush, the presidential palace and the tombs of the kings. But there was something about this place. You could tell that bad things had happened here, and indeed they had. It was here that many Taliban executions took place. The condemned man or woman was taken to the top diving board, and then either shot in the head or hanged in front of a crowd. 'For many Afghans,' the ambassador told me, 'it's a place of terrible memories.

'This is a broken country,' Cowper-Coles told me. The question was: how could it be fixed? 'We're here to help the Afghans help themselves. We're not here to colonize. What I see is that gradually, as you've seen happening in Helmand, our troops move out of a direct combat role and into a training and mentoring role.'

But what then, I wondered, in a country that is under the sway of local warlords and tribal elders? Surely they couldn't just be swept aside? The ambassador agreed. 'A strong centralized constitution is not necessarily right for this country. We've got to ensure that there are decent governors, and that the tribal elders are empowered.'

As for those warlords who remain actively involved in the drugs trade: 'Well,' Cowper-Coles told me, 'it's horses for courses. Some of them have really performed such atrocities and are responsible for such appalling murders and exploitation that they'll never be acceptable. But there are others where it's a much greyer issue and they need to be dealt into the settlement.'

And the Taliban? Could they ever really be part of this country's future? Cowper-Coles's view on this was enlightening. If Kabul fell again to the Taliban, he explained, 'the millions of women, the millions of girls who are back in school, back in work, back in public life, would be shut away again. Everything we've achieved since 2001 would be swept away.' But he was careful not to tar all members of the Taliban with the same brush. 'We need to recognize that there are many people supporting the Taliban who are simply local Pashtun religious nationalists who are in it because they are unemployed, because they're disillusioned with the Afghan government, not because they want to oppress the people. We need to reach out to them. There needs to be a proper process of reconciliation.'

Standing there by that swimming pool where so many terrible things had happened, I couldn't help hoping that this reconciliation came soon. I knew, though, that while the Taliban insurgency continued to rage in certain provinces, reconciliation was a long way off.

During my stay in Kabul our close protection team took us on a walkabout so that we could meet members of the local

348

population, to see if they were as positive about the presence of the ISAF forces as Cowper-Coles believed them to be. It was by no means a scientific survey, and we did come across a handful of locals who hankered after a return to the days of Taliban rule. But almost overwhelmingly, it appeared that the occupying force was welcomed.

In a village on the outskirts of Kabul, where new housing was being built brick by brick, I chatted to men, some with shaved faces and jeans. 'Foreign forces are good,' they told me. 'It's because of them that security is established. If they were not here it would be the same civil war and fighting.' What about the suicide bombers who plagued the city? 'It's un-Islamic. It's a wild act against humanity.'

I wondered if the locals could predict a time when the ISAF forces would leave and the ANA could keep the peace. 'One hundred per cent. Our hope is that the people of Afghanistan stand up on their own two feet and become self-sufficient. The assistance and cooperation of foreign forces are needed for the time being until our security forces are capable of standing on their own.'

In other words, we'll take your help while we need it, but once we're back on our own two feet—see ya later. And the truth is, I couldn't agree with them more. As Cowper-Coles said, we're not there to colonize: we're just there to help. (I also reminded myself, however, that there are many Western companies making money from the conflict in Afghanistan, from catering to construction to supplying hardware. It's in their interests for the war to continue . . .)

Before I left that village I was reminded of the fact that the Afghans, despite needing the help of outsiders, are far from helpless. I caught sight of a man watching us. His appearance was far from modern: he wore a black *dishdash* and sported a long, perfectly shaped beard. He was a mountain man, a sheep trader who brought his wares into Kabul on a regular basis. I went over to speak to him. Nearby were the footings for a building: an enormous hole, perhaps two storeys deep. The sides were sheer and there was no way of getting in and out of it. As we walked past, for some reason the microphone came off the boom and toppled into the hole.

The area was a building site and, as Westerners, our first thought was to go and find a ladder. We didn't get a chance. Without a word, the mountain man unwound his headgear, attached one of the children who were following us around to the end of it and lowered the kid into the hole. The child threw the part back up to me before the mountain man pulled him straight back up.

Once the kid was safely out of the hole, one of the close protection guys turned to me. 'Adapt and overcome,' he said.

Adapt and overcome: it was what the Afghan people had been doing for years. As I left Kabul I couldn't help thinking there was a lot more adapting and overcoming to be done in the future. But there was, at least, light at the end of the tunnel. Nobody seemed to think that the Taliban were likely to take back power in the city and that, to my mind, counted for a lot.

The same could not be said, however, of Helmand Province. Here the insurgency was as ferocious as ever, and now that my time in Kabul was over, I prepared to return.

19. PYRAMID HILL

For me, as for many people, Kajaki is a place of memories.

It was here, just over a year ago, that three soldiers from the Anglians had died in the friendly-fire incident in Mazdurak. It was here that I had spoken to their grieving colleagues. And it was from here that I had joined them in a mission to deny any equipment left behind in Mazdurak to the enemy.

Now, of course, the Anglians were long gone. Today, Kajaki was home to, among others, 45 Commando Royal Marines, Victor Company. The Marines' job was not to expand the FLET but to protect the dam which, when it is fully operational, will provide electricity to nearly 2 million people in southern Afghanistan. Maintaining the status quo is not straightforward. The area surrounding the base at Kajaki had always been littered with legacy mines, but I had heard that the threat from IEDs had hugely increased in the time that I had been away. The Taliban, it seemed, were starting to learn that they could not defeat the ISAF forces simply with guns, because we were always going to have greater and more advanced firepower than them. And so the war had become dirtier.

IEDs aren't like soldiers. They don't need

to be fed or watered. They don't need to be trained or counselled. They require no clothes or heat. They don't have to go off and pray. They don't have to sleep. They just sit there on the battlefield 24/7, waiting to do their devastating, deadly work. And having seen at Headley Court what IEDs can do to people, I was more than a little apprehensive about going out on the ground again in this dangerous part of a dangerous province.

It was warmer than Kabul, being further south, but never much warmer than 5 or 6 degrees—a big difference from the intense heat I'd experienced during the summer tours. We arrived at Kajaki from Camp Bastion by Chinook in the evening, having flown along the Helmand river and up over the dam before turning round to access the LZ. As soon as we were on the ground and unloaded, that impressive helicopter rose straight up into the sky like a flying saucer, disappearing mysteriously into the blackness of the encroaching night before skimming back to Bastion along the river, popping flares as it went, with its Apache escort flying high overhead.

The Marines were somehow different to the other guys I'd met. Whereas the soldiers I'd been with previously would come back from ops and—quite understandably—allow themselves a bit of down time playing cards or Nintendo or whatever floated their boat, many of the Marines couldn't sit still. They had to be doing something all the time: boxing with each other or making things or fixing things. They were forever tinkering with their vehicles; the thunderboxes had a huge excavation underneath them to act as a makeshift cesspit. The food at Kajaki was the best I'd ever eaten at a forward operating base. I don't know why—maybe because it was winter and the supply chain was better. (The Marines were quick to pull me up for using the wrong lingo in their presence: food was no longer 'scoff' but 'scran'; a cup of tea wasn't a 'brew' but a 'wet'.) All in all, the base was in much better nick than when I first went out.

Even though the Marines were different in some ways, they shared similar concerns to other soldiers I had met, the issue of pay being one of them. One lad, for instance, explained to me, as I chatted with the FSG one morning, that his missus back home worked in a call centre and earned more than he did. Their biggest fear was becoming an amputee. The same lad told me of a mate of his who was paralysed from the chest down at the age of twenty-one thanks to a previous tour of Afghanistan. I'd like to say I was surprised, but I wasn't. Amputation had already happened to several guys on this tour and given that they spent most of their time fighting in a minefield, it was a very pertinent fear.

The Marines had one advantage, however,

that the lads I'd met at Headley Court hadn't had. The WMIK Land Rovers, which offered scant protection against IEDs, had been replaced by the British-made Jackal. Wes, one of the FSG, showed me pictures of a Jackal he had been in when it had hit an IED. He and the other two lads had managed to escape pretty much unscathed. He laughed about having got a cracked rib. Then he gave me a tour of an actual vehicle. 'They're brilliant pieces of kit,' he told me. 'Compared to the old WMIKs they're a lot better. You hit a mine in one of the Jackals and you'll probably survive, just with cuts and bruises.' That was a definite improvement; but of course, you can't travel everywhere in a vehicle. An infantry soldier can't avoid moving on foot, and it wasn't long before I joined them doing just that.

My first excursion was to the northern FLET. No contact, but an interesting conversation with a local. When I asked him what would happen if he told us where the Taliban were, he gave me a sinister grin and slid his forefinger across his throat. Later, we learned from the interpreters that the enemy had spotted us: 'The American spies are here. We can see them. They're wearing dark colours and they've come to take the commander.'

The only people wearing dark colours— much to the Marines' amusement—were me and the cameraman Mark. Fan-fucking-tastic. The fact that the enemy thought we were spies coming to get them added a certain *je ne sais quoi* to our next excursion, which took place that afternoon.

Big Top is a Taliban stronghold to the south-west of the main base at Kajaki. It's reached by travelling down the 611 highway, and I was to accompany the FSG to this region while they provided cover to a contingent of ANA who were going into the green zone to talk to the locals. The Jackal was the vehicle of choice. Unfortunately there was not enough room in these three-man vehicles for the cameraman Mark and me to travel inside, so we were given the dubious pleasure of perching on the back, along with Wes, who was in the fifty-cal gunner's position.

Mark and I felt exposed, to say the least, stuck up there like a couple of coconuts in a shy.

'This doesn't look good,' Mark muttered in his Derry brogue.

'I'm not feeling too good, either,' I replied. We were like sitting ducks, only not as pretty.

The calm before the storm is always the worst. My brain started asking me questions.

Why are you here, Ross?
It was your stupid idea in the first place.
You're not doing this again.
Fuck me, I hope we don't go over an IED.
Fuck me, I hope I don't get shot.

356

Wes smiled at us. For him and his mates, this was an everyday danger; for us, it was a very special day—one we'd like to see the end of. I tried to stop thinking about the dangers and get on with the job in hand. It's at this moment that you tell yourself it's not going to happen to you, then try to stop your brain replying, 'Yeah, Ross, but that's what *everyone's* saying . . .'

Yeah, but . . . No, but . . . Yeah, but . . . No, but . . .

Progress, as always, was slow. Four hours to move 2 klicks. The Jackals had to stop at regular intervals so that the road ahead could be swept for mines. It had rained recently, which meant the guys checking the way ahead had to scrape back mud rather than dust. The job of a brave man. In time, we headed up towards the high ground so that the FSG would have an arc of fire over Big Top if necessary. But the Taliban knew that they used these locations, and as a result they were more likely to be IED'd.

Icom chatter. 'We're prepping the big thing up in the hills so that they never come back.'

Something big waiting for us? Or a big wind-up? No one knew. But it didn't help my state of mind.

I decided we should dismount at the bottom of a small hill overlooking Big Top. We would have to make it to the top by foot but before we could do this, our way ahead needed to be secured. Chalk lines—made by squirting white powder from a plastic bottle—were drawn to show the path that had been swept for mines. Step outside the lines and you're stepping into the unknown. Not a good idea.

Once the way ahead was cleared, we prepared to ascend.

Icom chatter: 'Engage them as soon as you see them.'

The lines were narrow, but I concentrated on staying within them. There was a strange stillness in the air. You could somehow just tell that things were about to kick off. There was no cover here—this wasn't like the green zone, where you could hide among the vegetation or the irrigation ditches. We were well and truly exposed.

Ahead of me were Scotty and Sven, in charge of the FSG. They stopped. 'Back off,' the instruction came. It meant they'd found something.

As we turned down the hill, the enemy could see their big surprise wasn't about to come off. They opened up with PKM rounds from the general direction of Big Top. Wes made it a two-way range by returning fire with his fifty-cal. I 'swastika'd'—army slang for the shape of your arms and legs when you're running like hell—back down the hill. I slammed right into Mark the cameraman, who was doing his best Bambi on ice impression. We dived, rounds still flying everywhere. A

358

voice from behind—Sven. 'It's all right, they're only over your head!' Thanks, Sven. Very reassuring!

The Jackal was at the bottom of the hill. All I could think of was getting to it, both because it offered cover and because we were out of the range of the enemy's trajectory when we were on the lower ground. Perhaps I should have stopped to help Mark up. I didn't. Self-interest kicked in. I pushed myself to my feet and continued to swastika down the hill. It was fight or flight—and flight had definitely taken over.

When you're under fire, the last thing you're thinking about is running between two narrow lines of chalk. My primary objective was to get behind the armour plating of the vehicle at the bottom of the hill.

I scooted outside the lines.

Sven's voice. Urgent. Hoarse. 'Ross! Stay on the track!'

The air was alive with rounds. I veered back on course, into the chalk lines, and sprinted to safety. Behind me Mark was running too, Sven carrying his camera. It was a huge relief to get the Jackal between us and the enemy.

The enemy fire subsided and the compounds from which we thought they were firing were hit by mortars. The FSG still needed to gain the high ground in order to support the troops going in; the route they were planning to take was barred because of the IED, so we turned round and looked for another way up. We travelled down to the compounds on the outskirts of Big Top, marking white lines all the way. Down one alley the Marines found another device—this was IED central—so we turned back again. Eventually they managed to find a suitable position and the ground troops moved in.

It was at just that moment, of course, that the Taliban decided they didn't want to play any more. No contact. From our point of advantage the FSG could see the enemy walking around Big Top; but none of them were carrying guns, so we couldn't engage them—even though we knew they were the people who had just been shooting at us. We even saw two of them order a taxi to take them home. As one of the guys said to me: can you believe the neck on that?

By now it was cold and we stayed up on that hill for four hours, after which time the ground troops started to leave Big Top while the FSG covered their withdrawal before heading back down. Mark and I had moved from Wes's Jackal to another one with a GMG gunner—Louis O'Brien—perched on the top. As we withdrew, the enemy opened up on us again. Wes's vehicle attracted most of the fire—thank God we had decided not to travel on the back of his Jackal, because the chances were that we'd have taken a hit. Louis opened up; more mortar rounds were called in to suppress the enemy fire and we eventually made it back to base. We heard that the Taliban were later boasting that they'd made us run away and destroyed five vehicles—total rubbish, but propaganda for any locals who happened to be listening in to their transmissions. Safely inside the base, Wes showed me just how close the contact had been. One of the rounds had hit the aerial of his Jackal, slicing off the top.

The lads laughed. So did I. We all realized, though, that but for a few inches, the aerial could have been one of them.

The base at Kajaki was a hell of a sight more comfortable than Musa Qala, but that didn't mean a good night's sleep was a given. That night, movement was spotted out on the ground: Taliban using the cover of darkness to plant more IEDs. The Marines weren't about to let that happen. Up at the observation posts at Sparrowhawk West and Athens, where the lads, as always, had been on constant watch all night, mortars were despatched. The enemy took cover in a bunker and suddenly the night sky was lit up by lumes to allow machine gunners to fire upon the enterprising Taliban. The mortars were re-zeroed to drop rounds on top of the bunker and yet again the Afghanistan night was filled with deafening explosions. It made a boring evening pass very quickly indeed. There were no confirmed kills; all we could do was hope that the intervention had stopped the enemy laying yet another of their hidden killers.

*   *   *

The following day we were up early, ready to accompany the Marines on their next mission: Operation Pyramid Hill. None of us knew, before we left, what a devastating day it would turn out to be.

The plan was this: to walk 3 klicks north-west of the main base and lie up above a village called Kahalabad. Once there, the Marines could expect to be contacted by the enemy. When that happened, they would return fire and go after their main target, a place called Kaji—a Taliban stronghold just across the wadi from Mazdurak.

As we approached Kahalabad, we trod as gingerly as ever inside the chalk lines. Accompanying us was a dog called Tangy that had befriended the troops and which had actually been there on my previous visit to Kajaki. The chalk lines, of course, meant nothing to him as he scampered all over the place. So far he had avoided stepping on a pressure pad. Must have been the luckiest dog alive. Our path took us uphill, into the high ground on Pyramid Hill. Another contingent of Marines, along with members of the ANA, were about 100 metres away across the wadi on top of a place known as Ant Hill. It was barren and exposed. We were in the line of fire

362

from the enemy stronghold of Kaji and that was just where we wanted to be: the laws of engagement stated that we couldn't fire upon them until they fired at us. Somewhere high above us, a B1 bomber was circling, ready to dump its ordnance on Kaji the moment we were engaged. But there was a time limit: eleven minutes. If we hadn't attracted enemy fire in that window, the B1 would have to be redeployed and would no longer be at our disposal.

The threat of IEDs was ever-present—the Taliban knew that the Marines used this piece of high ground, so it was regularly booby-trapped. It was hard work staying within the chalk lines; and nervy to say the least, knowing we were actively trying to attract enemy fire. When we reached the top of Pyramid Hill I was out of breath; but from here we had a good view of Kahalabad, Kaji and the mountains that surrounded us. It was a spectacular sight. The clouds bubbled and boiled around the rocky peaks as the morning sun glimmered over them. It was like something from *Lord of the Rings*, only with guns and fast air.

We waited. And as we waited, an explosion blasted through the air.

It didn't sound like any kind of ordnance I'd heard before and I couldn't tell which direction it had come from. There was a brief moment of silence.

'Anyone know what that was?' I asked.

Another pause. Then the shout came up.

'Contact IED. Ant Hill.' A device had exploded and that meant only one thing: someone, or something, had activated it.

I looked across the wadi. Sure enough, a plume of smoke was drifting across from Ant Hill. The smell of burnt chemicals hit my senses. Even from this distance we could tell it had been big. Soldiers had started scurrying around the brow of the hill. We heard shouts. 'Get over here now! Get a medic!'

And then the contact started.

The minute the Taliban's rounds flew towards us, the Marines had the right to fire back under the rules of engagement. The FSG, high up on a place called Essex Ridge, started to rain fire down on Kaji; and from Pyramid Hill came rounds from the GPMG. As the battle raged, I started to pick up bits of shouted information about the situation on Ant Hill. One casualty. A Chinook had been called in to casevac him to hospital as quickly as possible. We didn't know any more than that.

I could sense a change in the attitude of the lads around me. They were upset. Upset and angry. They were giving it everything they had on their attack on Kaji. Mortars were called in from the main base on enemy positions that the Marines had identified in Kahalabad while, at the foot of Ant Hill, medics

364

evacuated the casualty on a quad bike towards a landing zone at a safe distance from the battle.

As the fighting continued, word came through that the bomber was about to arrive. I could hear it in the distance, first a low rumble, and then louder. And louder.

Then it dropped its package.

I'd seen some bombs in my time in Afghanistan, but nothing like this one. As it splashed, it felt as though the whole world was shaking and the town of Kaji disappeared in a huge cloud of smoke and fire. The Taliban stronghold had just taken a direct hit with six 2,000-pound bombs. Believe me, that makes a very big bang. Enough to dampen the enthusiasm for the fight of whatever enemy was left, right?

Wrong.

Almost immediately, fifty-cal sniper rounds flew over my head. I'd just witnessed the biggest ordnance hit I'd ever seen, and still the Taliban were fighting. So, to follow up the destruction of the bombs, the Marines called in ground-launched missiles from a Guided Multiple Launch Rocket System (GMLRS) 30 klicks away at FOB Edinburgh in Musa Qala. This system, nicknamed the '70 km sniper', can deliver 200-pound warheads with pinpoint accuracy over huge distances, thanks to a GPS system built into the missiles. They go up so high that an air corridor has to be cleared, and then they nosedive directly from above the impact point, minimizing collateral damage. I watched as the missiles went about their work, causing a massive drifting of smoke over the Taliban stronghold and, finally, a silencing of their guns. Unbelievably, I saw two Taliban running from what was left of Kaji. They were clearly in the sights of the GPMG gunner in front of me. Everyone knew we'd suffered a casualty and the temptation to pull the trigger must have been overwhelming. However, true to the rules of engagement, he let them slip from his sights.

In operational terms the morning had been a success, but everyone's attention was now firmly focused on the casualty. The Medical Emergency Response Team was due to arrive any moment by Chinook; but the helicopter, of course, would be a perfect target for any Taliban who still had the appetite for a fight, so everyone was on alert and ready to suppress any fire directed at the MERT.

Mark and I started to hurry back down Pyramid Hill. We were still exposed, and on a steep gradient, so it would have been easy to slip out of the chalk lines. In the distance we saw the Chinook descending to pick up the casualty. All we could do was pray he'd be all right—whoever it was. We continued to extract, all the while concentrating on keeping in the narrow track, and eventually reached the bottom of Pyramid Hill in safety. One of

366

the guys, Corporal Matthew D'Arcy, was waiting for us. Breathless, I asked him if there was any news of the casualty.

D'Arcy's tone would have told me the worst had happened, even if his words hadn't. 'Cat E,' he said quietly. 'He's gone.'

'Cat E' was a NATO triage category. It meant the same as 'T4': the wounded Marine was dead. 'He died before we got back. The MERT came in 35 minutes. It was as good as gold. He'd lost just above the knee and lost an arm so it was massive trauma.'

The dead man was Travis Mackin, part of a small OMLT team, which was why he was accompanying the ANA up on to Ant Hill. He had celebrated his twenty-second birthday just four weeks previously.

There was an unbearably sombre mood around the camp in the wake of the operation as his friends came to terms with the death of a mate. Everyone knew that in the next few hours, his family would be receiving a knock on the door. The knock that they hoped they would never have to hear.

In the days that followed the operation, I took the opportunity to chat to some of the guys about their friend, especially Marines Adam Burke and Scott Gourley. They painted a picture of a man who was genuinely loved by everyone in the company; a man who seemed determined to live his life to the full. For Christmas he had grown a big orange beard and dressed up as Santa Claus, going all round the camp delivering presents to everyone, including the OC, the CSM and members of the Afghan National Army. He sounded to me like the kind of guy who had the ability to put a smile on the face of everyone he met.

But Travis Mackin wouldn't be able to do that any more. He wouldn't be able to do anything any more. In the harsh surroundings of the British base at Kajaki, I joined the men of Victor Company as they performed a memorial ceremony for their fallen friend. It was an incredible honour for me, a civvy, to be asked to stand in line with the soldiers at that service; to listen to the heartfelt words of his colleagues; to stand, humbled, as two lumes were sent up into the Afghan sky either side of a minute of silence as a final gesture of respect. As I stood there at that bleak outpost, and having been just 100 metres away from Travis Mackin when the IED went off, the full significance of a soldier's death was brought home to me. It doesn't seem at all right that, as the war in Afghanistan progresses, such deaths no longer make the front pages of our newspapers back home. It doesn't seem at all right that we are at risk of forgetting just what it is that these young men are sacrificing, so far from home, on our behalf.

Travis Mackin was the 139th British soldier to be killed in this conflict since 2001. As I prepared to leave Kajaki—and Afghanistan—

for the final time, I knew that he would not be
the last.

EPILOGUE

Afghanistan has changed me. But that's no surprise. It changes everybody.

I first came to Afghanistan to learn about the life of the ordinary soldier, to try to understand the pressures they are under on the most dangerous front line in the world today. I certainly did that. In my various trips to Helmand Province and elsewhere I met many soldiers who were risking their lives on a more-than-daily basis, on our behalf. That in itself is a pretty humbling experience. It was a privilege to witness their courage, tenacity and professionalism. And if this book and the films I have made serve no other purpose, I hope they demonstrate just what it is we are asking of these young men and women.

War isn't fought by pressing buttons miles from the battlefield. Far from it. In Afghanistan, as in many other areas of conflict, territory is only won and kept by men on the ground. An infantryman joining the army today can expect to spend two years on the front line during a 15-year service. If we expect our soldiers to put their lives on the line for us on a regular basis, it seems to me that we have to honour our side of the contract. They should be paid accordingly; they should be given proper, healthy food; they should have the best equipment available to them. Over the time I have been in Afghanistan I have heard these complaints countless times; but while the equipment is improving, the money and the food has stayed largely the same.

As I write this, the new American administration has approved a substantial deployment of extra troops to the region. This is a step in the right direction. Progress in Afghanistan can only be achieved if there are more ground troops, but this means other countries in ISAF pulling their weight. Certainly the British troops cannot do any more than they are doing. Between 2007 and 2008 the number of coalition forces injured in Afghanistan doubled; the number killed in action quadrupled. We can only hope that the arrival of more American forces reverses this worrying trajectory.

It seems to me that there must also be a change in the rules of engagement, if only in certain areas. During my final trip to Kajaki, the Royal Marines knew that the town of Kaji was populated entirely by Taliban militants; and yet they had to use themselves as human bait, to attract the enemy's fire, before they could attack. The human cost was too high, as I'm sure the family and friends of Travis Mackin would testify.

Some people estimate that we will remain in Afghanistan for another ten years, others for another 15. The building of Camp Bastion 2 suggests to me that the British have a long-term strategy in Afghanistan. But this is an expensive war both in terms of money and in terms of lives lost. Is it worth it? It's unrealistic to believe that Afghan warlords won't control the poppy harvest or have influence in certain areas of the government; it's unrealistic to believe that corruption will be eradicated. Acknowledging these facts, and controlling them at an acceptable level, is to my mind the only way of ensuring that the Afghans, in the long term, have a peaceful life; and that the conflict, in the long term, has an end.

The effects of this war, however, on many of the men and families involved in it will be far longer lasting than the war itself. This is the first generation of soldiers for a long time to experience such intense fighting for such long periods. Post-traumatic stress disorder can take five or ten years to develop. Only time will tell the full long-term effects of their experiences in Afghanistan.

I personally have nothing but admiration for everyone I met in the armed forces, some of whom have become personal friends and will be for life. But as I sit in London writing these words, I am very aware of the people who didn't make it back. They should never be forgotten.

GLOSSARY

2ic	second in command
556	5.56 millimetre round
ANA	Afghan National Army
ANP	Afghan National Police
CLU	command launch unit
CO	commanding officer, commander of a large military unit (*see also OC*)
DC	district centre
dick, dicker	observe, observer
FIBUA	fighting in a built-up area (*also known as FISH*)
FISH	fighting in somebody's house (*see FIBUA*)
FLET	forward line of enemy troops
FOB	forward operating base
FOO	forward observing officer
FSG	fire support group
GMG	grenade machine gun
GMLRS	guided multiple launch rocket system
GPMG	general purpose machine gun
HE	high explosive
Hesco	large collapsible wire mesh and heavy-duty fabric container which, filled with earth or sand, is used to construct protective barriers

IDF	indirect fire, ordnance not fired directly at a target, for example mortar rounds
IED	improvised explosive device
ISAF	International Security Assistance Force, the NATO-led United Nations security and development mission in Afghanistan
Jackal	British all-terrain four-wheel-drive military vehicle introduced to replace the WMIK Land Rover *(see WMIK)*
LZ	landing zone
Mastiff	British heavily armoured six-wheel-drive patrol vehicle derived from the American Cougar family of vehicles
MERT	medical emergency response team
Minimi	Belgian-manufactured light machine gun used by the British Army
NAAFI	Navy, Army and Air Force Institutes, the organization that runs recreational facilities and shops for the British armed forces
NDS	Afghan special police
OC	officer commanding, commander of a small military unit (less than battalion size) *(see also CO)*
OMLT	operational mentor and liaison

	team
OP	observation post
Pinzgauer	all-terrain British military truck
PKM	Russian-made general purpose machine gun used by the Taliban
REMF	rear-echelon motherfucker
RPG	rocket-propelled grenade
RV	rendezvous
SA80 A2	standard rifle of the British Army
sit rep	situation report
Viking	amphibious armoured all-terrain vehicle consisting of two tracked units linked by a steering mechanism
WMIK	Weapons Mount Installation Kit, a stripped-down Land Rover fitted with roll bars and weapons mounts

AUTHOR'S NOTE

I am totally indebted to the professionalism and friendship of the crews who accompanied me on my trips to Afghanistan. On Herrick 6: John Conroy, Andrew Thompson, James Snowden and Fred Scott; on Herrick 8 Matt Bennett, Jonathan Young and Anuar Arroyo; on Herrick 9 Matt Bennett and Mark McCauley.

ACKNOWLEDGEMENTS

I once again would like to thank the following people: Clive Tulloh, my co-executive producer, who was always at the end of the phone when I was getting shot at; Adam Parfitt, without whose help this book would not have been written; my editor Katy Follain for her continuing enthusiasm and professionalism; Lord Waheed Alli for all his advice and kindness; the whole team at Sky and Tiger Aspect; and Wendy Banks, for organizing my life.